LIVING LANGUAGE®

COMPLETE
BRAZILIAN
PORTUGUESE
THE BASICS

Written by
Dulce Marcello

Edited by
Christopher A. Warnasch

ACKNOWLEDGMENTS

Thanks to the Living Language team: Tom Russell, Nicole Benhabib, Christopher Warnasch, Zviezdana Verzich, Suzanne McQuade, Shaina Malkin, Elham Shabahat, Sophie Chin, Denise De Gennaro, Linda Schmidt, Alison Skrabek, Lisbeth Dyer, and Tom Marshall.

Editor: Christopher A. Warnasch
Production Editor: Lisbeth Dyer
Production Manager: Thomas Marshall
Interior Design: Sophie Ye Chin

First Edition

ISBN: 978-1-4000-2419-3

Library of Congress Cataloging-in-Publication Data available upon request.

This book is available at special discounts for bulk purchases for sales promotions or premiums. Special editions, including personalized covers, excerpts of existing books, and corporate imprints, can be created in large quantities for special needs. For more information, write to Special Markets/Premium Sales, 1745 Broadway, MD 6-2, New York, New York 10019 or e-mail specialmarkets@randomhouse.com.

PRINTED IN THE UNITED STATES OF AMERICA

10 9 8

COURSE OUTLINE

Welcome to *Living Language Complete Brazilian Portuguese: The Basics!* We know you're ready to jump right in and start learning Brazilian Portuguese, but before you do, you may want to spend some time familiarizing yourself with the structure of this course. This will make it easier for you to find your way around, and will really help you get the most out of your studies.

UNITS AND LESSONS

Living Language Complete Brazilian Portuguese: The Basics is a course in Brazilian Portuguese that includes ten *Units,* each of which focuses on a certain practical topic, from talking about yourself and making introductions to asking directions and going shopping. Each Unit is divided into *Lessons* that follow four simple steps:

1. *Words,* featuring the essential vocabulary you need to talk about the topic of the Unit;

2. *Phrases,* bringing words together into more complex structures and introducing a few idiomatic expressions;

3. *Sentences,* expanding on the vocabulary and phrases from previous lessons, using the grammar you've learned to form complete sentences; and,

4. *Conversations,* highlighting how everything works together in a realistic conversational dialogue that brings everything in the Unit together.

The lessons each comprise the following sections:

WORD LIST/PHRASE LIST/SENTENCE LIST/CONVERSATION

Every lesson begins with a list of words, phrases, or sentences, or a dialogue. The grammar and exercises will be based on these components, so it's important to spend as much time reading and rereading these as possible before getting into the heart of the lesson.

NOTES

A brief section may appear after the list or dialogue to highlight any points of interest in the language or culture.

NUTS & BOLTS

This is the nitty-gritty of each lesson, where you'll learn the grammar of the language, the nuts and bolts that hold the pieces together. Pay close attention to these sections; this is where you'll get the most out of the language and learn what you need to learn to become truly proficient in Portuguese.

PRACTICE

It's important to practice what you've learned on a regular basis. You'll find practice sections throughout each lesson; take your time to complete these exercises before moving on to the next section. How well you do on each practice will determine whether or not you need to review a particular grammar point before you move on.

TIP!

In order to enhance your experience, you'll find several tips for learning Portuguese throughout the course. This could be a tip on a specific grammar point, additional vocabulary related to the lesson topic, or a tip on language learning in general. For more practical advice, you can also refer to the *Language learning tips* section that follows this introduction.

CULTURE NOTES AND LANGUAGE LINKS

Becoming familiar with the culture of Portuguese-speaking countries is nearly as essential to language learning as grammar. These sections allow you to get to know these cultures better through facts about Portuguese-speaking countries and other bits of cultural information. You'll also find the links to various websites you can visit on the internet to learn more about a particular country or custom, or to find a language learning tool that may come in handy.

DISCOVERY ACTIVITY

Discovery activities are another chance for you to put your new language to use. They will often require you to go out into the world and interact with other Portuguese speakers, or simply to use the resources around your own home to practice your Portuguese.

UNIT ESSENTIALS

Finally, each Unit ends with a review of the most essential vocabulary and phrases. Make sure you're familiar with these phrases, as well as their structure, before moving on to the next Unit.

The coursebook also contains *Summary of Portuguese grammar* and *Internet resources* sections to be used for further reference.

LEARNER'S DICTIONARY

If you've purchased this book as a part of the complete audio package, you also received a Learner's Dictionary with more than 20,000 of the most frequently used Portuguese words, phrases, and idiomatic expressions. Use it as a reference any time you're at a loss for words in the exercises and discovery activities, or as a supplemental study aid. This dictionary is ideal for beginner or intermediate level learners of Portuguese.

AUDIO

This course works best when used along with the four audio CDs included in the complete course package. These CDs feature all the word lists, phrase lists, sentence lists, and dialogues from each unit, as well as key examples from the *Nuts & bolts* sections. This audio can be used along with the book, or on the go for hands-free practice.

And it's as easy as that! To get even more out of *Living Language Complete Brazilian Portuguese: The Basics,* you may want to read the *Language learning tips* section that follows this introduction. If you're confident that you know all you need to know to get started and prefer to head straight to Unit 1, you can always come back to this section for tips on getting more out of your learning experience.

Good luck!

If you're not sure about the best way to learn a new language, take a moment to read this section. It includes lots of helpful tips and practical advice on studying languages in general, improving vocabulary, mastering grammar, using audio, doing exercises, and expanding your learning experience. All of this will make learning more effective and more fun.

GENERAL TIPS

Let's start with some general points to keep in mind about learning a new language.

1. FIND YOUR PACE

The most important thing to keep in mind is that you should always proceed at your own pace. Don't feel pressured into thinking that you only have one chance to digest information before moving on to new material. Read and listen to parts of lessons or entire lessons as many times as it takes to make you feel comfortable with the material. Regular repetition is the key to learning any new language, so don't be afraid to cover material again, and again, and again!

2. TAKE NOTES

Use a notebook or start a language journal so you can have something to take with you. Each lesson contains material that you'll learn much more quickly and effectively if you write it down, or rephrase it in your own words once you've understood it. That includes vocabulary, grammar points and examples, expressions from dialogues, and anything else that you find noteworthy. Take your notes with you to review wherever you have time to kill—on the bus or train, waiting at the airport, while dinner is cooking, or whenever you can find the time. Remember—practice (and lots of review!) makes perfect when it comes to learning languages.

3. Make a regular commitment

Make time for your new language. The concept of "hours of exposure" is key to learning a language. When you expose yourself to a new language frequently, you'll pick it up more easily. On the other hand, the longer the intervals between your exposure to a language, the more you'll forget. It's best to set time aside regularly for yourself. Imagine that you're enrolled in a class that takes place at certain regular times during the week, and set that time aside. Or use your lunch break. It's better to spend less time several days a week than a large chunk of time once or twice a week. In other words, spending thirty or forty minutes on Monday, Tuesday, Wednesday, Friday, and Sunday will be better than spending two and a half or three hours just on Saturday.

4. Don't have unrealistic expectations

Don't expect to start speaking a new language as if it were your native language. It's certainly possible for adults to learn new languages with amazing fluency, but that's not a realistic immediate goal for most people. Instead, make a commitment to become "functional" in a new language, and start to set small goals: getting by in most daily activities, talking about yourself and asking about others, following TV and movies, reading a newspaper, expressing your ideas in basic language, and learning creative strategies for getting the most out of the language you know. Functional doesn't mean perfectly native fluent, but it's a great accomplishment!

5. Don't get hung up on pronunciation

"Losing the accent" is one of the most challenging parts of learning a language. If you think about celebrities, scientists, or political figures whose native language isn't English, they probably have a pretty recognizable accent. But that hasn't kept them from becoming celebrities, scientists, or political figures. Really young children are able to learn the sounds of any language in the world, and they can reproduce them perfectly. That's part of the process of learning a native language. In an adult, or even in an older child, this ability has diminished, so if you agonize over sounding like a native speaker in your new language, you're just setting yourself up for disappointment. That's not to say that you can't learn pronunciation well. Even adults can get pretty far through mimicking the sounds that they hear. So, listen carefully to the audio several times. Listening is a very important part of this process: you can't reproduce a sound until you learn to distinguish the sound. Then mimic what you hear. Don't be afraid of sounding strange. Just keep at it, and soon enough you'll develop good pronunciation.

6. DON'T BE SHY

Learning a new language inevitably involves speaking out loud, and it involves making mistakes before you get better. Don't be afraid of sounding strange, or awkward, or silly. You won't: you'll impress people with your attempts. The more you speak, and the more you interact, the faster you'll learn to correct the mistakes you do make.

TIPS ON LEARNING VOCABULARY

You obviously need to learn new words in order to speak a new language. Even though that may seem straightforward compared with learning how to actually put those words together in sentences, it's really not as simple as it appears. Memorizing words is difficult, even just memorizing words in the short term. But long term memorization takes a lot of practice and repetition. You won't learn vocabulary simply by reading through the vocabulary lists once or twice. You need to practice.

There are a few different ways to "lodge" a word in your memory, and some methods may work better for you than others. The best thing to do is to try a few different methods until you feel that one is right for you. Here are a few suggestions and pointers:

1. AUDIO REPETITION

Fix your eye on the written form of a word, and listen to the audio several times. Remind yourself of the English translation as you do this.

2. SPOKEN REPETITION

Say a word several times aloud, keeping your eye on the written word as you hear yourself speak it. It's not a race—don't rush to blurt out the word over and over again so fast that you're distorting its pronunciation. Just repeat it, slowly and naturally, being careful to pronounce it as well as you can. And run your eye over the shape of the word each time you say it. You'll be stimulating two of your senses at once that way—hearing and sight—so you'll double the impact on your memory.

3. WRITTEN REPETITION

Write a word over and over again across a page, speaking it slowly and carefully each time you write it. Don't be afraid to fill up entire sheets of paper with your new vocabulary words.

4. FLASH CARDS

They may seem childish, but they're effective. Cut out small pieces of paper (no need to spend a lot of money on index cards) and write the English word on one side and the new word on the other. Just this act alone will put a few words in your mind. Then read through your "deck" of cards. First go from the target (new) language into English—that's easier. Turn the target language side face up, read each card, and guess at its meaning. Once you've guessed, turn the card over to see if you're right. If you are, set the card aside in your "learned" pile. If you're wrong, repeat the word and its meaning and then put it at the bottom of your "to learn" pile. Continue through until you've moved all of the cards into your "learned" pile.

Once you've completed the whole deck from your target language into English, turn the deck over and try to go from English into your target language. You'll see that this is harder, but also a better test of whether or not you've really mastered a word.

5. MNEMONICS

A mnemonic is a device or a trick to trigger your memory, like "King Phillip Came Over From Great Spain," which you may have learned in high school biology to remember that species are classified into <u>k</u>ingdom, <u>p</u>hylum, <u>c</u>lass, <u>o</u>rder, <u>f</u>amily, genus, and <u>s</u>pecies. They work well for vocabulary, too. When you hear and read a new word, look to see if it sounds like anything–a place, a name, a nonsense phrase. Then form an image of that place or person or even nonsense scenario in your head. Imagine it as you say and read the new word. Remember that the more sense triggers you have–hearing, reading, writing, speaking, imagining a crazy image–the better you'll remember.

6. Groups

Vocabulary should be learned in small and logically connected groups whenever possible. Most of the vocabulary lists in this course are already organized this way. Don't try to tackle a whole list at once. Choose your method–repeating a word out loud, writing it across a page, etc., and practice with a small group.

7. Practice

Don't just learn a word out of context and leave it hanging there. Go back and practice it in the context provided in this course. If the word appears in a dialogue, read it in the full sentence and call to mind an image of that sentence. If possible, substitute other vocabulary words into the same sentence structure ("John goes to the *library*" instead of "John goes to the *store*"). As you advance through the course, try writing your own simple examples of words in context.

8. Come back to it

This is the key to learning vocabulary–not just holding it temporarily in your short term memory, but making it stick in your long term memory. Go back over old lists, old decks of flash cards you made, or old example sentences. Listen to vocabulary audio from previous lessons. Pull up crazy mnemonic devices you created at some point earlier in your studies. And always be on the lookout for old words appearing again throughout the course.

TIPS ON USING AUDIO

The audio in this course doesn't only let you hear how native speakers pronounce the words you're learning, but it also serves as a second kind of input to your learning experience. The printed words serve as visual input, and the audio serves as *auditory* input. There are a few different strategies that you can use to get the most out of the audio. First, use the audio while you're looking at a word or sentence. Listen to it a few times along with the visual input of seeing the material. Then, look away and just listen to the audio on its own. You can also use the audio from previously studied lessons as a way to review. Put the audio on your computer or an MP3 player and take it along with you in your car, on the train, while you walk, while you jog, or anywhere you have free time. Remember that the more exposure you have to and contact you have with your target language, the better you'll learn.

TIPS ON USING DIALOGUES

Dialogues are a great way to see language in action, as it's really used by people in realistic situations. To get the most out of a dialogue as a language student, think of it as a cycle rather than a linear passage. First read through the dialogue once in the target language to get the gist. Don't agonize over the details just yet. Then, go back and read through a second time, but focus on individual sentences. Look for new words or new constructions. Challenge yourself to figure out what they mean by the context of the dialogue. After all, that's something you'll be doing a lot of in the real world, so it's a good skill to develop! Once you've worked out the details, read the dialogue again from start to finish. Now that you're very familiar with the dialogue, turn on the audio and listen to it as you read. Don't try to repeat yet; just listen and read along. This will build your listening comprehension. Then, go back and listen again, but this time pause to repeat the phrases or sentences that you're hearing and reading. This will build your spoken proficiency and pronunciation. Now listen again without the aid of the printed dialogue. By now you'll know many of the lines inside out, and any new vocabulary or constructions will be very familiar.

TIPS ON DOING EXERCISES

The exercises are meant to give you a chance to practice the vocabulary and structures that you learn in each lesson, and of course to test yourself on retention. Take the time to write out the entire sentences to get the most out of the practice. Don't limit yourself to just reading and writing. Read the sentences and answers aloud, so you'll also be practicing pronunciation and spoken proficiency. As you gain more confidence, try to adapt the practice sentences by substituting different vocabulary or grammatical constructions, too. Be creative, and push the practices as far as you can to get the most out of them.

TIPS ON LEARNING GRAMMAR

Each grammar point is designed to be as small and digestible as possible, while at the same time complete enough to teach you what you need to know. The explanations are intended to be simple and straightforward, but one of the best things you can do is to take notes on each grammar section, putting the explanations into your own words, and then copying the example sentences or tables slowly and carefully. This will do two things. It will give you a nice clear notebook that you can take with you so you can review and practice, and it will also force you to take enough time with each section so that it's really driven home. Of course, a lot of grammar is memorization—verb endings, irregular forms, pronouns, and so on. So a lot of the vocabulary learning tips will come in handy for learning grammar, too.

I. AUDIO REPETITION

Listen to the audio several times while you're looking at the words or sentences. For example, for a verb conjugation, listen to all of the forms several times, reading along to activate your visual memory as well.

2. SPOKEN REPETITION

Listen to the audio and repeat several times for practice. For example, to learn the conjugation of an irregular verb, repeat all of the forms of the verb until you're able to produce them without looking at the screen. It's a little bit like memorizing lines for a play—practice until you can make it sound natural. Practice the example sentences that way as well, focusing of course on the grammar section at hand.

3. WRITTEN REPETITION

Write the new forms again and again, saying them slowly and carefully as well. Do this until you're able to produce all of the forms without any help.

4. FLASH CARDS

Copy the grammar point, whether it's a list of pronouns, a conjugation, or a list of irregular forms, on a flash card. Stick the cards in your pocket so you can practice them when you have time to kill. Glance over the cards, saying the forms to yourself several times, and when you're ready to test yourself, flip the card over and see if you can produce all of the information.

5. GRAMMAR IN THE WILD

Do you want to see an amazing number of example sentences that use some particular grammatical form? Well, just type that form into a search engine. Pick a few of the examples you find at random, and copy them down into your notebook or language journal. Pick them apart, look up words you don't know, and try to figure out the other grammatical constructions. You may not get everything 100% correct, but you'll definitely learn and practice in the process.

6. COME BACK TO IT

Just like vocabulary, grammar is best learned through repetition and review. Go back over your notes, go back to previous lessons and read over the grammar sections, listen to the audio, or check out the relevant section in the grammar summary. Even after you've completed lessons, it's never a bad idea to go back and keep the "old" grammar fresh.

HOW TO EXPAND YOUR LEARNING EXPERIENCE

Your experience with your new language should not be limited to this course alone. Like anything, learning a language will be more enjoyable if you're able to make it a part of your life in some way. And you'd be surprised to know how easily you can do that these days!

1. USE THE INTERNET

The internet is an absolutely amazing resource for people learning new languages. You're never more than a few clicks away from online newspapers, magazines, reference material, cultural sites, travel and tourism sites, images, sounds, and so much more. Develop your own list of favorite sites that match your needs and interests, whether it's business, cooking, fashion, film, kayaking, rock climbing, or . . . well, you get the picture. Use search engines creatively to find examples of vocabulary or grammar "in the wild." Find a favorite blog or periodical and take the time to work your way through an article or entry. Think of what you use the internet for in English, and look for similar sites in your target language.

2. CHECK OUT COMMUNITY RESOURCES

Depending on where you live, there may be plenty of practice opportunities in your own community. There may be a cultural organization or social club where people meet. There may be a local college or university with a department that hosts cultural events such as films or discussion groups. There may be a restaurant where you can go for a good meal and a chance to practice a bit of your target language. Of course, you can find a lot of this information online, and there are sites that allow groups of people to get organized and meet to pursue their interests.

3. FOREIGN FILMS

Films are a wonderful way to practice hearing and understanding a new language. With English subtitles, pause, and rewind, they're practically really long dialogues with pictures! Not to mention the cultural insight and experience they provide. And nowadays it's simple to rent foreign DVDs online or even access films online. So, if you're starting to learn a new language today, go online and rent yourself some movies that you can watch over the next few weeks and months.

4. Music

Even if you have a horrible singing voice, music is a great way to learn new vocabulary. After hearing a song just a few times, the lyrics somehow manage to plant themselves in the mind. And with the internet, it's often very easy to find the entire lyric sheet for a song online, print it out, and have it ready for whenever you're alone and feel like singing.

5. Television

If you have access to television programming in the language you're studying, including of course anything you can find on the internet, take advantage of that! You'll most likely hear very natural and colloquial language, including idiomatic expressions and rapid speech, all of which will be a healthy challenge for your comprehension skills. But the visual cues, including body language and gestures, will help. Plus, you'll get to see how the language interacts with the culture, which is also a very important part of learning a language.

6. Food

A great way to learn a language is through the cuisine. What could be better than going out and trying new dishes at a restaurant with the intention of practicing your newly acquired language? Go to a restaurant, and if the names of the dishes are printed in the target language, try to decipher them. Then try to order in the target language, provided of course that your server speaks the language! At the very least you'll learn a few new vocabulary items, not to mention sample some wonderful new food.

Portuguese words are written phonetically for the most part, which means that you pronounce words the way they're written. Of course, they're not written in English, so you have to learn the sounds that each letter or letter combination stands for in Portuguese before the phonetic spelling will make any sense to you. This will happen gradually as you learn, but to get you started, here's a summary of Brazilian Portuguese spelling and pronunciation. Don't try to commit everything to memory right now, and don't worry about what the words mean. The purpose of this overview is just to give you a general sense so you can get started without being completely baffled by the words that you see. You can—and should—come back to this section as you progress through the course, as Portuguese pronunciation becomes more intuitive for you.

Let's start with the vowels. There are three important distinctions to understand about Portuguese vowels. First, vowels may be either oral (pronounced with the airflow coming completely through the mouth) or nasal (pronounced with the airflow coming partially through the nose). We'll start with the oral vowels below, and then we'll return to the nasal vowels afterward. The second distinction is between "open" and "closed" vowels. An open vowel is pronounced with the jaw lower, so there's more of an opening for the air to pass through. A closed vowel is pronounced with the jaw higher or closer to the roof of the mouth, so there's a smaller opening for the air to pass through. English has this distinction in, for example, *seek* (closed) vs. *sick* (open) or *take* (closed) vs. *tech* (open). The vowels **a, e,** and **o** in Portuguese have both open and closed varieties. Sometimes that's marked with an accent; **á, é,** and **ó** are all open vowels in stressed syllables, and **â, ê,** and **ô** are all closed vowels in stressed syllables. But usually there's no written indication of whether a vowel is open or closed. That means that **a** can have two pronunciations, either open or closed, but **á** will always be open, and **â** will always be closed. There is no open/closed distinction in **i** or **u**. The third distinction is between stressed and unstressed vowels. The rules for word stress in Portuguese are regular, but they can affect the pronunciation of vowels. We'll come back to the rules for stress later, but first let's look at each vowel separately:

a	Open when stressed or before stressed syllables: like *a* in *father.*	**fase, vale, gato, caro, pensar, comentar, Brasil, travar**
a	Closed when unstressed or word final: like *a* in *sofa.*	**mesa, Ana, raça, costas, dia, América, Amazônia**
á	Always stressed and open, like *a* in *father.*	**pá, comissário, catástrofe, decálogo, mármore**
â	Always stressed and closed, like *a* in *ant.*	**câmara, ânsia, alfândega, cerâmica, lâmpada**
e	Open: like *e* in *best.*	**festa, dez, completo, velho, guerra, pedra, metro**
e	Closed: similar to *ay* in *day,* but clipped. Sometimes like *i* in *routine.*	**selo, medo, verde, vendedor, mentir, de, me, se, lhe, fase, importante, teatro, compreender, feliz, menino, enorme, exame**

é	Always stressed and open, like *e* in *best.*	**pé, fé, décimo, férias, tépido**
ê	Always stressed and closed, like *ay* in *day* but clipped.	**você, estêncil, competência, Gênova, decênio**
i	Like *i* in *routine.* Accent does not alter pronunciation.	**filha, ficar, Brasil, dizer, piscina, carícia, físico, particípio**
o	Mostly in stressed syllable: open, like *o* in *off* (Northeastern U.S. pronunciation).	**costa, porta, grota, olhos, bota**
o	Closed: like *o* in *go,* but clipped.	**boca, ovelha, polvo, português**
o	In common monosyllabic words, in unstressed word-final position, before a stressed **i,** or when reduced: like *oo* in *loot,* but clipped.	**o, os, do, branco, livro, falo, cozinha, tenho, gostamos**

ó	Always stressed and open, like *o* in *off* (Northeastern U.S. pronunciation).	só, avó, geológico, paródia, microscópio
ô	Always stressed and closed, like *o* in *go* but clipped.	alô, pôr, cômico, fôlego, anônimo, avô
u	Like the *oo* in *loot*, but clipped. Accent does not alter pronunciation.	puro, júri, duro, rural, músico, múltiplo

NASAL VOWELS

If you speak French, the distinction between oral and nasal vowels will be familiar to you. But actually, since you speak English, it's familiar to you as well, but you may not realize it. Say the words *dope, dote, dome,* and *don't* aloud. Now, pinch your nose closed as you say them aloud again. *Dope* and *dote* are unaffected, but it's impossible to pronounce *dome* and *don't* if you block your nose. That's because the *-m* and *-n* make the vowel *o* nasal in those words. This is exactly the same in Portuguese; **-n** and **-m** at the end of a syllable or word nasalize the preceding vowel, and in fact **-n** and **-m** are not really pronounced on their own. They only affect the pronunciation of the vowel before them. The other way that nasal vowels are marked is with the tilde, but this is only used with ã or õ.

ã, an, am	Like *u* in *thunder* or *hunh?*	alemã, manhã, canta, branco, alfândega, ambos, ambição
en, em	Like *ai* in *faint* or *paint*.	bem, jovem, homens, tem, quarenta, frente, tempo
in, im	Like *ea* in *cleaned*.	sim, fim, ginga, limpa, lindo, simpático, saltimbanco
õ, an, om	Like *o* in *don't* or *won't*.	onde, montar, bom, contar, pompom, fonte
un, um	Like *oo* in *swoons* or *loomed*.	um, uns, duns, cumprir, tumba, punctura

But be careful. If a vowel is followed by -n or -m and then another vowel in the middle of a word, the n or m is actually at the beginning of the next syllable, so it doesn't nasalize the preceding vowel. Compare these pairs of words. The first one has a nasal vowel, and the second doesn't.

limpar–limar; simples–símile; grande–grana; pompa–pomar

DIPHTHONGS
A diphthong is a combination of two vowels that make one sound together. Diphthongs in English are *oy*, *ay*, and *ow*, among others. Portuguese has a lot of diphthongs, both oral and nasal, but if you know the pronunciation of the individual vowels, it's pretty easy to figure out how the combinations are pronounced. Let's start with oral diphthongs:

ai	Like *ai* in *aisle*.	mais, caipirinha, aipo, pai
au	Like *ou* in *out*.	Paulo, autor, auto, mau
ei	Like *ey* in *they*.	peixe, fáceis, feira, seis

éi	Similar to *ei*, but with an open *e*, like *Betty* without B and *tt*.	**hotéis, papéis, pincéis, réis**
eu	Like *a* in *gate* followed by *oo* in *boot*.	**seu, meu, neutro, neurose**
éu	Similar to **eu**, but with an open *eh*.	**chapéu, céu, réu, léu**
oi	Like *oy* in *boy*.	**sois, dois, depois, oito**
ói	Similar to **oi**, but with an open *o* as in *off*.	**espanhóis, dói, sóis, rouxinóis**
ou	Like *ou* in *soul* or *o* in *go*, with the *w* sound at the end.	**vou, sou, falou, outono**

If unstressed **i** comes before another vowel, it's pronounced like a **y**:

iate, iene, viu, Glória, Cecília, Maurício

If unstressed **u** comes before another vowel, it's pronounced like a **w**:

muito, fui, ruivo, puir

But in the combinations **gue, gui, que,** and **qui,** the **u** is only there to keep the hard g and k sounds (see **g** and **q** under consonants):

Português, guerra, guia, quem, querer, aqui, quilo

NASAL DIPHTHONGS

ão	Similar to *ou* in *hound*.	**não, João, capitão, verão**
ãe	Like *u* in *thunder* followed immediately by the *e* in *get*.	**pães, mãe, capitães, cães**
õe	Like *o* in *don't*, followed by *e* in *get*.	**põe, aviões, posições, ambições**

CONSONANTS

Now let's look at the consonants. The consonants **b, f, m, n, p,** and **v** are pronounced similarly in English and in Portuguese:

boca, boa, feira, falar, muito, almoçar, não, pena, papel, pesado, vou, avó

Just keep in mind that **m** and **n** at the end of a syllable or a word nasalize the preceding vowel, and aren't really pronounced on their own:

bom, tem, algum, lomba, ponte, lançar, convenção, ante

There are a few points to be made about the other consonants, so let's look at each one on its own:

c	Before **a, o, u,** and consonants other than **h,** like *k* in *kite*.	**caro, causa, cônsul, capital, cujo, cloro, recruta**
c	Before **e** and **i,** like *c* in *center*.	**cidade, central, cesto, especial, céu, décimo**

ç	Like *s* in *see*.	açúcar, moço, lançar, nação, caça, movediço
ch	Like *ch* in *machine*.	chamar, chegar, bochecha, flecha, rocha
d	Before **a, o, u,** and other consonants, like *d* in *dog*.	da, dançar, dor, domingo, duma, drama
d	Before **e** and **i,** close to *j* in *jar*.	dizer, dia, divertir, saudade, cidade, bondade, vontade, diâmetro, divórcio
g	Before **a, o, u** and other consonants, like *g* in *go*.	galo, gato, gola, goma, gula, glaciar, global, grão, grave, magnífico
g	Before **e** and **i,** like *s* in *pleasure*.	gelo, gênio, plagiar, mágico, garagem, giz, gema
gu	Before **a,** like *gw* in *Gwen*.	guaraná, guarda, guardar, guatemalteco
gu	Before **e** and **i,** like *g* in *go*.	lânguido, guerra, guia, joguete, seguido, preguiça, guincho
h	Silent.	hotel, haver, homem, hesitar, hoje, horrível, hóspede
j	Like *s* in *pleasure*.	jogo, jantar, jardim, joça, jeito, granja, enjôo
l	Usually close to the *l* in *lead*, but with the tongue further forward.	lenha, lavar, liso, geológico, dólar, alcance

l	At the end of a word, softened, similar to *w* in *we*.	**final, Brasil, decimal, hotel, favorável, boçal, servil**
lh	Like *lli* in *million*.	**lhama, lhes, lhano, milho, milhão, calhau**
nh	Like *ni* in *onion*.	**espanhol, ranheta, canhão, canhota, lenho**
qu	Before **a** and **o**, like *qu* in *quota*.	**qual, quadra, quanto, quatro, quota, quotidiano**
qu	Before **e** and **i**, like *k* in *kite*.	**quem, querido, quieto, quilo, quina, arquiteto**
r	At the beginning of a word, like a breathy *h*. (Trilled in some parts of Brazil.)	**raça, reserva, roupa, rosa, rio, rua, ruído**
r	In the middle of a word between vowels, like a tap or flap against the ridge behind the top teeth.	**para, pêra, duro, careta, zero, caro**

r	At the end of a syllable (before another consonant), like a breathy *h,* or a flap in some parts of Brazil.	**carne, porta, Marte, forte, fôrma, dormir**
r	At the end of a word, like a breathy *h,* or a flap in some parts of Brazil.	**bar, pôr, parar, senhor, chegar, falar**
rr	Like a breathy *h.* (Trilled in some parts of Brazil.)	**emperrado, serrano, jorro, barra, arroz, borracha**
s	At the beginning of a word or after another consonant, like *s* in *see.*	**saco, sexto, sobre, ensejo, insistir, insônia, mensagem**
s	Between vowels, as *z* in *zipper.*	**rosa, frase, pisada, vaso, mesa, tese**
s	Before **b, d, ge, gi, j, l, m, n, r, v,** or **z,** as *z* in *zipper.*	**mesmo, esmeralda, esboço, desvio, resvalar, pasmoso**

s	Before hard c, hard g, f, p, qu, and t, and in final position, like *s* in *see*.	gesto, esquema, asco, esposo, destino, asfaltar, resgatar, resquício, canetas, hotéis, livros
ss	Like *ss* in *message*.	gesso, passar, esse, classe, tossir, nosso
t	Before a, o, u, and other consonants, like *t* in *take*.	tarde, talo, todo, tocar, tubo, tropical, trem, atacar, plantar
t	Before e and i, like the *ch* in *choose*.	feirante, tinta, tirar, tia, brilhante, importante
x	Usually like *sh* in *shoe*.	caixa, peixe, debuxo, xícara, baixo, mexer
x	Can also be pronounced like *z* in *zipper*, *s* in *see*, or *x* in *taxi*.	exame, existir, exercício, máximo, próximo, trouxe, táxi, fixo
z	Usually like *z* in *zipper*, but at the end of a word, like *s* in *see* or *s* in *measure*.	fazer, zona, zorro, zero, feliz, capaz, rapaz, rudez

Word stress

Words ending in **-a, -e, -o,** or the consonants **-s, -m,** or **-ns** are usually stressed on the penultimate (second-to-last) syllable:

gato, elefante, branca, Estados Unidos, restaurante, carro, garagem, falam, homens

Words ending in **-i, -u** (or **-i** or **-u** followed by **-m** or **-s**), or a diphthong, including the nasals (or a diphthong followed by **-s**), are stressed on the last syllable:

hotel, nação, alemã, depois, aqui, tabu, tabus, anual, Isabel, regular, cantar, português

If a word does not follow one of the two rules above, a written accent marks the syllable that is stressed. The accute accent on **í** or **ú** simply marks stress, but on **á, é,** or **ó** it marks both stress and an open vowel.

fácil, agradável, música, automóvel, físico, área

The circumflex on **â, ê,** or **ô** represents a stressed closed vowel.

você, cônsul, câmara, ânsia, bisavô, alfândega, Amazônia, epidêmico

The grave accent is only used over the letter **à** in certain contractions. It doesn't change the stress of a word:

à, às, àquela

UNIT 1
Saying hello

Oi! *(Hi!)*

In Unit 1, you'll learn how to introduce yourself, how to say where you're from, and how to ask for basic information about other people. Naturally, you'll learn greetings and other courtesy expressions, along with the basics of Portuguese grammar, including gender, articles, and the verb **ser** *(to be)*. Are you ready?

Lesson 1 (words)

Each unit begins with a lesson that focuses on words. The words will be used throughout the unit, so familiarize yourself with them. For advice on learning new vocabulary, consult the *Language learning tips* section at the beginning of this program.

WORD LIST 1

professor *(m.)*	*teacher*
professora *(f.)*	*teacher*
o/a/os/as	*the*
e	*and*
médico	*doctor*
estudante *(m./f.)*	*student*
escritório	*office*
casa	*house*
bem	*well, fine*
bom *(m.)*, **boa** *(f.)*	*good*
pequeno	*small*
muito	*very*

The following abbreviations will be used in this course: *(m.)* = masculine, *(f.)* = feminine, *(sg.)* = singular, *(pl.)* = plural, *(fml.)* = formal/polite, *(infml.)* = informal.

NUTS & BOLTS 1

GENDER OF NOUNS AND DEFINITE ARTICLES

As you know, a noun refers to a person, place, or thing. Nouns in both English and Portuguese can be singular or plural, but in Portuguese all nouns also have grammatical gender, either masculine or feminine. The definite article *(the)* reflects the gender of the noun. **O** is masculine, and **a** is feminine. Take a look at the following examples.

masculine	feminine
o brasileiro *(the Brazilian man)*	**a brasileira** *(the Brazilian woman)*
o italiano *(the Italian man)*	**a italiana** *(the Italian woman)*
o japonês *(the Japanese man)*	**a japonesa** *(the Japanese woman)*
o professor *(the male teacher)*	**a professora** *(the female teacher)*
o médico *(the male physician)*	**a médica** *(the female physician)*
o secretário *(the male secretary)*	**a secretária** *(the female secretary)*
o homem *(the man)*	**a mulher** *(the woman)*
o carro *(the car)*	**a casa** *(the house)*
o hotel *(the hotel)*	**a praia** *(the beach)*
o apartamento *(the apartment)*	**a caneta** *(the pen)*
o cão *(the dog)*	**a mesa** *(the table)*

masculine	feminine
o açúcar *(the sugar)*	a cama *(the bed)*
o relógio *(the clock/watch)*	a mala *(the suitcase)*

As you can see, nouns that end in -o are typically masculine, and nouns that end in -a are typically feminine. But there are some exceptions such as o dia *(the day)* and o turista *(the male tourist)*. Nouns that end in -e may be either masculine or feminine, such as o estudante (the male student) and a estudante *(the female student)*. Nouns ending in consonants are usually masculine: o motor *(the engine)*, o lápis *(the pencil)*, and o jornal *(the newspaper)*. But a mulher *(the woman)* is a common exception. Nouns that refer to people usually match the natural gender.

The definite articles o and a, which are used much more often in Portuguese than *the* is in English, will always tell you the gender of the noun, so when you learn new vocabulary you should learn each noun with its article.

PRACTICE 1
Give the correct definite article, o or a.

1. _____ restaurante *(the restaurant)*

2. _____ escritório *(the office)*

3. _____ igreja *(the church)*

4. _____ americano *(the American man)*

5. _____ francesa *(the French woman)*

6. _____ enfermeira *(the female nurse)*

7. _____ água *(the water)*

8. _____ café *(the coffee)*

9. _____ açúcar *(the sugar)*

10. _____ praia *(the beach)*

WORD LIST 2

o marido	*the husband*
a mulher	*the wife/woman*
a criança	*the child (m./f.)*
os livros	*the books*
ou	*or*
o jornal	*the newspaper*
a profissão	*the occupation*
também	*too, also*
o celular	*the cell phone*
onde	*where*
Tchau!	*Bye! (infml.)*
Oi!	*Hi! (infml.)*
Até logo!	*Bye! (fml.)*
pouco	*little*

NUTS & BOLTS 2

PLURAL OF NOUNS AND DEFINITE ARTICLES

To form the plural of most nouns ending in a vowel, just add -s, like in English. There are also plural forms of the definite articles, **os** and **as.**

o livro/os livros *(the book/s)*	a camisa/as camisas *(the shirt/s)*
o escritório/os escritórios *(the office/s)*	a criança/as crianças *(the child/children)*

If a word ends in **-ão,** change it to **-ões.**

o avião/os aviões *(the airplane/s)*	a ação/as ações *(the action/s)*

There are some exceptions that have to be learned on a case-by-case basis.

o pão/os pães *(the bread/s)*	o alemão/os alemães *(the German/s)*

Nouns ending in -m change the -m to -n and add -s.

o homem/os homens *(the man/men)*	o som/os sons *(the sound/s)*

Nouns ending in -r, -z, and -s add -es.

o doutor/os doutores *(the doctor/s)*	a luz/as luzes *(the light/s)*
o professor/os professores *(the teacher/s)*	o mês/os meses *(the month/s)*

And finally, nouns ending in -l drop the -l and add -is. An accent mark is often added to show the stress.

a capital/as capitais *(the capital/s)*	o espanhol/os espanhóis *(the Spaniard/s)*
o hotel/os hotéis *(the hotel/s)*	o papel/os papéis *(the paper/s)*

PRACTICE 2
Translate the following:

1. os hotéis

2. os carros

3. as praias

4. os livros

5. os escritórios

Now give the plural forms of these nouns.

6. a ação

7. o homem

8. o jornal

9. o mês

10. o professor

ANSWERS

PRACTICE 1: 1. o; **2.** o; **3.** a; **4.** o; **5.** a; **6.** a; **7.** a; **8.** o; **9.** o; **10.** a

PRACTICE 2: 1. the hotels; **2.** the cars; **3.** the beaches; **4.** the books; **5.** the offices; **6.** as ações; **7.** os homens; **8.** os jornais; **9.** os meses; **10.** os professores.

———————— Lesson 2 (phrases) ————————

PHRASE LIST 1

a mulher e o homem	*the woman and the man*
sou americano	*I'm American (m.)*
ela é italiana	*she's Italian*
sou casada	*I'm married (f.)*
daqui	*from here*
Que legal!	*How nice! (infml.)*
e você?	*and you?*
este/esta é	*this is (m./f.)*
estes/estas são	*these are (m./f.)*

Muito prazer!	It's a pleasure!
o meu amigo	my friend (m.)
a nossa diretora	our director (f.)
Adoro Nova Iorque.	I love New York.
a casa grande	the big house
o apartamento pequeno	the small apartment

NUTS & BOLTS 1
SUBJECT PRONOUNS

Here are the subject pronouns in Portuguese.

eu	I
você	you (sg.)
ele	he, it
ela	she, it
nós	we
vocês	you (pl.)
eles	they (m.)
elas	they (f.)

Notice that there are two forms of *you* in Portuguese, singular and plural. In fact, you'll also come across **tu** (sg., infml.) in Portugal, as well as the archaic **vós** (pl., infml.) in literature and poetry. Also notice that in Portuguese the third person plural *they* has both a masculine and a feminine form. For mixed groups of people, use the masculine. Finally, keep in mind that all nouns have gender, so **ele** can mean *it* for a masculine noun, and **ela** can mean *it* for a feminine noun. The same is true of **eles** and **elas** in the plural.

Elas são japonesas.

They are Japanese. (Referring to two or more Japanese women)

Eles são franceses.

They are French. (Referring to two or more French men, or to a mixed group)

O jornal? Ele está aqui.

The newspaper? It's here.

PRACTICE 1

Replace each phrase with a subject pronoun.

Ex: Eu e Paulo

nós

1. Pedro
2. Mariana
3. Mariana e Sofia
4. Eu, Mariana, e Pedro

5. Pedro e Paulo
6. Mariana e Pedro
7. Pedro, Mariana, e Sofia
8. Você, Mariana, e Paulo

PHRASE LIST 2

bom dia	*good morning*
boa tarde	*good afternoon*
boa noite	*good evening, good night*
até mais	*see you later*
tudo bem	*everything's fine*
Como vai?	*How are you?*
o novo engenheiro	*the new engineer (m.)*
a nova arquiteta	*the new architect (f.)*
os velhos amigos	*the old friends*
o homem alto	*the tall man*
muito obrigado/muito obrigada	*thank you very much (m./f.)*

de nada	*you're welcome*
de Los Angeles	*from Los Angeles*
com licença	*excuse me*

NUTS & BOLTS 2
SER *(TO BE)*

Now, let's look at one of the most important verbs, **ser** *(to be)*.

eu sou	*I am*
você é	*you are*
ele é	*he is*
ela é	*she is*
nós somos	*we are*
vocês são	*you are*
eles são	*they are (m. or mixed)*
elas são	*they are (f.)*

As in English, **ser** can be used to express nationality or place of origin with the preposition **de** *(of)*.

Eu sou italiano.
I'm Italian.

Ele é de Nova Iorque.
He's from New York.

It's also used to give professions and occupations and to describe inherent characteristics of people, places, and things.

Eu sou turista.
I'm a tourist.

Pedro é professor.
Pedro's a teacher.

O Brasil é grande.
Brazil is big.

Ana é casada.
Ana is married.

One thing to keep in mind is that **ser** is not used in Portuguese to express location or changing qualities of people or things. There's another verb that's used to do that, which we'll come back to later.

PRACTICE 2
Complete with the correct form of the verb **ser**.

1. Ele _____ brasileiro. *(He's Brazilian.)*

2. Você _____ de Los Angeles. *(You're from Los Angeles.)*

3. Helena _____ professora. *(Helena is a teacher.)*

4. Eu _____ casado. *(I'm married.)*

5. A casa _____ grande. *(The house is big.)*

6. Você _____ o novo médico. *(You're the new doctor.)*

7. Tom _____ meu amigo. *(Tom is my friend.)*

8. Ela _____ americana. *(She's American.)*

9. Nós _____ aqui. *(We're here.)*

10. Elas _____ de Nova Iorque. *(They're from New York. [f.])*

ANSWERS
PRACTICE 1: 1. Ele; **2.** Ela; **3.** Elas; **4.** Nós; **5.** Eles; **6.** Eles; **7.** Eles; **8.** Vocês

PRACTICE 2: 1. é; **2.** é; **3.** é; **4.** sou; **5.** é; **6.** é; **7.** é; **8.** é; **9.** somos; **10.** são

SENTENCE LIST 1

Este é meu amigo Roberto.	*This is my friend Roberto.*
Eu sou americana.	*I am American. (f.)*
Eu sou de Nova Iorque.	*I'm from New York.*
Você é do Rio?	*Are you from Rio?*
Nós não somos do Rio.	*We're not from Rio.*
Eu nasci em Curitiba.	*I was born in Curitiba.*
De onde você é?	*Where are you from?*
Eu sou casado.	*I am married. (m.)*
Ele é solteiro.	*He's single.*
Elas são daqui.	*They're from here. (f.)*

NUTS & BOLTS 1
NUMBERS 1–20

1	um/uma *(m./f.)*	9	nove
2	dois/duas *(m./f.)*	10	dez
3	três	11	onze
4	quatro	12	doze
5	cinco	13	treze
6	seis	14	quatorze
7	sete	15	quinze
8	oito	16	dezessis

17	dezessete	19	dezenove
18	dezoito	20	vinte

Notice that the numbers *one* and *two* have both masculine and feminine forms. So you'd say **uma mulher e um homem** *(one woman and one man)* and **duas casas e dois carros** *(two houses and two cars).*

PRACTICE 1

Complete each sentence with the correct form of the verb **ser.**

1. Nós _____ de Nova Iorque. _____ americanos. *(We're from New York. We're Americans.)*

2. Pedro e Mariana _____ casados. Eles não _____ solteiros. *(Pedro and Maria are married. They're not single.)*

3. Os dois amigos _____ estudantes. *(The two friends are students.)*

4. Os três estudantes _____ da Califórnia? *(Are the three friends from California?)*

5. As duas professoras _____ italianas. *(The two teachers are Italian. [f.])*

SENTENCE LIST 2

Gostaria de apresentá-lo ao Sr. José Luís.	I'd like to introduce you to Mr. José Luís.
Ouvi falar que é muito grande.	I've heard it's very big.
Muito prazer em conhecê-lo também.	It's a pleasure to meet you, too.
Nós somos de São Paulo.	We're from São Paulo. (m.)
Elas são italianas.	They're Italian. (f.)
Ele é nosso gerente de vendas.	He's our sales manager.

Como você se chama?	*What's your name?*
Esta loja é grande.	*This store is big.*
Estas ruas são estreitas.	*These streets are narrow.*
Não conheço os Estados Unidos.	*I don't know the United States.*

NUTS & BOLTS 2
NEGATION

To form a negative sentence, just put **não** *(not)* before the verb.

Eu não sou brasileiro.
I'm not Brazilian.

Ela não é arquiteta.
She's not an architect.

Nós não somos casados.
We're not married.

Notice that when answering a question in the negative, you'll use **não** twice: **Você é brasileiro? Não, não sou brasileiro. Eu sou americano.** *(Are you Brazilian? No, I'm not Brazilian. I'm American.)* The first **não** means *no,* and the second one means *not.*

PRACTICE 2

Answer these questions in the negative.

1. Pedro é casado? *(Is Pedro married?)*

2. Os jornais são americanos? *(Are the newspapers American?)*

3. Você é de São Paulo? *(Are you from São Paulo?)*

4. Vocês são do Paraná? *(Are you [pl.] from Paraná?)*

5. Carolina é de Boston? *(Is Carolina from Boston?)*

6. As crianças são francesas? *(Are the children French?)*

Cool link

Go to www.fas.harvard.edu/~rll/resources/portuguese/resources
_portuguese.html

Click on *Language Resources,* and you'll find online dictionaries, translators, grammar explanations, and a wealth of other links that will help you learn Portuguese. It's always a great idea to play with the dictionaries and translators, because this increases your vocabulary. Start a Portuguese Journal and write down the new words and expressions you discover. As you learn how to use verbs and form more complex sentences, you can even start jotting down a few sentences about your day, your family, your job . . . your life, in Portuguese!

ANSWERS
PRACTICE 1: **1.** somos, somos; **2.** são, são; **3.** são; **4.** são; **5.** são

PRACTICE 2: **1.** Não, Pedro não é casado. **2.** Não, os jornais não são americanos. **3.** Não, eu não sou de São Paulo. **4.** Não, nós não somos do Paraná. **5.** Não, Carolina não é de Boston. **6.** Não, as crianças não são francesas.

——————— Lesson 4 (conversations) ———————

CONVERSATION 1
Listen in as Cláudia, Paul, and Eduardo greet one another at the office.

Eduardo: Bom dia, Dona Cláudia. Gostaria de apresentá-la ao Senhor Paul Jones. O Seu Paul é o nosso novo arquiteto. Ele é de Los Angeles.

Cláudia: Como vai, Seu Paul. Muito prazer em conhecê-lo.

Paul: O prazer é todo meu.

Eduardo:	Seu Paul, a Dona Cláudia é nossa diretora de vendas.
Paul:	A senhora é do Rio?
Cláudia:	Não, não sou. Eu sou italiana, sou de Milão.
Eduardo:	A Dona Cláudia trabalha na nossa filial de São Paulo.
Paul:	Não conheço São Paulo, mas ouvi falar que é uma cidade muito grande.
Cláudia:	É verdade. Com licença, mas preciso ir agora. Até logo.

Eduardo:	*Good morning, Ms. Claudia. I'd like to introduce you to Mr. Paul Jones. He's our new architect. He's from Los Angeles.*
Claudia:	*How are you, Mr. Jones? It's a pleasure to meet you.*
Paul:	*The pleasure is all mine.*
Eduardo:	*Paul, Ms. Claudia is our sales director.*
Paul:	*Are you from Rio?*
Claudia:	*No, I'm not. I'm Italian. I'm from Milan.*
Eduardo:	*Ms. Claudia works in our São Paulo branch.*
Paul:	*I've never been to São Paulo, but I've heard it's a very big city.*
Claudia:	*That's true. Excuse me, but I have to go now. See you soon.*

NOTES

Although Brazilians are, in general, informal people, a certain level of formality is required when addressing an older person or someone of a higher professional status. Titles such as **Senhor/Senhores** *(Mr., sg./pl.)*, **Senhora/Senhoras** *(Mrs., sg./pl.)*, **Seu** *(Mr., Sir)*, and **Dona** *(Mrs., Ms., Ma'am)* are used. **Seu** and **Dona** are commonly used in speech, and they're usually followed by a first name. In writing, the abbreviations **Sr.** *(Mr.)* and **Sra.** *(Mrs.)* are used. Also note that in formal conversation, **o Senhor** and **a Senhora** are used in place of **você**, and **os Senhores** and **as Senhoras** in place of **vocês**.

NUTS & BOLTS 1
Pronunciation and special symbols

You've probably noticed that some words in Portuguese use special orthographic symbols or accents. The **til** *(tilde)* indicates a nasal vowel: **não** *(no)*, **ações** *(actions)*. The **acento agudo** *(acute accent)* is used to show stress, and in the case of **á, é,** and **ó** to also mark an open vowel: **possível** *(possible)*, **único** *(exclusive)*, **herói** *(hero)*, **nós** *(we)*, **chá** *(tea)*, **café** *(coffee)*. The **acento circunflexo** *(circumflex accent)* is used to show that a vowel is stressed and closed: **você** *(you)*, **avô** *(grandfather)*, **lâmpada** *(lamp)*. The **acento grave** *(grave accent)* is only used to distinguish certain words: **a** *(the)*, **à** *(to the)*. And the **cedilha** *(cedilla)* is used on **ç** before **a, o,** and **u** to indicate the sound *s* as in *see:* **açúcar** *(sugar)*. Notice that the second **c** in **açúcar** is pronounced as *k* in *kite*.

PRACTICE 1
Answer the questions with a complete sentence following the cues provided.

Ex. Você e de Roma? (Não, de Milão.)

Não, eu não sou de Roma. Eu sou de Milão.

1. O Senhor e de São Paulo? (Não, de Miami.)
2. Você é de Paris? (Não, de Londres.)
3. Ela é da Califórnia? (Não, da Bahia.)
4. Dona Claudia é a nova gerente? (Não, nova diretora.)
5. Eles são espanhóis? (Não, alemães.)

CONVERSATION 2
Listen to Felipe as he introduces his American friend, Paul, to Ana.

Felipe: Oi, Ana. Tudo bem?

Ana: Bem, e você?

Felipe: Também. Ana, este é meu amigo Paul. Ele é americano.

Ana: Oi, Paul. Prazer.

Paul: O prazer é meu.

Ana: De onde você é?

Paul: Eu sou de Nova Iorque.

Ana: Que legal! Adoro Nova Iorque.

Paul: E você, Ana? Você é do Rio?

Ana: Não, não sou daqui. Eu nasci em Curitiba, sou do Paraná. Bem, preciso ir. Até mais.

Felipe e Paul: Tchau, Ana.

Felipe: Hi, Ana. How's everything?

Ana: Fine, and you?

Felipe: Fine, too. Ana, this is my friend Paul. He's American.

Ana: Hi, Paul. It's a pleasure to meet you.

Paul: The pleasure is mine.

Ana: Where are you from?

Paul: I'm from New York.

Ana: That's nice! I love New York.

Paul: And you, Ana? Are you from Rio?

Ana: No, I'm not from here. I was born in Curitiba, I'm from Paraná. Well, I have to go. See you later.

Felipe and Paul: Bye, Ana.

NUTS & BOLTS 2

ASKING YES/NO QUESTIONS

To ask a simple yes/no question in Portuguese, just use the same word order as in a statement, but with question intonation.

Elas são colombianas?

Are they Colombian?

Eles são suíços?

Are they Swiss?

Ela é arquiteta?

Is she an architect?

PRACTICE 2

Complete the informal dialogue with these expressions:

Bem, e você? De onde você é? Oi, prazer. Você é americano? Até mais

> Felipe: Oi, Mariana. Tudo bem?
> Mariana: 1_____
> Felipe: Também. Este é meu amigo Bill.
> Mariana: 2_____
> Bill: O prazer é meu.
> Mariana: 3_____
> Bill: Não, não sou americano.
> Mariana: 4_____
> Bill: Sou da Inglaterra, sou inglês.
> Mariana: Preciso ir. 5_____

Discovery activity

Go around your house and pick out ten or fifteen objects that are important fixtures in your everyday life. Look up their Portuguese equivalents in a dictionary or online reference, and write the new words on labels. Then, label the objects, along with **o** or **a**, depending on gender. You could also practice the plurals. For example, on the refrigerator put a note that says **a geladeira/as geladeiras**. Every time you see the Portuguese words, say them aloud for practice. Before you know it, you'll have added those words to your vocabulary.

ANSWERS

PRACTICE 1: 1. Não, eu não sou de São Paulo. Eu sou de Miami. **2.** Não, eu não sou de Paris. Eu sou de Londres. **3.** Não, ela não é da Califórnia. Ela é da Bahia. **4.** Não, ela não é a nova gerente. Ela é a nova diretora. **5.** Não, eles não são espanhóis, Eles são alemães.

PRACTICE 2: 1. Bem, e você? **2.** Oi, prazer. **3.** Você é americano? **4.** De onde você é? **5.** Até mais.

UNIT 1 ESSENTIALS

Como vai?

How are you?

Até logo.

Bye.

Ele é professor.

He is a teacher.

Eu sou americano.

I am American.

Você é do Rio?

Are you from Rio?

Elas são casadas.

They are married.

De onde vocês são?

Where are you from?

A senhora é a nova arquiteta?

Are you the new architect?

O senhor não é o novo professor?

Aren't you the new teacher?

A Dona Mariana é de São Paulo.

Ms. Mariana is from São Paulo.

Com licença.

Excuse me.

Gostaria de apresentá-lo ao Seu Ricardo.

I'd like to introduce you to Mr. Ricardo.

Muito prazer em conhecê-lo.

It's a pleasure to meet you.

Obrigado/a.

Thank you. (m./f.)

De nada.

You're welcome.

Unit 2
Talking about the family

Tudo bem? In Unit 2 you'll learn how to talk about your family and your home, so you'll learn a lot of very useful vocabulary. You'll also learn how to use adjectives to describe people and things, and possessives, so you'll be able to talk about your family and ask about someone else's. Ready?

——————————— Lesson 5 (words) ———————————

WORD LIST 1
Don't forget that **o** is *the* (m.) and **a** is *the* (f.). With these articles, you'll be able to tell the gender of nouns in the vocabulary lists.

o pai, a mãe	*father, mother*
o filho, a filha	*son, daughter*
o primo, a prima	*cousin*
o irmão, a irmã	*brother, sister*
o avô, a avó	*grandfather, grandmother*
o tio, a tia	*uncle, aunt*
o sobrinho, a sobrinha	*nephew, niece*
o marido	*husband*
a mulher	*wife, woman*
a gente	*people, we (conversational)*
a pessoa, as pessoas	*person, people*

NOTES

A gente literally means *the people,* but it's also used in informal conversation to mean *we:* **a gente é da Argentina** *(we are from Argentina),* **a gente é estudante** *(we are students).* Compare this to **a pessoa** *(person)* and **as pessoas** *(people, more than one individual per-*

son). To talk about people, as in a group of people from a country, use **o povo: o povo brasileiro é feliz** *(Brazilians are a happy people).*

NUTS & BOLTS 1
INDEFINITE ARTICLES
Just as in English, there are two kinds of articles in Portuguese, definite and indefinite.

You already know the definite articles **o, a, os, as** *(the),* so now let's look at the indefinite articles and learn how to use them.

	singular	plural
masculine	**um** *(a/an)*	**uns** *(some)*
feminine	**uma** *(a/an)*	**umas** *(some)*

The singulars can be translated as *a* or *an*: **um quarto** *(a bedroom),* **um banheiro** *(a bathroom),* **um gabinete** *(a cabinet),* **uma estante** *(a bookcase),* **uma cama** *(a bed),* **uma chave** *(a key).* The plurals can be translated as some: **uns quartos** *(some bedrooms),* **uns banheiros** *(some bathrooms),* **uns gabinetes** *(some cabinets),* **umas estantes** *(some bookcases),* **umas camas** *(some beds),* **umas chaves** *(some keys).*

PRACTICE 1
Choose the indefinite article for each of the following nouns, and then translate.

1. professora
2. escritórios
3. hotel
4. canetas
5. mesa

6. jornais
7. camisas
8. dias
9. pessoas
10. turista

WORD LIST 2

o quarto	*bedroom*
o computador	*computer*
o toca CD	*CD player*
a televisão/a TV	*television/TV*
o sofá	*sofa*
a cadeira	*chair*
a mesa	*table*
a sala	*living room*
a cozinha	*kitchen*
o banheiro	*bathroom*
a janela	*window*
a porta	*door*
a piscina	*swimming pool*
Tudo bem?	*How's it going?/How are you doing?*
Puxa!	*Wow!/Gee!/Oh, no!*
Que pena!	*What a pity!/That's too bad!*

NUTS & BOLTS 2

Há *(THERE IS/THERE ARE)*

Há means both *there is* and *there are*. Note that there's no pronoun like *there* used.

Há uma casa. Não há uma casa. Há uma casa?
There's a house. There isn't a house. Is there a house?

Há vinte quartos no hotel.
There are twenty bedrooms in the hotel.

Há uns americanos na casa.
There are some Americans in the house.

PRACTICE 2

Form sentences with **há** and the following nouns. Then, form questions and give the answers in the negative with **não**.

Ex. uma casa

Há uma casa. Há uma casa? Não, não há uma casa.

1. uns hotéis *(some hotels)*
2. umas chaves *(some keys)*
3. uma piscina *(a pool)*
4. uma pessoa *(a person)*
5. uns americanos *(some Americans)*

Culture note

The Brazilian family is a very tightly knit group. This can be seen in a few ways. For example, children typically live with their parents until they get married, and even then, in some less prosperous households, the newlyweds will live with one set of in-laws. Also, Brazilians don't usually "go off" to college. They stay in their hometown, and they choose a university they can attend while living with their parents who, in most cases, would not have it any other way, especially where daughters are concerned. Finally, families typically get together every Sunday for a lunch with a large part of the extended family. This usually starts at around 1:00 P.M., and it goes on until the soccer games begin on TV around 3:00 P.M.

ANSWERS

PRACTICE 1: 1. uma professora (a teacher); **2.** uns escritórios (some offices); **3.** um hotel (a hotel); **4.** umas canetas (some pens); **5.** uma mesa (a table); **6.** uns jornais (some newspapers); **7.** umas camisas (some shirts); **8.** uns dias (some days); **9.** umas pessoas (some people); **10.** um turista (a male tourist) or uma turista (a female tourist)

PRACTICE 2: 1. Há uns hotéis. Há uns hotéis? Não, não há uns hotéis. **2.** Há umas chaves. Há umas chaves? Não, não há umas chaves. **3.** Há uma piscina. Há uma piscina? Não, não há uma piscina. **4.** Há uma pessoa. Há uma pessoa? Não, não há uma pessoa. **5.** Há uns americanos. Há uns americanos? Não, não há uns americanos.

PHRASE LIST 1

Está certo.	*Okay./It's all right.*
Como está?	*How are you doing?*
Está tudo bem?	*Is everything all right?*
Você está bem?	*Are you well?*
Você está pronto?	*Are you ready?*
Está quente.	*It's hot.*
Está frio.	*It's cold.*
o ar condicionado	*air conditioning*
o aquecimento central	*central heating*
Estou aqui.	*I'm here.*
uma casa grande	*a big house*
uma rua estreita	*a narrow street*
a avenida comprida	*the long avenue*
uns computadores novos	*some new computers*
um sofá confortável	*a comfortable sofa*
uma cozinha ótima	*a great kitchen*
a banheira grande	*the big bathtub*
o banheiro limpo	*the clean bathroom*

NUTS & BOLTS 1

ESTAR *(TO BE)*

In Unit 1, you learned that the verb **ser (eu sou, você e, ele/ela é, nós somos, vocês são, ele/ela são)** is used to talk about places of origin, to state professions and occupations, and to describe inherent characteristics of people, places, or things. **Estar** also means *to be,* but it is used a bit differently. First, let's see its forms.

eu estou	nós estamos
você está	vocês estão
ele/ela está	eles/elas estão

Estar is used to express locations and temporary qualities or states, while ser is used to express more permanent characteristics. Compare está frio *(it's cold)* with Alaska é frio *(Alaska is cold)*. Here are some other examples of estar.

Eu estou aqui.
I'm here.

Nós estamos bem.
We're fine.

Está quente.
It's hot.

PRACTICE 1

Complete each sentence with the correct form of estar.

1a. Você _____ pronto? *(Are you ready?)*

1b. Não, não _____ pronto. *(No, I'm not ready.)*

2a. O gato e o cachorro _____ na sala? *(Are the cat and the dog in the living room?)*

2b. Não, eles não _____ na sala, eles _____ no quarto. *(No, they're not in the living room, they're in the bedroom.)*

3a. A: Você e a Carolina _____ na França? *(Are you and Carolina in France?)*

3b. Não, nós não _____ na França, nós _____ na Espanha. *(No, we're not in France, we're in Spain.)*

4a. O quarto _____ quente? *(Is the bedroom hot?)*

4b. Não, o quarto não _____ quente, o quarto _____ frio. *(No, the bedroom is not hot, the bedroom is cold.)*

5a. Os carros _____ aqui? *(Are the cars here?)*

5b. Não, os carros não _____ aqui, os carros _____ na garagem. *(No, the cars aren't here, the cars are in the garage.)*

PHRASE LIST 2

os cabelos castanhos	*the brown hair*
os cabelos grisalhos	*the gray hair*
os olhos escuros	*the dark eyes*
a mulher jovem	*the young woman*
a poltrona confortável	*the comfortable armchair*
as mesas redondas	*the round tables*
os carros importados	*the imported cars*
o vizinho amigável	*the friendly neighbor*
o livro velho	*the old book*
as primas francesas	*the French cousins*
as pessoas altas	*the tall people*
as caixas quadradas	*the square boxes*

NUTS & BOLTS 2

ADJECTIVE AGREEMENT

When you use an adjective to describe a noun in Portuguese, you have to make the adjective agree with the noun. That usually means that adjectives will have the familiar endings -o (m. sg.), -a (f. sg.), -os (m. pl.) and -as (f. pl.). Take a look at these examples, and notice that the adjective typically follows the noun in Portuguese.

	singular	plural
masculine	**o carro pequeno** *(the small car)*	**os carros pequenos** *(the small cars)*
feminine	**a casa pequena** *(the small house)*	**as casas pequenas** *(the small houses)*

This is the typical pattern of endings for adjectives that end in -o in the masculine singular form, which is what you'll see in dictionaries, because it's considered the basic form. Some other examples are: **o livro velho** *(the old book)*, **os livros velhos** *(the old* *books)*, **a filha bonita** *(the pretty daughter)*, **as filhas bonitas** *(the pretty daughters)*, **o barco rápido** *(the fast boat)*, **os barcos rápidos** *(the fast boats)*, **a revista nova** *(the new magazine)*, and **as revistas novas** *(the new magazines).* There are a few irregular adjectives, for example **bom** *(good)* and **mau** *(bad).*

o filme bom *(the good film)*	**os filmes bons** *(the good films)*
a festa boa *(the good party)*	**as festas boas** *(the good parties)*
o menino mau *(the bad boy)*	**os meninos maus** *(the bad boys)*
a menina má *(the bad girl)*	**as meninas más** *(the bad girls)*

Adjectives that end in **-e** or in a consonant usually have just one form for the singular, and one form for the plural. Just as is the case with nouns, if an adjective ends in **-l** in the singular, it will drop the **-l** and add **-is,** and if it ends in **-m** in the singular, it will end in **-ns** in the plural.

o banheiro grande *(the big bathroom)*	**os banheiros grandes** *(the big bathrooms)*
a banheira grande *(the big bathtub)*	**as banheiras grandes** *(the big bathtubs)*
a cadeira confortável *(the comfortable chair)*	**as cadeiras confortáveis** *(the comfortable chairs)*
o sofá confortável *(the comfortable sofa)*	**os sofás confortáveis** *(the comfortable sofas)*
o café ruim *(the bad coffee)*	**os cafés ruins** *(the bad coffees)*
a maçã ruim *(the bad apple)*	**as maçãs ruins** *(the bad apples)*

PRACTICE 2

Fill in the blanks with one of the following adjectives: **cheias** *(full)*, **boa** *(good)*, **fechados** *(closed)*, **altas** *(tall)*, **caro** *(expensive)*, **frio** *(cold)*, **confortável** *(comfortable)*, **redondas** *(round)*, **americana** *(American)*, **castanhos** *(brown)*.

1. As mesas são _____.

2. Os cabelos são _____.

3. O café não está _____, o café está quente.

4. Os bancos estão _____.

5. Há umas mulheres _____ na loja.

6. O BMW é um carro _____.

7. A revista "Time" é inglesa? Não, a revista "Time" é _____.

8. Há uma cama _____?

9. As xícaras estão _____? Não, as xícaras estão vazias.

10. A praia é _____? Não, a praia é ruim.

Cool link

Check out the following link to the CIA World Factbook. It has a wealth of facts, figures and updated information on Brazil.

https://cia.gov/cia/publications/factbook/geos/br.html

And here's a link to the same information on Portugal.

https://cia.gov/cia/publications/factbook/geos/po.html

But don't stop there! There are plenty of other Portuguese-speaking countries to explore: Angola, Cape Verde, East Timor, Guinea-Bissau, Mozambique, and São Tomé and Príncipe.

ANSWERS
PRACTICE 1: 1a. está; **1b.** estou; **2a.** estão; **2b.** estão, estão; **3a.** estão; **3b.** estamos, estamos; **4a.** está; **4b.** está, está; **5a.** estão; **5b.** estão, estão

PRACTICE 2: 1. redondas; **2.** castanhos; **3.** frio; **4.** fechados; **5.** altas; **6.** caro; **7.** americana; **8.** confortável; **9.** cheias; **10.** boa

---
Lesson 7 (sentences)

SENTENCE LIST 1

O meu passaporte é americano.	*My passport is American.*
A minha mulher é advogada.	*My wife is a lawyer.*
Os meus olhos são castanhos.	*My eyes are brown.*
As minhas primas são solteiras.	*My cousins are single. (f.)*
Os meus pais são velhos.	*My parents are old.*
O meu país é moderno.	*My country is modern.*
Os seus documentos estão em ordem.	*Your documents are in order.*
Os nossos pratos são velhos.	*Our plates are old.*
As nossas amigas são húngaras.	*Our friends are Hungarian.*
A sua colher está suja.	*Your spoon is dirty.*
As nossas facas estão limpas.	*Our knives are clean.*

NUTS & BOLTS 1
POSSESSIVE ADJECTIVES (I)
A possessive adjective is a kind of adjective that shows possession, like the English *my, your, her, our,* and so on. A possessive pronoun is similar, but it actually stands in for a noun, like *mine, yours, hers, ours,* and so on. Thankfully, possessive nouns and pronouns in Portuguese have the same forms:

Possessive adjectives	Possessive pronouns
o meu livro *(my book)*	**O livro é meu.** *(The book is mine.)*
os meus livros *(my books)*	**Os livros são meus.** *(The books are mine.)*
o seu livro *(your book)*	**O livro é seu.** *(The book is yours.)*
os seus livros *(your books)*	**Os livros são seus.** *(The books are yours.)*
os nossos livros *(our books)*	**Os livros são nossos.** *(The books are ours.)*

As you can probably guess, possessives have to agree in number and gender. But keep in mind that they agree with the thing possessed, rather than the possessor. Below you'll see the full chart for *my, your,* and *our.* We'll come back to the forms for *his, her,* and *their* a bit later.

Singular	Plural
o meu carro *(my car)*	**os meus carros** *(my cars)*
a minha casa *(my house)*	**as minhas casas** *(my houses)*
o seu carro *(your car)*	**os seus carros** *(your cars)*
a sua casa *(your house)*	**as suas casas** *(your houses)*
o nosso carro *(our car)*	**os nossos carros** *(our cars)*
a nossa casa *(our house)*	**as nossas casas** *(our houses)*

The use of the article with the possessive adjective is optional, but most native speakers use it. However, with possessive pronouns it is usually omitted: **o meu carro é importado, o carro importado é meu** *(my car is imported, the imported car is mine).*

PRACTICE 1
Use the translations to fill in the blanks with the correct possessive.

1. A _____ tia é americana. *(My aunt is American.)*

2. O _____ tio é brasileiro. *(My uncle is Brazilian.)*

3. Os _____ irmãos são altos. *(My brothers are tall.)*

4. As _____ irmãs são jovens. *(My sisters are young.)*

5. Os _____ pais são brasileiros? *(Are your parents Brazilian?)*

6. O _____ carro e importado? *(Is your car imported?)*

7. A _____ poltrona e confortável? *(Is your armchair comfortable?)*

8. As _____ praias são lindas. *(Our beaches are beautiful.)*

9. Os _____ escritórios são modernos. *(Our offices are modern.)*

10. A _____ professora é legal. *(Our teacher is nice.)*

SENTENCE LIST 2

Os nossos maridos estão aqui.	*Our husbands are here.*
A minha prima é italiana.	*My cousin is Italian.*
A minha prima está em casa.	*My cousin is at home.*
O banheiro está ocupado.	*The bathroom is occupied.*
O meu quarto é pequeno, mas é confortável.	*My room is small, but it is comfortable.*
Os sofás são caros, mas são lindos.	*The sofas are expensive, but they are nice.*
Os seus olhos são castanhos?	*Are your eyes brown?*

O meu carro está na minha casa.	*My car is in my house.*
O meu quarto não está limpo.	*My room is not clean.*
Os nossos quartos são ótimos.	*Our rooms are great.*

NUTS & BOLTS 2
SER vs. ESTAR

Let's take a moment to compare **ser** and **estar,** both of which mean *to be.* **Ser** is used to express inherent or more or less permanent qualities, including nationalities, occupations, and fixed or geographical locations. It is also used to express possession and to tell the time.

O Sr. Pedro é professor, e a Dona Mariana é doutora.
Mr. Pedro is a teacher, and Ms. Mariana is a doctor.

A porta é grande.
The door is big.

Maria é alta.
Maria is tall.

Eu sou americana.
I am American. (f.)

A Itália é na Europa.
Italy is in Europe.

O escritório é na Rua Dutra.
The office is on Dutra Street.

O livro é meu.
The book is mine.

É uma hora.
It's one o'clock.

Estar is used to express more temporary or changeable characteristics, like transient conditions or states, temporary locations, and the weather.

A porta está aberta.
The door is open.

Maria está doente.
Maria is sick.

O lápis está na mesa.
The pencil is on the table.

O carro está na Rua Dutra.
The car is on Dutra Street.

Está quente.
It's hot.

PRACTICE 2

Choose **ser** or **estar** in each of the sentences below.

1. A piscina (está/é) cheia.

2. Peter e John (são/estão) americanos.

3. Como você (está/é)? Eu (estou/sou) bem.

4. As minhas irmãs (são/estão) altas.

5. O seu pai (está/é) engenheiro ou arquiteto?

6. O copo (está/é) meu ou seu?

7. Eu (estou/sou) na praia.

8. A praia de Copacabana (está/é) no Rio de Janeiro.

9. Eu e meu marido (estamos/somos) no hotel.

10. O seu café (está/é) quente? Não, meu café (está/é) frio.

Discovery activity

Make a list of things you're surrounded by in your daily life, in other words, nouns that you see in your house, at the office, on the street, etc. Then think of adjectives that you could use to describe them. Make phrases such as **o carro novo** *(the new car)*, being careful of course to use the right adjective agreement. Then decide whether you're describing a permanent characteristic or a more temporary situation, and add the verb **ser** or **estar** to form complete sentences. Use your dictionary or an online reference to help you expand your vocabulary.

ANSWERS
PRACTICE 1: minha; **2.** meu; **3.** meus; **4.** minhas; **5.** seus; **6.** seu; **7.** sua; **8.** nossas; **9.** nossos; **10.** nossa

PRACTICE 2: **1.** está; **2.** são; **3.** está, estou; **4.** são; **5.** é; **6.** é; **7.** estou; **8.** é; **9.** estamos; **10.** está, está

——————— Lesson 8 (conversations) ———————

CONVERSATION 1
Listen in as Márcia and Ricardo talk on their cell phones about a house for rent.

> Márcia: Alô querido. Eu estou na casa. Ela é clara e grande.
>
> Ricardo: Há armários nos quartos?
>
> Márcia: Sim, há armários grandes nos três quartos, e também na cozinha.
>
> Ricardo: E, há lugar para os nossos carros?
>
> Márcia: Sim, há uma garagem grande para dois carros.
>
> Ricardo: E, há estantes para os meus livros?
>
> Márcia: Sim, há muitas estantes. Há estantes nos quartos, e nas duas salas.
>
> Ricardo: Duas salas? Há duas salas na casa?

Márcia:	Sim, há duas salas e há até uma piscina! A casa é perfeita. Estou muito feliz.
Ricardo:	E o aluguel? O aluguel é caro?
Márcia:	Alô. Alô. Ricardo? A ligação está ruim!

Márcia:	*Hello, baby. I'm at the house. It's bright and big.*
Ricardo:	*Are there closets in the bedrooms?*
Márcia:	*Yes, there are big closets in the three bedrooms, and also in the kitchen.*
Ricardo:	*And is there room for our cars?*
Márcia:	*Yes, there's a big two-car garage.*
Ricardo:	*And, are there bookcases for my books?*
Márcia:	*Yes, there are lots of bookcases. There are bookcases in the bedrooms and in the two living rooms.*
Ricardo:	*Two living rooms? There are two living rooms in the house?*
Márcia:	*Yes, there are two living rooms, and there's even a swimming pool! The house is perfect. I'm very happy.*
Ricardo:	*And the rent? Is the rent expensive?*
Márcia:	*Hello. Hello. Ricardo? The connection is bad!*

NUTS & BOLTS 1
POSSESSIVE ADJECTIVES (2)

You've already learned the first and second person possessives, so now let's look at other third person possessives, which correspond to *his, her,* and *their.* You know that **seu, seus, sua,** or **suas** can mean *your,* but they can also mean *his, her,* or *their.* So, **o seu carro é bom** can be translated as *your car is good, his car is good, her car is good,* or *their car is good.* To avoid misunderstanding, instead of **seu** you can use the noun with a definite article, followed by **dele** *(his, of him),* **dela** *(her, of her),* **deles** *(their, of them, m.),* or **delas** *(their, of them, f.).* Let's see how that works.

o seu carro	o carro dele	*his car*
o seu carro	o carro dela	*her car*

o seu carro	o carro deles	*their (m. or mixed) car*
o seu carro	o carro delas	*their (f.) car*

as suas casas	as casas dele	*his houses*
as suas casas	as casas dela	*her houses*
as suas casas	as casas deles	*their (m. or mixed) houses*
as suas casas	as casas delas	*their (f.) houses*

Just like the other possessive adjectives, **dele, dela, deles,** and **delas** can be used as possessive pronouns: **o carro é dela** *(the car is hers)*. Let's look at some example sentences.

A advogada está no seu escritório.
The lawyer is in your/his/her/their office.

A advogada está no escritório dela.
The lawyer is in her office.

Os engenheiros estão nos seus escritórios.
The engineers are in your/his/her/their offices.

Os engenheiros estão nos escritórios deles.
The engineers are in their (own) offices.

Os engenheiros estão no escritório dela.
The engineers are in her office.

Os engenheiros estão no escritório dele.
The engineers are in his office.

PRACTICE 1

Follow the cues to find the correct possessive adjective.

Ex: (livros/meu e meu marido)

Os nossos livros.

1. casas/Marina e Pedro
2. estantes/Ricardo
3. estantes/Carolina
4. filhos/Carolina e Ricardo
5. primas/Ricardo

6. mãe/minha e sua
7. pai/meu e seu
8. quartos/Marina
9. quadros/Pedro
10. amigas/Mariana, Pedro e Carolina

CONVERSATION 2

Listen in while Luiza shows Carolina a picture taken a week earlier at her family reunion.

Luiza: Olhe a foto. Nós estamos na casa de praia.

Carolina: Você está ótima na foto! E as outras pessoas, quem são?

Luiza: A mulher loira é a minha mãe.

Carolina: Puxa, ela é jovem! E o homem alto de cabelos grisalhos?

Luiza: Ele é o meu pai. Ele está tão feliz!

Carolina: Os seus pais são muito elegantes. Quem são as crianças?

Luiza: Eles são os meus sobrinhos. Eles são os filhos do meu irmão Rafael.

Carolina: O seu irmão é muito atraente. Que pena que ele é casado!

Luiza: A mulher dele é muito bonita também. Olhe, ela está aqui. Ela é a morena de cabelos compridos.

Carolina: E o seu marido? Ele não está na foto?
Luiza: Não, ele não está na foto. Ele é o fotógrafo!

Luiza: *Look at the picture. We're at the beach house.*
Carolina: *You look great in the photograph! And the other people, who are they?*
Luiza: *The blond woman is my mother.*
Carolina: *Wow! She looks young. And the tall man with gray hair?*
Luiza: *He's my father. He is so happy!*
Carolina: *Your parents are very elegant. Who are the children?*
Luiza: *They're my nephews. They're my brother Rafael's sons.*
Carolina: *Your brother is very attractive! Too bad he's married!*
Luiza: *His wife is very pretty, too. Look, she's here. She's the brunette with long hair.*
Carolina: *And your husband? Isn't he in the picture?*
Luiza: *He isn't in the picture. He's the photographer!*

NUTS & BOLTS 2
THE NUMBERS 20–100

20	vinte	32	trinta e dois/duas
21	vinte e um/uma	33	trinta e três
22	vinte e dois/duas	40	quarenta
23	vinte e três	50	cinqüenta
30	trinta	60	sessenta
31	trinta e um/uma	70	setenta

80	oitenta	101	cento e um/uma
90	noventa	102	cento e dois/duas
100	cem	103	cento e três

In Unit 1 you learned that **um** *(one)* and **dois** *(two)* have both masculine and feminine forms. The same is true of higher numbers with **um** or **dois**.

Há vinte e duas portas, e há trinta e dois carros.
There are twenty-two doors, and there are thirty-two cars.

PRACTICE 2
Translate these sentences, writing out the numbers.

1. There are forty-two people.

2. There are fifty-one male engineers and sixty-two female architects.

3. There are seventy-two books.

4. There are eighty-one chairs.

5. There are one hundred one women.

6. His forty-two shirts.

7. Her sixty-one pens.

8. His and her fifty-two magazines.

Tip!

As you learned in Unit 1, entering new words into a journal can be a great way to expand your vocabulary. Now try adding to those words. Use a number or an adjective, or use the new word in a sentence. Then write the translation, and add notes on any important information about the new word, like the pronunciation, gender, and so on. Next, think of a synonym and an antonym. You'll see that in no time, you'll have acquired an amazing range of new words. It's easier to learn words when they're linked to others (i.e., chunks of language) than when they stand alone, because it's easier to remember things in context.

ANSWERS
PRACTICE 1: 1. as casas deles; **2.** as estantes dele; **3.** as estantes dela; **4.** os filhos deles; **5.** as primas dele; **6.** nossa mãe; **7.** nosso pai; **8.** os quartos dela; **9.** os quadros dele; **10.** as amigas deles

PRACTICE 2: 1. Há a quarenta e duas pessoas. **2.** Há cinqüenta e um engenheiros e sessenta e duas arquitetas. **3.** Há setenta e dois livros. **4.** Há oitenta e uma cadeiras. **5.** Há cento e uma mulheres. **6.** As quarenta e duas camisas dele. **7.** As sessenta e uma canetas dela. **8.** As cinqüenta e duas revistas deles.

UNIT 2 ESSENTIALS
Há vinte quartos no hotel.
There are twenty rooms in the hotel.

Há uma pessoa no escritório.
There's a person in the office.

Há uns quadros caros nas paredes.
There are some expensive paintings on the walls.

Há vinte e uma revistas e trinta e dois livros na estante.
There are twenty-one magazines and thirty-two books on the bookcase.

O quarto não está quente, o quarto está frio.
The room is not hot, it's cold.

O Alaska não é quente, o Alaska é frio.
Alaska is not hot, Alaska is cold.

O meu quarto é pequeno, mas confortável.
My room is small, but comfortable.

Os nossos colegas estão nos escritórios deles.
Our colleagues are in their offices.

O seu irmão é muito atraente.
Your brother is very attractive.

O carro dela é caro, mas o carro dele é barato.
Her car is expensive, but his car is cheap.

Os nossos filhos são jovens e bonitos.
Our sons/children are young and pretty.

Os nossos quartos são pequenos, mas estão limpos.
Our rooms are small, but they are clean.

Há armários grandes nos três quartos e até uma piscina.
There are big closets in the three bedrooms and even a swimming pool.

Os meus pais estão muito felizes.
My parents are very happy.

Tudo bem? Tudo bem.
How are you doing? I'm fine.

UNIT 3
Everyday life

In Unit 3 you'll learn some new verbs that you'll be able to use to talk about your everyday life. You'll learn how to express your likes and dislikes, and you'll also learn how to ask and give information using question words, such as *what, when,* and *where.* Finally, you'll learn that very useful skill, how to tell time. **Que legal!** *(How cool!)*

—————————— Lessons 9 (words) ——————————

WORD LIST 1

a hora	*hour*
a manhã	*morning*
a tarde	*afternoon*
a noite	*night*
atrasado/a	*late*
adiantado/a	*early*
na hora	*on time*
o relógio	*clock/watch*
todo/s	*every*
o minuto	*minute*
o segundo	*second*
quase	*almost*
hoje	*today*
a atividade	*activity*
a aula	*lesson/class*
a academia	*gym*
o despertador	*alarm clock*
o rádio-relógio	*clock radio*

NUTS & BOLTS 1
TELLING TIME

The word **hora/s** means *hour/s,* and it's also used to ask for and give the time: **Que horas são?** *(What time is it?)* To answer just use **é** for 1:00 and **são** for 2:00 or higher: **É uma hora.** *(It's one o'clock.)* **São duas horas.** *(It's two o'clock.)* Because **hora** is feminine, you have to use the feminine forms **uma** and **duas.** Just like in English, you can specify that a time is *in the early morning* (midnight to 6:00 A.M.) with **da madrugada,** *in the morning* with **da manhã,** *in the afternoon* with **da tarde,** and *in the evening* or *at night* with **da noite.**

São três da madrugada.

It's three in the (early) morning.

São dez da manhã.

It's ten in the morning.

São quatro da tarde.

It's four in the afternoon.

São sete da noite.

It's seven in the evening.

São onze da noite.

It's eleven at night.

To say that it's half past an hour, use **e meia** *(and a half).* To say that it's a quarter past an hour, use **e quinze.** To say that it's quarter to an hour use **quinze para as ...**

São cinco e meia da tarde.

It's 5:30 in the afternoon.

São onze e quinze da manhã.

It's 11:15 in the morning.

São quinze para as dez da noite.

It's 9:45 at night.

To express other times between the hours, use **e** *(and)* for minutes after the hour, and **faltam . . . para** or just **para** for minutes before the hour:

É uma e cinco.
It's 1:05.

São quatro e vinte.
It's 4:20.

Faltam dez para as duas.
It's ten to two.

São vinte para as sete.
It's twenty to seven.

Notice that you have three possible ways of expressing a time like 9:50: **São nove e cinqüenta.** *(It's nine fifty.)* **São dez para as nove.** *(It's ten to ten.)* **Faltam dez para as nove.** *(It's ten minutes before ten.)* One more thing to keep in mind is that the 24-hour clock, or "military" time, is also used for official times or schedules. So, you'll see 13:00 for 1:00 P.M., 15:00 for 3:00 P.M., and so on.

PRACTICE 1
Translate the following.

1. What time is it?

2. It's 10:30.

3. It's 3:15.

4. It's 8:30.

5. It's 3:50. *(Use* faltam.*)*

6. It's 12:30 A.M. *(Use* meia.*)*

7. It's 10:45.

8. It's 1:05 in the afternoon.

WORD LIST 2

depois	*after*
antes	*before*
o café da manhã	*breakfast*
o chuveiro	*shower*

o banho	*bath*
a escova de dentes	*toothbrush*
a pasta de dentes	*toothpaste*
a escova de cabelo	*hairbrush*
o sabonete	*soap*
a garrafa de cerveja	*beer bottle*
o frasco de xampu	*shampoo bottle*
o aparelho de barbear	*razor*
a xícara de café	*coffee cup*
a colher de sopa	*soup spoon*
o copo de vinho	*wineglass*

NUTS & BOLTS 2
THE PREPOSTION DE *(OF)*

A very common and useful preposition in Portuguese is **de,** meaning *of* or *from,* as in: **Eu sou de Nova Iorque.** *(I'm from New York.)* When **de** comes right before a definite article, it forms a contraction: **do (de + o), da (de + a), dos (de + os)** and **das (de + as).** You'll see these contractions a lot in expressions of time or origin, because Portuguese uses definite articles much more often than English does. But note that the definite article isn't used with place names that begin with **São, Santo,** or **Santa,** or with foreign names.

Nós somos do Rio, ele é de São Paulo, e ela é de Chicago.
We're from Rio, he's from São Paulo, and she's from Chicago.

Os meus pais são dos Estados Unidos.
My parents are from the United States.

O seu casaco é da Itália?
Is your coat from Italy?

Minha aula é das seis às sete.
My class is from 6:00 to 7:00.

Notice in the last example the form **às** *(to the)*. It's a contract. with the preposition **a** *(to, at)*, but we'll come back to that. **De** also used to show possession or association:

Esse é o novo carro do Marco.
This is Marco's new car.

O carro do meu pai é branco.
My father's car is white.

Os amigos do meu irmão são legais.
My brother's friends are nice.

De is also used to show contents, to indicate what something is made of, and in the equivalent of compound noun constructions.

Eu gostaria de um copo de vinho, por favor.
I'd like a glass of wine, please.

As prateleiras da estante são de madeira.
The shelves of the bookcase are made of wood.

Eu gostaria de uma nova toalha de banho, por favor.
I'd like a new bath towel, please.

Finally, **de** is used with means of transportation: **de trem** *(by train)*, **de avião** *(by plane)*, **de ônibus** *(by bus)*, **de carro** *(by car)*, **de navio** *(by ship)*, but **a pé** *(on foot)*.

PRACTICE 2
Complete with the appropriate form of **de**.

1. Eles são _____ Nova Iorque. *(They're from New York City.)*

2. Meu amigo é _____ Califórnia. *(My friend is from California.)*

3. As camisas são _____ Paris? Não, as camisas são _____ Barcelona. *(Are the shirts from Paris? No, the shirts are from Barcelona.)*

4. Os copos _____ vinho são _____ minhas amigas. *(The glasses of wine are my friends'.)*

5. O diretor _____ marketing é _____ Japão. *(The marketing director is from Japan.)*

6. Os livros _____ matemática são _____ escola. *(The mathematics books are the school's.)*

7. Os copos _____ suco são _____ estudantes. *(The glasses of juice are the students'.)*

8. Este é o telefone _____ hotel? Não, este é o telefone _____ minha casa. *(Is this the hotel's phone number? No, this is my home phone number.)*

9. A que horas é o café _____ manhã? É_____ das oito às dez da manhã. *(What time is breakfast? It's from 8:00 to 10:00 in the morning.)*

10. As toalhas _____ banho _____ hotel são _____ algodão. *(The hotel bath towels are made of cotton.)*

Culture note

Different cultures have very different relationships with the clock. Of course, statements like "Brazilians are not punctual" are gross generalizations, and they're unfair to the countless individuals who pay careful attention to being on time. But still, speaking in generalizations, it's probably fair to say that punctuality is not as prized a character trait in Brazil as it is in many English-speaking cultures. This observation is the fodder of anthropology papers, psychological analyses, cross-cultural studies, and of course jokes made at the expense of Cariocas, the inhabitants of Rio de Janeiro, who are perhaps the Brazilian champions of tardiness. Paulistas, people from São Paulo and the traditional rivals of Cariocas, would like to think of themselves as punctual, but their punctuality would probably still not pass muster with most Americans. There may be some perfectly understandable reasons for this tendency toward tardiness. For example, traffic in most big cities is chaotic, and traffic delays are often offered as excuses for tardiness. Setting aside the question of whether traffic is *really* behind all of the tardiness, a good piece of advice is that you should expect some degree of tardiness when making appointments with Brazilians for social events. For example, Brazilians usually arrive 30 minutes late for dinner at someone's home, and possibly one hour late for a party. The etiquette for social situations is: **antes tarde do que nunca** *(better late than never!)*

Keep in mind, though, these rules don't apply to business situations. If you're traveling to Brazil on business, you should be on time for your appointments, and you should expect Brazilians to be on time as well. In that respect Brazil follows global business norms; punctuality is expected.

ANSWERS
PRACTICE 1: 1. Que horas são? **2.** São dez e trinta./São dez e meia. **3.** São três e quinze. **4.** São oito e trinta./São oito e meia. **5.** Faltam dez para as quatro. **6.** É meia noite e meia. **7.** São dez e quarenta e cinco./São quinze para as onze. **8.** É uma e cinco da tarde.

PRACTICE 2: 1. de; **2.** da; **3.** de, de; **4.** de, das; **5.** de, do; **6.** de, da; **7.** de, dos; **8.** do, da; **9.** da, das; **10.** de, do, de

─────────────── Lesson 10 (phrases) ───────────────

PHRASE LIST 1

estar atrasado para	*to be late for*
trabalhar muito	*to work a lot*
estudar inglês	*to study English*
morar no Rio	*to live in Rio*

falar português	to speak Portuguese
viajar de trem	to travel by train
encontrar os amigos	to see friends
tirar fotos	to take photos
acordar cedo	to wake up early
combinar encontros	to make plans to meet
tirar férias	to take vacations
entrar no Banco 24 Horas	to go to the ATM
conversar no bar	to talk in a bar
parar no sinal vermelho	to stop at the red light
mandar flores	to send flowers

NUTS & BOLTS 1
REGULAR -AR VERBS

In Portuguese, most regular infinitives (the *to* form of verbs) end in **-ar, -er,** or **-ir.** Each type of infinitive follows a certain conjugation, or pattern of endings, to show agreement with a subject, like the English *you speak* and *she speaks.* In this lesson we'll start with the conjugation of **-ar** verbs such as **falar** *(to speak).*

eu falo	*I speak*	nós falamos	*we speak*
(tu falas)	*you speak*	(vós falais)	*you speak*
você fala	*you speak*	vocês falam	*you speak*
o senhor fala	*you speak (fml. m.)*	os senhores falam	*you speak (fml. m.)*
a senhora fala	*you speak (fml. f.)*	as senhoras falam	*you speak (fml. f.)*
ele fala	*he speaks*	eles falam	*they speak (m./mixed)*
ela fala	*she speaks*	elas falam	*they speak (f.)*

As you can see, to conjugate an -ar verb in the simple present, you take off the -ar and add certain endings depending on the subject. Note that the forms in parentheses are not used in Brazil. In Portugal **tu** *(you)* is used in very informal speech, between members of a family and close friends. In Brazil people use **você** *(you)* when talking to friends, people the same age, and younger people. In the plural, **vocês** is used in both Brazil and Portugal, and **vós** is considered fairly archaic and rarely used. Also note that both countries use **o senhor, a senhora, os senhores,** and **as senhoras** as the less familiar and more polite forms. So, if we take away the less common forms, there are only five forms that you need to focus on: the infinitive, two singular forms, and two plural forms. Let's look at them with another verb, **estudar** *(to study).*

eu estudo	nós estudamos
você, ele, ela, o senhor, a senhora estuda	eles, elas, vocês, os senhores, as senhoras estudam

Let's see some examples. Note that you can usually drop the pronouns **eu** and **nós,** because it's plain from the ending who the subject is.

Estudo inglês.
I study English.

Você fala português.
You speak Portuguese.

Estudamos inglês.
We study English.

Freqüentemente falamos de livros.
We often speak about books.

Here are some more common and useful -ar verbs. They're all conjugated in exactly the same way as **falar** and **estudar**.

morar	*to live*	**conversar**	*to talk*
trabalhar	*to work*	**parar**	*to stop*
viajar	*to travel*	**olhar**	*to look at*
encontrar	*to find, to meet up*	**chamar**	*to call*
tirar	*to take out or off*	**começar**	*to begin, to start*
acordar	*to wake up*	**terminar**	*to finish*
combinar	*to make plans*	**mandar**	*to send*
entrar	*to enter, to go in*	**usar**	*to use*

Don't forget that questions use the same word order, and **não** *(not)* is placed before the verb in negative sentences.

Você mora aqui?
Do you live here?

Você não mora aqui.
You don't live here.

Notice that the Portuguese simple present can be translated differently in English, according to context.

Eu falo francês e italiano.
I speak French and Italian.

Eu falo português neste momento.
Right now I'm speaking Portuguese.

Sim, é verdade. Eu realmente falo português!
Yes, it's true. I do speak Portuguese!

PRACTICE 1
Supply the correct form of the verbs in parentheses.

1. Eu _____ (acordar) às seis e meia todos os dias. *(I wake up at 6:30 every day.)*

2. As atividades _____ (começar) às sete da noite? *(Do the activities start at 7:00 P.M.?)*

3. Eu e meus amigos _____ (combinar) uma festa. *(My friends and I make plans for a party.)*

4. A aula de português _____ (terminar) às quatorze horas. *(The Portuguese lesson ends at 2:00 P.M.)*

5. O advogado _____ (mandar) o contrato. *(The lawyer sends the agreement.)*

6. A senhora _____ (trabalhar) aqui? *(Do you work here?)*

7. Os carros _____ (parar) no sinal vermelho. *(The cars stop at the red light.)*

8. Eu _____ (tirar) fotos dos meus amigos. *(I take pictures of my friends.)*

9. Os turistas _____ (olhar) os monumentos. *(The tourists look at the monuments.)*

10. Brasileiros não _____ (chegar) adiantados, brasileiros _____ (chegar) atrasados. *(Brazilians don't arrive early; Brazilians arrive late.)*

PHRASE LIST 2

gostar de . . .	*to like . . .*
gosto de . . .	*I like . . .*
gostar de vinho	*to like wine*
gostar de leite	*to like milk*
não gostar de sorvete	*to not like ice cream*
gostar dos amigos	*to like friends*
amar nossos filhos	*to love our children*
odiar trânsito	*to hate traffic*
não agüentar	*can't stand*
adorar viajar	*to love to travel*
demora?	*does it take long?*
é só?	*is that all?*
geralmente cedo	*usually early*
nunca tarde	*never late*
estar sem tempo	*to not have time*

NUTS & BOLTS 2

THE VERB GOSTAR DE *(TO LIKE)*

The regular verb **gostar de** is used to talk about things you like, or in the negative, things you dislike. **Gostar** is conjugated as a regular **-ar** verb, so the four main conjugated forms that you need to know are **gosto, gosta, gostamos,** and **gostam.** The thing that is liked or disliked is always introduced by the preposition **de.** That can be either a noun or a verb.

Eu gosto de vinho tinto.
I like red wine.

Eu gosto de acordar cedo.
I like to wake up early.

Eu não gosto de chegar atrasado.
I don't like to arrive late.

Don't forget the contractions of **de** with definite articles **(do, da, dos, das)** are used to talk about specific things, but when you're talking about likes or dislikes in general, just use **de.**

Eu gosto do meu amigo, Paulo.
I like my friend, Paulo.

Ele gosta da casa dele.
He likes his house.

Você gosta de livros de mistério?
Do you like mystery books?

PRACTICE 2

Fill in the blanks with the verb **gostar** using the correct form of the preposition **de.**

1. Brasileiros _____ praia. *(Brazilians like the beach.)*

2. Ele _____ Praia de Copacabana. *(He likes Copacabana Beach.)*

3. Nós não _____ chegar atrasados. *(We don't like to arrive late.)*

4. Crianças não _____ estudar gramática. *(Children don't like to study grammar.)*

5. Vocês _____ diretora de marketing? *(Do you like the marketing director?)*

6. As minhas amigas _____ minha casa de praia. *(My friends like my beach house.)*

7. Você _____ trabalhar no banco? *(Do you like to work at the bank?)*

8. Geralmente, professores não _____ alunos atrasados. *(Usually, teachers don't like late students.)*

9. Ele _____ cerveja, mas ela _____ vinho. *(He likes beer, but she likes wine.)*

10. Eu não _____ meu apartamento, mas _____ sua casa. *(I don't like my apartment, but I like your house.)*

Discovery activity

Make a list of things you like, love, dislike, hate, or can't stand. Use the expressions **eu gosto de** ... *(I like ...)*, **eu não gosto de** ... *(I don't like ...)*, **eu não suporto** ... *(I can't stand ...)*, **eu adoro** ... *(I love ...* , used for things), **eu amo** ... *(I love ...* , used for people), and **eu odeio** ... *(I hate ...)* Then, interview a friend, and add his or her preferences, changing the verb forms of course. Finally, make a list comparing both.

ANSWERS

PRACTICE 1: 1. acordo; 2. começam; 3. combinamos; 4. termina; 5. manda; 6. trabalha; 7. param; 8. tiro; 9. olham; 10. chegam, chegam

PRACTICE 2: 1. gostam de; 2. gosta da; 3. gostamos de; 4. gostam de; 5. gosta da; 6. gosta da; 7. gosta de; 8. gostam de; 9. gosta de, gosta de; 10. gosto do; gosto da

---

——————— Lesson 11 (sentences) ———————

SENTENCE LIST 1

Quando ele estuda?	*When does he study?*
Ele estuda de noite.	*He studies at night.*
Onde vocês moram?	*Where do you live?*
Nós moramos na Rua Pamplona, número 26.	*We live at 26 Pamplona Street.*
Por que ela estuda português?	*Why does she study Portuguese?*
Ela estuda português porque gosta.	*She studies Portuguese because she likes it.*
O que vocês estudam?	*What do you study?*
Estudamos português.	*We study Portuguese.*
Como elas viajam?	*How do they travel?*
Elas viajam de trem.	*They travel by train.*
A professora está atrasada.	*The teacher is late.*

O avião está adiantado.	*The plane is early.*
O relógio está adiantado.	*The clock is fast.*
Meu relógio está atrasado.	*My watch is slow.*
Mariana adora festas.	*Mariana loves parties.*
Mariana ama Paulo.	*Mariana loves Paulo.*
Eu odeio trânsito.	*I hate traffic.*
Nós não suportamos o calor.	*We can't stand the heat.*

NUTS & BOLTS 1
QUESTION WORDS

You already know how to ask simple yes-no questions in Portuguese, so now let's look at questions with question words. We'll begin with **o que** *(what)*, **quando** *(when)*, **onde** *(where)*, **por que** *(why)* and **como** *(how)*. Notice that unlike in English, you never have to use an auxiliary verb like *do* or *does*. Just begin your question with the question word.

O que você odeia?
What do you hate?

Quando você viaja?
When do you travel?

Onde você trabalha?
Where do you work?

Por que você está atrasado?
Why are you late?

Como você acorda?
How do you wake up?

Notice that **por que** *(why)* is two separate words. The answer, *because*, is one word: **porque**. **Por que você está atrasado? Eu estou atrasado porque o trânsito está ruim.** *(Why are you late? I'm late because traffic is bad.)*

PRACTICE 1

Complete the following questions with the right question word or phrase: **Quando, Como, Onde, Por que, O que.**

1. _____ você estuda português? Na universidade. *(Where are you studying Portuguese? At the university.)*

2. _____ o avião chega? Às 21:00. *(When does the plane get in? At 9:00 P.M.)*

3. _____ vocês chegam atrasados? Porque não usamos despertador. *(Why do you arrive late? Because we don't use an alarm clock.)*

4. _____nós acordamos? Usamos um rádio-relógio. *(How do we wake up? We use a clock radio.)*

5. _____ela estuda na universidade? Ela estuda arquitetura. *(What does she study at the university? She studies architecture.)*

SENTENCE LIST 2

Como é seu sobrenome?	*What's your last name?*
Meu sobrenome é Smith.	*My last name is Smith.*
O que você faz de manhã?	*What do you do in the morning?*
Eu acordo às seis, tomo banho, depois tomo café da manhã, e estudo português.	*I wake up at 6:00, take a shower, then I have breakfast, and I study Portuguese.*
O que você faz no seu tempo livre?	*What do you do in your free time?*
Eu faço muitas coisas interessantes no meu tempo livre.	*I do lots of interesting things in my free time.*
Eles fazem muitas perguntas sobre o meu dia a dia.	*They ask a lot of questions about my daily routine.*
A minha amiga está combinando um cinema para as oito da noite.	*My friend is making plans to go to the movies at 8:00 P.M.*

A diretora marca a reunião para as dez da manhã.	The director is scheduling the meeting for 10:00 A.M.
Faz tempo que eu não encontro meus amigos.	I haven't seen my friends in a long time.
Vocês gostam de fazer esporte?	Do you like to play sports?
Ele faz negócios com o Japão.	He does business with Japan.
A Estrela faz brinquedos.	Estrela makes toys.

NUTS & BOLTS 2
THE VERB FAZER *(TO DO, TO MAKE)*

Let's take a look at the conjugation of the very common irregular verb **fazer** *(to do, to make)*.

eu faço	nós fazemos
você faz	vocês fazem
ele/ela faz	eles/elas fazem

Fazer can be translated in a few different ways.

O que você faz de manhã?
What do you do in the morning?

Eu faço café.
I make coffee.

O que o seu pai faz?
What does your father do (as a profession)?

As crianças fazem academia, e também fazem aulas de inglês.
The children go to the gym, and they also take English classes.

Eu não faço universidade, faço colegial.
I'm not in the university, I'm in high school.

A nossa empresa faz negócios com a China.

Our company does business with China.

Ele faz bagunça.

He's making a mess.

Os trabalhadores fazem muito barulho.

The workers make a lot of noise.

Another common use of **fazer** is in the expression **faz tempo que.** . . . This can be translated as something along the lines of "it's been a while/a long time since . . ."

Faz tempo que não encontro meus amigos.

It's been a while since I've seen my friends./I haven't seen my friends in a long time.

Faz tempo que você trabalha aqui?

Have you worked here long?/Has it been a while since you've been working here?

Sim, faz tempo que trabalho aqui.

Yes, I've worked here for a long time./Yes, it's been a while that I've been working here.

Não, não faz tempo, faz um ano.

No, I haven't worked here for long; it's been one year.

Faz três anos que trabalho aqui.

I've worked here for three years.

PRACTICE 2

Match the question in the left column with the most appropriate answer in the right column.

1. O que a sua empresa faz?	A. Ela é médica.
2. O que você faz na universidade?	B. Com gim e vermute.

3. Quando ele faz a lição de casa?	C. Sim, faz cinco anos.
4. Eles fazem negócios com a Europa?	D. Na Sala 1.
5. O que a sua mãe faz?	E. Automóveis.
6. Como você prepara um martini?	F. Não, só com a Ásia.
7. Faz tempo que você mora no Rio?	G. De noite.
8. Onde ele faz a reunião?	H. Medicina.

Cool links

www.brasilemb.org/	Brazilian Embassy, for information on visas and documents you need when traveling to Brazil.
www.braziltour.com/site/en/home/index.php	Brazilian Tourism, the official website for tourism with information and cultural tips in English.
www.portugal.org/index.shtml	Official website for information on Portugal.

ANSWERS

PRACTICE 1: **1.** Onde; **2.** Quando; **3.** Por que; **4.** Como; **5.** O que

PRACTICE 2: **1.** E; **2.** H; **3.** G; **4.** F; **5.** A; **6.** B; **7.** C; **8.** D

———————— Lesson 12 (conversations) ————————

CONVERSATION 1

Listen in while Flávia answers some questions for a cell phone survey.

Entrevistador:	**Com licença. Posso fazer algumas perguntas para uma pesquisa?**
Flávia:	**Depende. Demora muito? Eu estou sem tempo.**
Entrevistador:	**Só alguns minutos.**
Flávia:	**Sobre o que é a pesquisa?**
Entrevistador:	**A pesquisa é sobre como você usa o seu celular. Você trabalha?**
Flávia:	**Não, não trabalho, sou estudante.**
Entrevistador:	**Que horas você acorda?**
Flávia:	**Geralmente, eu acordo às seis e meia, mas nos fins de semana eu acordo entre nove e dez da manhã.**
Entrevistador:	**Como você gosta de acordar? Você usa radio-relógio, despertador ou celular?**
Flávia:	**Eu uso o meu celular.**
Entrevistador:	**Quando você usa mais o seu celular?**
Flávia:	**Quando combino encontros com meus amigos.**
Entrevistador:	**E com quem você conversa mais tempo no celular? Com a sua família ou com os seus amigos?**
Flávia:	**Eu converso mais com meus amigos.**
Entrevistador:	**Você manda mensagens de texto?**
Flávia:	**Sim, claro.**

Entrevistador:	Para quem você manda mais mensagens de texto?
Flávia:	Acho que mando mais mensagens de texto para minha família.
Entrevistador:	É só. Muito obrigado.
Flávia:	De nada.

Interviewer:	Excuse me, can I ask you some questions for a survey?
Flávia:	It depends. I don't have much time. Does it take long?
Interviewer:	Only a couple of minutes.
Flávia:	What's the survey about?
Interviewer:	The survey is about how you use your cell phone. Do you work?
Flávia:	No, I don't work. I'm a student.
Interviewer:	What time do you wake up?
Flávia:	I usually wake up at 6:30, but on weekends I wake up between 9:00 and 10:00.
Interviewer:	How do you prefer to wake up? Do you use a clock radio, alarm clock, or your cell phone?
Flávia:	I use my cell phone.
Interviewer:	When do you use your cell phone the most?
Flávia:	When I make plans to see my friends.
Interviewer:	Who do you speak with the most on your cell phone?
Flávia:	I speak with my friends the most.
Interviewer:	Who do you send text messages to?
Flávia:	I send text messages to my family.
Interviewer:	That's all. Thank you very much.
Flávia:	You're welcome.

NUTS & BOLTS 1
MORE QUESTION WORDS

Let's look at a few more common question words, starting with **quantos** (m.) and **quantas** (f.), which are used to mean *how many* with plural nouns.

Quantos livros você quer?
How many books do you want?

Quantas casas ele visita?
How many houses does he visit?

The phrase **quantas vezes** *(how many times)* is useful.

Quantas vezes por semana você estuda português?
How many times a week do you study Portuguese?

Quantas vezes por ano eles viajam para a Europa?
How many times a year do they travel to Europe?

Quanto (m.) and **quanta** (f.) are used to mean *how much,* and they're used with singular mass nouns, like *time, money, water,* etc.

Quanto tempo dura o filme?
How long does the film last?

Quanta gasolina o carro consome?
How much gasoline does the car consume?

The phrases **quanto custa?** *(how much does it cost?)* and **quanto custam?** *(how much do they cost?)* are very useful.

Quanto custa o anel?
How much does the ring cost?

Quanto custam as garrafas de vinho?
How much are the bottles of wine?

Quem is used to mean *who,* and **de quem** means *whose.*

Quem estuda alemão?
Who studies German?

De quem é o casaco?
Whose coat is it?

And finally, to ask questions with *which*, use **qual**:

Qual trem chega de São Paulo?
Which train is arriving from São Paulo?

Qual casa é a sua?
Which is your house?

One point to keep in mind is that you can't separate a question word from a preposition in Portuguese, as you can in English.

Sobre o que é a pesquisa?
What is the survey about?/About what is the survey?

Para quem são as flores?
Who are the flowers for?/For whom are the flowers?

Com quem você conversa?
Who are you talking with?/With whom are you talking?

PRACTICE 1

Use the following question words to complete the questions.
Quanto, Que horas, Quantas, Como, O que, Com quem, Sobre o que, Por que.

1. _____ você acorda? Acordo às seis todos os dias.

2. _____ eles fazem de manhã? Eles trabalham.

3. _____ vocês viajam para o Japão? Viajamos de avião.

4. _____ perguntas o médico faz? Ele faz muitas perguntas.

5. _____ o diretor estuda chinês? Porque ele faz negócios com a China.

6. _____ custa o carro? É barato ou caro? O carro é barato.

7. _____ você conversa? Com as minhas amigas?

8. _____ vocês conversam. Nós conversamos sobre os nossos namorados.

CONVERSATION 2
Listen in as two old friends catch up.

Paulo: Oi, quanto tempo! Que legal encontrar você aqui! Tudo bem?

Roberto: Tudo bem. Faz tempo, mesmo. Como vai sua mulher, a Ana?

Paulo: Ela está bem. E a sua mulher, como vai?

Roberto: Ela está ótima. Ela está feliz com a casa nova.

Paulo: Vocês mudaram? Onde vocês moram agora?

Roberto: Sim, nos mudamos. Agora moramos no Morumbi. A casa é muito boa e muito grande. Quando você e a Glória vão nos fazer uma visita?

Paulo: Em breve, espero. Você ainda trabalha na mesma empresa?

Roberto: Sim, ainda trabalho no Banco do Brasil. E você? Onde você trabalha agora?

Paulo: Agora trabalho no Museu de Arte Moderna, o MASP. Eu gosto do meu novo emprego. Tenho muitos benefícios, e tenho tempo livre para fazer outras coisas. Por exemplo, eu faço um curso de fotografia. Agora quando eu viajo, eu tiro fotos incríveis. O que você faz no seu tempo livre?

Roberto: Que tempo livre? Eu só trabalho. Às vezes, das oito da manhã até às oito da noite. Nunca tenho tempo para tirar férias ou fazer cursos.

Paulo: Que vida dura! Mas, é bom falar com você de novo. Lembranças à sua mulher.

Paulo:	Hi. It's been a long time! How nice to run into you here! How are you doing?
Roberto:	Fine. It's really been a long time. How's your wife, Ana?
Paulo:	She's great. She's happy about the new house.
Roberto:	Did you move? Where do you live now?
Paulo:	Yes, we've moved. Now we live in Morumbi. It's a very nice, big house. When are you and Glória coming to visit?
Paulo:	Soon, I hope. Do you still work at the same company?
Roberto:	Yes, I still work at Banco do Brasil. And you? Where do you work now?
Paulo:	Now I work at the Museum of Modern Art, MASP. I like my new job. There are lots of benefits, and I have free time to do other things. For example, I'm taking a photography course. Now when I travel, I take incredible pictures. What do you do in your free time?
Roberto:	What free time? All I do is work, sometimes from eight in the morning to eight at night. I never have time to take vacations or take courses.
Paulo:	What a hard life! But it's good to talk to you again. Send my regards to your wife.

NUTS & BOLTS 2

THE VERB TER (TO HAVE)

The verb **ter** is irregular, and it's found in many common expressions, as you'll see below. First, let's look at its conjugation.

eu tenho	nós temos
você tem	vocês têm
ele/ela tem	eles/elas têm

Notice that the second and third person plural forms, **vocês têm** and **eles têm,** are written with the circumflex accent to distinguish them from the singular forms. Now let's look at the uses of **ter.** First, it's used to express possession, like English:

Eu não tenho telefone celular.
I don't have a cell phone.

Ela tem três irmãos.
She has three brothers.

But **ter** is also used to talk about age.

Quantos anos você tem?
How old are you?

Eu tenho vinte e cinco anos.
I'm twenty-five years old.

There are a lot of other common expressions in Portuguese that use the verb **ter: ter medo** *(to be afraid),* **ter fome** *(to be hungry),* **ter sede** *(to be thirsty),* **ter sorte** *(to be lucky),* **ter azar** *(to have bad luck),* **ter razão** *(to be right),* **ter certeza** *(to be sure),* **ter saudade** *(to miss someone or something; to have a feeling of nostalgia).*

Quem tem medo de escuro?
Who's afraid of the dark?

Eu não tenho fome, mas tenho sede.
I'm not hungry, but I'm thirsty.

Eles têm azar quando jogam pôquer.
They're unlucky when they play poker.

Você tem razão, o filme começa às oito e não às sete.
You're right, the film starts at 8:00, and not at 7:00.

Nós temos saudade do Brasil.
We miss Brazil.

PRACTICE 2
Complete each sentence with the correct form of the verb **ter**.

1. Ele _____ sessenta e três.

2. Mariana _____ muito dinheiro.

3. Nós não _____ quando acordamos.

4. Os professores não _____ os livros; a loja _____os livros.

5. Nós não _____ muito tempo. Quanto tempo demora?

6. Vocês _____certeza do endereço?

7. O Brasil _____muitas cidades grandes.

8. Eu_____uma surpresa para você!

9. Quando eles_____aulas de português?

10. Eu _____um presente para vocês!

Tip!

Listening to and singing along with Brazilian **bossa nova** is an excellent way to improve your vocabulary while developing your pronunciation and intonation. In fact, you probably already know a little bossa nova, like **Garota de Ipanema** *(Girl from Ipanema)*, **Águas de Março** *(Waters of March)*, **Insensatez** *(How Insensitive)*, and **Desafinado** *(Out of Tune)*. It's relatively easy to sing along to bossa nova because of its slow and melodious cadence, and it certainly is a lot of fun, so try to get a bossa nova CD that comes with the lyrics, or download a song and do an internet search for its lyrics. To get you started, here are a few links that will give you great information, a bit of history, and suggestions for good musicians to help you fall in love with this uniquely Brazilian musical style, if you haven't already!

http://www.allaboutjazz.com/php/article.php?id=251

http://en.wikipedia.org/wiki/Brazilian_jazz

http://en.wikipedia.org/wiki/Bossa_nova

ANSWERS
PRACTICE 1: 1. Que horas; **2.** O que; **3.** Como; **4.** Quantas; **5.** Por que; **6.** Quanto; **7.** Com quem; **8.** Sobre o que

PRACTICE 2: 1. tem; **2.** tem; **3.** temos; **4.** têm, tem; **5.** temos; **6.** têm; **7.** tem; **8.** tenho; **9.** têm; **10.** tenho

UNIT 3 ESSENTIALS
Os nossos amigos estão atrasados.
Our friends are late.

O avião está adiantado.
The plane is early.

Que horas são?
What time is it?

Minha aula é das seis às sete.
My class is from 6:00 to 7:00.

Eu gostaria de uma nova toalha de banho, por favor.
May I have a new bath towel, please?

Você mora aqui?
Do you live here?

Eu não agüento o calor.
I can't stand the heat.

Eu gosto de acordar cedo.
I like to wake up early.

Por que você está atrasado?
Why are you late?

Onde você trabalha?
Where do you work?

Eu faço muitas coisas interessantes no meu tempo livre.
I do lots of interesting things in my free time.

Faz tempo que você trabalha aqui?

Have you worked here long?/Has it been a while since you've been working here?

Quantos livros você quer?

How many books do you want?

Quanta gasolina o carro consome?

How much gasoline does the car consume?

Quantos anos você tem?

How old are you?

Unit 4
Talking about health

In this unit you'll learn how to talk about your health, which means you'll learn important vocabulary related to the human body. Unit 4 also covers the regular verbs ending in -**er,** and the equivalents of *need to, have to, want to, can,* and *should.* Finally, you'll learn important expressions that use **estar,** as well as the demonstratives *this, that, these,* and *those.* **Saúde!** *(To your health!)*

——————— Lessons 13 (words) ———————

WORD LIST 1

a saúde	*health*
a cabeça	*head*
a boca	*mouth*
o olho	*eye*
a orelha	*ear*
o nariz	*nose*
a garganta	*throat*
o pescoço	*neck*
a perna	*leg*
o rosto	*face*
o braço	*arm*
o pé	*foot*
a mão	*hand*
o estômago	*stomach*
o dente	*tooth*
o dedo	*finger/toe*
o coração	*heart*

o pulmão	*lung*
o sangue	*blood*
o osso	*bone*

NUTS & BOLTS 1
NUMBERS 100 AND ABOVE

In Unit 2, Lesson 8, you learned that the number for 100 is **cem,** 101 is **cento e um** (masculine) or **cento e uma** (feminine), 102 is **cento e dois/duas,** 103 is **cento e três,** and so on. The same happens to the other numbers in the hundreds:

duzentos/as–200	quatrocentos/as–400
duzentos e doze–212	quinhentos/as–500
duzentos e cinqüenta–250	seiscentos/as–600
duzentas e oitenta–280	setecentos/as–700
trezentos/as–300	oitocentos/as–800
trezentas e uma–301	novecentos/as–900

Este livro tem mais de quatrocentas páginas.
This book has more than 400 pages.

Há mais de cento e noventa nações no mundo.
There are more than 190 nations in the world.

There's only one form for **mil** *(one thousand),* but there's a singular and plural for both **milhão** *(million)* and **bilhão** *(billion).*

mil–1,000	dez mil e duzentos/as–10,200
dois/duas mil–2,000	cem mil e um (uma)–100,001

duzentos mil e um (uma)–200,001	dois milhões–2,000,000
trezentos mil, cento e dois–300,102	quatro milhões–4,000,000
um milhão–1,000,000	um bilhão–1,000,000,000
um milhão e duzentos/as mil–1,200,000	dois bilhões–2,000,000,000

Notice that **e** *(and)* is used to separate the hundreds, tens and units.

um milhão, cento e vinte e nove mil, trezentos e quarenta e seis

1,129,346

quatro bilhões, duzentos milhões, oitocentos e quarenta e oito

4,200,000,848

If you follow **milhão, bilhão,** or **trilhão** *(trillion)* directly by a noun, introduce that noun with **de** *(of).*

um milhão de pessoas– *a million people*	**um milhão e seiscentas mil pessoas–***one million, six hundred thousand people*
um bilhão de estrelas– *a billion stars*	**um bilhão e trezentos mil dólares–**$1,000,300,000.00

Also note that in written Portuguese, periods are used to separate hundreds, thousands, millions, and so on, and commas are used before decimal places. So, $1.300.000,00 is the Portuguese equivalent of $1,300,000.00. Some other useful vocabulary related to numbers is: **uma dezena** *(ten)*, **uma dúzia** *(one dozen)*, **uma centena** *(one hundred)*, and **os/as milhares** *(one thousand)*

PRACTICE 1
Match column A and column B.

Column A	Column B
1. cento e dois	A. 210.000
2. vinte e quatro	B. 36
3. dois milhões e trezentos mil	C. 35.000
4. três dúzias	D. 102
5. trezentos e trinta	E. 30
6. uma dúzia	F. 24
7. dois mil	G. 330
8. três dezenas	H. 2.000
9. trinta e cinco mil	I. 1.200.000
10. um milhão e duzentos mil	J. 12
11. duzentos e dez mil	K. 2.300.000

WORD LIST 2

o remédio	*medicine*
a vitamina	*vitamin*
a consulta médica	*doctor's appointment*
a receita médica	*medical prescription*
o pronto socorro	*emergency room*

em forma	*fit, in shape*
a disposição	*state of mind, condition, disposition*
cansado(a)	*tired*
a injeção	*injection*
a dor	*ache, pain*
doente	*sick, ill (adjective)*
a infecção	*infection*
a gripe	*flu*
o resfriado	*a cold*
a aspirina	*aspirin*
o curativo Band-Aid®	*adhesive bandage Band-Aid®*
o xarope	*cough syrup*
o colírio	*eye drops*

NUTS & BOLTS 2
DEMONSTRATIVES

Demonstratives are words that point to something, like *this, that, these,* and *those* in English. Portuguese demonstratives agree in gender and number with the nouns they refer to. Just like in English, their forms vary according to distance, but there are actually three distinctions made in Portuguese.

masculine	feminine	
este	esta	*this*
esse	essa	*that*
aquele	aquela	*that (over there)*
estes	estas	*these*
esses	essas	*that*
aqueles	aquelas	*that (over there)*

The forms **este, esta, estes,** and **estas** refer to something that is near both the speaker and the person spoken to. They're the equivalents of *this* or *these.*

Este remédio é para resfriado?
Is this a cold medicine?

Estas meias são de fibra natural?
Are these socks made of natural fibers?

The forms **esse, essa, esses,** and **essas** refer to something near or related to the person being spoken to, but not near the speaker. The most natural translation for this situation is *that* or *those.*

Essa receita médica é a minha?
Is that prescription (you're holding) mine?

Esses jornais são locais?
Are those newspapers local?

Finally, **aquele, aquela, aqueles,** and **aquelas** refer to something that is remote or unrelated to both the speaker and the person spoken to.

Quem é aquela mulher?
Who is that woman (across the street)?

Aqueles jogadores de futebol são ótimos.
Those soccer players (out on the field) are great.

All of these demonstratives can be used as adjectives, in other words right before a noun as in all of the examples above, or on their own as pronouns.

Estes aqui são meus e aqueles com você são seus.
These here are mine, and those with you are yours.

Este homem é jovem, mas aquele lá é velho.

This man is young, but that one over there is old.

Of course, sometimes you may not know what exactly you're referring to, so you won't know if it's masculine or feminine. In this case, there are special neuter, invariable forms of the demonstratives: **isto** *(this thing here)*, **isso** *(that thing you have)*, and **aquilo** *(that thing over there)*.

O que é isto aqui?

What is this (thing) here?

O que é isso?

What is that (thing) right there?

O que é aquilo?

What is that (thing) over there?

Now that you've learned the different forms, it's worth pointing out that in informal, spoken Brazilian Portuguese not much attention is paid to the differences between **esse** and **este, essa** and **esta,** or **isso** and **isto.** So either **este** or **esse** is used to refer to something near and **aquele** to something far. Another important point to make is that demonstratives form contractions with **de.** But they're simple—they just consist of the regular forms of the demonstratives, with **d-** added at the beginning: **deste, desta, desse, dessa, daquele, daqueles, disto, disso,** and so on.

Onde é a piscina desse hotel?

Where is this hotel's swimming pool?

Quem é o diretor daquela empresa?

Who's the director of that company?

Eu gosto disso, mas não gosto daquilo.

I like this, but I don't like that.

PRACTICE 2

Fill in the blanks with one of the demonstratives. Use the translation to guide you.

1. Pedro, _____ é minha amiga, Mariana. *(Pedro, this here is my friend, Mariana.)*

2. Ele quer _____ documentos? *(Does he want those documents over there?)*

3. _____ lojas estão abertas? *(Are those stores over there open?)*

4. _____ sapatos são caros. *(These shoes I'm wearing are expensive.)*

5. _____ flores na minha mão são perfumadas. *(These flowers I'm holding are fragrant.)*

6. Pedro, _____ é seu amigo, Ricardo? *(Pedro, is that your friend, Ricardo, with you?)*

7. _____ carteira é cara? *(Is that wallet you have expensive?)*

Cool link

Both Brazil and Portugal use the metric system for measurements, which means grams and kilos for weight, liters for liquids, kilometers for distance, and Celsius for temperature. You may remember some of this from the United States' attempt to go metric in the late 1970s, or maybe that was before your time. In any event, most of the world is metric, so it's a great idea to memorize at least a few basic metric equivalents. Below you'll find some useful websites that will help you convert weights and measures, temperatures and areas.

www.metric-conversions.org/#

www.worldwidemetric.com/metcal.htm

And if you're really interested in the metric system:

http://en.wikipedia.org/wiki/SI

http://en.wikipedia.org/wiki/Metrication_in_the_United_States

--------- Lesson 14 (phrases) ---------

PHRASE LIST 1

a dor de cabeça	*headache*
a dor de garganta	*sore throat*
o nariz entupido	*stuffy nose*
os pés inchados	*swollen feet*
tomar remédios	*to take medicine*
o exame médico geral	*medical checkup*
o conselho do amigo	*a friend's advice*
as recomendações do médico	*the doctor's suggestions/advice*
Isso dói!	*That hurts!*
manter a forma	*to keep fit, to stay in shape*
perder peso	*to lose weight*
engordar	*to gain weight*
ter alergias	*to have allergies*
Volte aqui.	*Come back.*
doença contagiosa	*contagious disease*
Estimo as suas melhoras.	*I hope you get better soon.*
contra indicação	*warning (contraindication)*

NUTS & BOLTS 1
REGULAR -ER VERBS
You've already learned that regular **-ar** verbs are conjugated with the endings **-o, -a, -amos,** and **-am.** The second group of regular

verbs in Portuguese are the **-er** verbs, and the **-er** endings are very similar to -ar endings, except **e** replaces **a**. Let's look at an example verb, **entender** *(to understand)*.

eu entend<u>o</u>	nós entend<u>emos</u>
você entend<u>e</u>	vocês entend<u>em</u>
ele/ela entend<u>e</u>	eles/elas entend<u>em</u>

Some other important verbs ending in **-er** are the following.

escrever *(to write)*	resolver *(to solve)*
beber *(to drink)*	morrer *(to die)*
comer *(to eat)*	viver *(to live)*
correr *(to run)*	devolver *(to give back)*
perceber *(to notice)*	aprender *(to learn)*
esconder *(to hide)*	receber *(to receive)*

Eu não entendo a pergunta.
I don't understand the question.

Nós aprendemos português.
We learn Portuguese.

Você come demais!
You eat too much!

Quantas pessoas vivem aqui?
How many people live here?

PRACTICE 1
Fill in the blanks with the correct form of the verb indicated in the translation.

1. Os atletas _____ a maratona de Nova York. *(The athletes run the NY Marathon.)*

2. Os meninos _____ leite de manhã. *(The children drink milk in the morning.)*

3. As plantas não _____sem água. *(Plants don't live without water.)*

4. O professor de matemática _____ o problema no quadro. *(The math teacher solves the problem on the board.)*

5. Você _____ que eu perdi cinco quilos? *(Do you notice that I lost 5 kilos?)*

6. O cachorro _____ o osso no jardim. *(The dog hides the bone in the garden.)*

7. Eu _____ português para viajar para o Brasil. *(I'm learning Portuguese to travel to Brazil.)*

8. Eu não _____ cerveja porque não gosto de bebidas alcoólicas. *(I don't drink beer because I don't like alcoholic beverages.)*

9. Nós _____ uma língua estrangeira. *(We're learning a foreign language.)*

10. Mariana _____ a lista dos convidados. *(Mariana is writing the guest list.)*

11. O que os seus filhos _____ de manhã? *(What do your children eat in the morning?)*

12. Os adultos _____ as emoções. *(Adults hide their emotions.)*

PHRASE LIST 2

tudo azul	*everything's fine (infml.)*
biblioteca pública	*public library*

caminhar bastante	*to walk a lot*
beber muito líquido	*to drink plenty of liquids*
levantar pesos	*to lift weights*
fazer ioga	*to do yoga*
fazer exercícios	*to exercise*
em pouco tempo	*in no time/in little time*
de três em três horas	*every three hours*
um dia sim outro não	*every other day*
ser vegetariana	*to be vegetarian*
sem energia para nada	*without any energy*
melhorar	*to get better*
ler a bula	*to read the instructions (for medicine)*
comer frutas e verduras	*to eat fruits and vegetables*
estar doente	*to be sick*
ser saudável	*to be healthy*
estar com febre	*to have a fever*
estar com tosse	*to have a cough*
estar com dor de cabeça	*to have a headache*
estar com pressa	*to be in a hurry*
estar com medo	*to be afraid*

NOTES

Did you notice two time expressions above? Some other common time expressions are: **logo/em breve/daqui a pouco** *(soon)*, até *(until)*, **uma vez/duas vezes/três vezes** *(once/twice/three times)*, às vezes *(sometimes)*, **algumas vezes** *(a few times)*.

NUTS & BOLTS 2

THE VERBS VER *(TO SEE)* AND LER *(TO READ)*

Here are the conjugations of two more common irregular verbs. First is **ver** *(to see)*.

eu vejo	nós vemos
você vê	vocês vêem
ele/ela vê	eles/elas vêem

And here is **ler** *(to read)*.

eu leio	nós lemos
você lê	vocês lêem
ele/ela lê	eles/elas lêem

Note that the second and third person plural forms double the **e**, and that there is a circumflex on the first **e**.

Você vê aquele homem?
Do you see that man?

Eu vejo muitos filmes bons.
I see a lot of good movies.

Nós não lemos muito na aula.
We don't read very much in class.

PRACTICE 2
Fill in the blanks with the verb **ver** *(to see)*:

1. Quantas vezes por ano você _____ o médico?

2. Eles _____ o dentista duas vezes por ano.

3. Nós não _____ o diretor de manhã.

4. Suzana _____ a sua amiga na festa.

5. As crianças choram quando não _____ os pais.

6. Pedro e Mariana, vocês _____ aquele cachorro?

7. Os turistas sempre _____ as praias bonitas.

Fill in the blanks with the verb **ler** *(to read)*:

8. O médico _____ a bula do remédio.

9. Quantos livros você _____ por ano?

10. Mariana não _____ as instruções da máquina fotográfica dela.

11. Nós ainda não _____ o contrato.

12. Eu _____ dois jornais por dia.

13. Felipe e Pedro não _____ revistas, mas _____ jornais.

14. O professor _____ as provas dos alunos.

15. Você _____ as receitas do médico?

Tip!

Watching movies in the original language is enjoyable, and it will help you improve your listening comprehension in an entertaining way. Rent DVDs in Portuguese, and to begin, watch the film with the English subtitles. Just relax, take in the rhythm and cadence of the language, and try to see how much you're able to pick up. Next, select a three- to four-minute segment to watch with the English subtitles. Finally, go back and watch the same segment without the subtitles. Do that as many times, and with as many segments, as you want. On top of being a fun and entertaining way to learn a foreign language, the films listed below will give you an excellent opportunity to learn more about Brazil.

Dona Flor e Seus Dois Maridos (Dona Flor and Her Two Husbands), directed by Bruno Barreto; *Central do Brasil* (Central Station), directed by Walter Salles; *2 Filhos de Francisco—A História de Zezé di Camargo & Lúciano* (Two Sons of Francisco—The Story of Zezé di Camargo and Lúciano), directed by Breno Silveira; *O Que É Isso, Companheiro?* (Four Days in September), directed by Bruno Barreto; *Orfeu Negro* (Black Orpheus), directed by Marcel Camus.

ANSWERS

PRACTICE 1: 1. correm; **2.** bebem; **3.** vivem; **4.** resolve; **5.** percebe; **6.** esconde; **7.** aprendo; **8.** bebo; **9.** aprendemos; **10.** escreve; **11.** comem; **12.** escondem

PRACTICE 2: 1. vê; **2.** vêem; **3.** vemos; **4.** vê; **5.** vêem; **6.** vêem; **7.** vêem; **8.** lê; **9.** lê; **10.** lê; **11.** lemos; **12.** leio; **13.** lêem, lêem; **14.** lê; **15.** lê

Lesson 15 (sentences)

SENTENCE LIST 1

Nós não estamos com sono.	*We're not sleepy.*
Vocês estão com fome?	*Are you hungry?*
Elas estão com vontade de comer pizza.	*They feel like eating pizza.*
O paciente está com dor de cabeça.	*The patient has a headache.*
O meu filho está com febre.	*My son has a fever.*
Os animais estão com sede.	*The animals are thirsty.*
Os executivos estão com pressa.	*The businessmen are in a hurry.*
A garota está sem vontade de estudar.	*The girl doesn't feel like studying.*
O rapaz não está com medo.	*The young man is not afraid.*
Por que o funcionário está com vergonha?	*Why is the employee embarrassed?*
A professora está sem paciência.	*The teacher has no patience.*
Ele está com dor de barriga.	*He has a stomachache.*
As crianças estão com tosse.	*The children have a cough.*
As minhas pernas doem.	*My legs hurt.*
A minha cabeça dói.	*My head hurts.*

| **Aspirina é bom para dor de dente?** | *Is aspirin good for toothaches?* |
| **Você tem dor de cabeça?** | *Do you have a headache?* |

NOTES:

Here are some idiomatic expressions with body parts.

Mariana não pára de falar! Ela fala pelos cotovelos.

Mariana won't stop talking. She really talks a lot. (lit., talks through her elbows)

Pedro está com dor-de-cotovelo porque não tem mais namorada.

Pedro has been feeling blue because he's lost his girlfriend.

Ela é meu braço direito; sem ela não faço nada.

She's my right arm; I can't do anything without her.

Ele não entende o filme porque o filme não tem pé nem cabeça.

He can't understand the movie because it doesn't make sense.

Você pode contar os seus problemas; sou todo ouvidos!

You can tell me your problems; I'm all ears!

NUTS & BOLTS 1
EXPRESSIONS WITH ESTAR COM

Estar com *(to be with)* is used to express a momentary or fleeting feeling:

Estou com dor de cabeça.

I have a headache.

As crianças estão com fome.

The children are hungry.

In Unit 3 you learned some expressions with the verb **ter,** for example **eu tenho fome** *(I'm hungry).* **Estar com** is used to talk about something a person is feeling at a particular moment, while **ter** is used to talk about more general feelings.

Eu estou com sede, preciso tomar água.

I'm thirsty, I need to drink water.

Eu tenho sede quando faço ginástica.

I get thirsty when I work out.

Another useful expression with **estar** is **estar com vontade de +** infinitive, which means *to feel like doing something*. A related expressions is **estar sem vontade de.**

Eu estou com vontade de comer pizza.

I feel like eating pizza.

Nós não estamos com vontade de viajar de ônibus.

We don't feel like traveling by bus.

Estou sem vontade de acordar cedo.

I don't feel like waking up early.

Ela está sem vontade de ler este livro.

She doesn't feel like reading this book.

Some other expressions with **estar com** are: **estar com febre** *(to have a fever)*, **estar com pressa** *(to be in a hurry)*, **estar com tosse** *(to have a cough)*, **estar com dor de dente** *(to have a toothache)*, **estar com medo** *(to be afraid)*, **estar com sede** *(to be thirsty)*, and **estar com dor de cabeça** *(to have a headache)*.

PRACTICE 1

Complete the sentences with the following expressions: **com febre, com pressa, com tosse, com vontade, com dor de dente, com medo, com dor de cabeça.**

1. Sua testa está quente. Você está _____. *(Your forehead is hot. You have a fever.)*

2. Onde está o telefone do dentista? Estou _____. *(Where's the dentist's phone number? I have a toothache.)*

3. Táxi! Rápido! Estou _____! *(Taxi! Quick! I'm in a hurry!)*

4. O que você está _____ de fazer? *(What do you feel like doing?)*

5. Ele toma xarope porque está _____. *(He's taking cough medicine because he has a cough.)*

6. Nós tomamos aspirina porque estamos _____. *(We're taking aspirin because we have a headache.)*

7. Ela chama a polícia porque está _____. *(She's calling the police because she's afraid.)*

Now complete each sentence with **ter** or **estar com**:

8. Quando eu acordo, eu _____ sede. *(I feel thirsty when I wake up.)*

9. Ela compra uma garrafa de água porque _____ sede. *(She's buying a bottle of water because she's thirsty.)*

10. Quando as crianças estão sozinhas, elas _____ medo. *(When children are alone they are scared.)*

11. Olhe! Um cachorro! _____ medo. *(Look! A dog! I'm scared.)*

12. Não gosto de cantar em público porque _____ vergonha. *(I don't like to sing in public because I feel embarrassed.)*

13. O menino _____ vergonha porque não conhece os outros alunos. *(The boy is embarrassed because he doesn't know the other students.)*

SENTENCE LIST 2

Qual é o problema?	*What's the matter?*
O que você tem?	*What's the matter with you?*
Como você se sente?	*How do you feel?*
Eu não me sinto bem.	*I don't feel very well.*
Estou mal.	*I feel terrible.*

Meu corpo está dolorido.	*My body aches.*
Perder peso é difícil.	*Losing weight is hard.*
Emagrecer não é fácil.	*Losing weight isn't easy.*
Nadar é bom para saúde.	*Swimming is good for your health.*
Dançar é divertido.	*Dancing is fun.*
Andar de ônibus é tedioso.	*Riding a bus is boring.*
Fumar é proibido.	*Smoking is prohibited.*
Beber e dirigir é perigoso.	*Drinking and driving is dangerous.*
Aprender português é importante.	*Learning Portuguese is important.*
Correr a maratona é cansativo.	*Running the marathon is tiring.*

NUTS & BOLTS 2

THE INFINITIVE AS A NOUN

In English, when you begin a sentence with a verb used as a noun, you will generally use the *-ing* form, also known as the gerund. For example, *to swim* is a verb, but as a noun you'd say *swimming is fun*. In Portuguese, you use the infinitive.

Nadar é divertido.
Swimming is fun.

Aprender português é importante.
Learning Portuguese is important.

Cozinhar não é tedioso.
Cooking is not boring.

Manter a forma é difícil?
Is staying in shape difficult?

Can you guess the gender of infinitives used as nouns by looking at the adjectives above? That's right, they're masculine, so the adjectives take the masculine singular forms.

PRACTICE 2

Answer the following questions using the adjectives in parentheses as a cue.

1. Por que ele não trabalha na polícia? Porque_____. (perigoso)

2. Por que ela faz ginástica? Porque_____. (saudável)

3. Porque nós dançamos? Porque _____. (divertido)

4. Porque ele visita o médico uma vez por ano? Porque _____. (importante)

5. Porque ela não perde peso? Porque _____. (difícil)

6. Por que eles não fumam no restaurante? Porque_____. (proibido)

7. Por que eles não trabalham até à meia noite? Porque_____. (cansativo)

8. Por que Pedro não estuda inglês na Inglaterra? Porque_____. (caro)

ANSWERS

PRACTICE 1: **1.** com febre; **2.** com dor de dente; **3.** com pressa; **4.** com vontade; **5.** com tosse; **6.** com dor de cabeça; **7.** com medo; **8.** tenho; **9.** está com; **10.** têm; **11.** estou com; **12.** tenho; **13.** está com

PRACTICE 2: **1.** trabalhar na polícia é perigoso; **2.** fazer ginástica é saudável; **3.** dançar é divertido; **4.** visitar o médico é importante; **5.** perder peso é difícil; **6.** fumar é proibido; **7.** trabalhar até à meia noite é cansativo; **8.** estudar na Inglaterra é caro

———————— Lesson 16 (conversations) ————————

CONVERSATION 1

Marisa is talking to Vera, her personal trainer, at the gym.

      Vera: **Oi, como está? Tudo legal?**
Marisa: **Não, não estou bem. Estou cansada e sem disposição para nada. Ultimamente, acordo**

sem energia. Hoje, não estou com vontade de
fazer ginástica.

Vera: Você deve tomar as vitaminas Energex—
trabalhar e ficar em forma é mais fácil com
Energex.

Marisa: Onde eu posso comprar essas vitaminas?

Vera: Você pode comprar Energex aqui na academia
ou na farmácia. Mas lembre-se, você também
deve fazer ginástica, comer frutas e verduras, e
beber bastante água. Em pouco tempo, você
vai ver a diferença!

Marisa: E, quantas vitaminas devo tomar por dia?

Vera: Você pode tomar duas ou três.

Marisa: Vera, Energex tem alguma contra-indicação?

Vera: Não, não tem, é 100% (cem por cento) natural.

Marisa: Obrigada, vou experimentar.

Vera: *Hi, how's everything?*

Marisa: *I don't feel well. I'm tired and don't feel like (doing)
anything. Lately, I wake up with no energy. Today, I
don't feel like working out.*

Vera: *You should take Energex vitamins—working and
staying fit is easier with Energex.*

Marisa: *Where can I buy these vitamins?*

Vera: *You can buy Energex here at the gym, or at the
pharmacy. But remember, you should also work out, eat
fruits and vegetables, and drink plenty of liquids. In no
time, you'll see the difference!*

Marisa: *How many vitamins should I take a day?*

Vera: *You can take two or three.*

Marisa: *Does Energex have any (drug interaction)
warnings?*

Vera: *No, it doesn't. It's 100% natural.*

Marisa: *Thanks, I'll try it.*

NOTES

The verb **perder** *(to lose)* is irregular and is conjugated as follows.

eu perco	nós perdemos
você perde	vocês perdem
ele/ela perde	eles/elas perdem

You'll be studying the verb **ficar** *(to stay, remain, be located,* etc.) in a later lesson. For now, notice that **ficar em forma** means *to get fit* or *to get in shape.*

In Brazil you have **farmácias** *(pharmacies),* and **drogarias** *(drugstores).* In big cities they offer almost the same range of goods and products as their American counterparts. But in small towns, pharmacies only provide the traditional assortment of medicine and health-related items.

NUTS & BOLTS 1

DEVER *(SHOULD)* AND PODER *(CAN)*

The verbs **dever** *(should)* and **poder** *(can)* are used with another verb in the infinitive, just as in English:

Ele deve estudar mais.

He should study more.

Nós podemos comprar uma casa na praia.

We can buy a beach house.

Here are the full conjugations of **dever** and **poder,** used with the infinitive **falar** as an example.

eu devo falar *(I should speak)*	nós devemos falar *(we should speak)*
você deve falar *(you should speak)*	vocês devem falar *(you should speak)*

ele/ela deve falar *(he/she should speak)*	**eles/elas devem falar** *(they should speak)*
eu posso falar *(I can speak)*	**nós podemos falar** *(we can speak)*
você pode falar *(you can speak)*	**vocês podem falar** *(all of you can speak)*
ele/ela pode falar *(he/she can speak)*	**eles/elas podem falar** *(they can speak)*

PRACTICE 1

Fill in the blanks with the correct form of the verb given in parentheses. Translate your answers. See if you can guess the meanings of unfamiliar words by context, or look them up.

1. Você _____ devolver o presente? (poder)

2. As crianças não _____ correr na rua. (dever)

3. Eu não _____ resolver o problema. (poder)

4. Ela não _____ esconder o rosto. (poder)

5. O gerente _____ receber o relatório. (dever)

6. A aluna _____ responder. (dever)

7. O que eles _____ beber? (poder)

8. Quando eu _____ chegar? (dever)

9. Nós _____ ver a praia. (poder)

10. O que os alunos _____ ler? (dever)

CONVERSATION 2

Listen to a conversation between Felipe and his doctor, Dr. Benjamin.

Dr. Benjamin: Boa tarde, seu Felipe. Qual é o problema? O que o senhor tem?

Felipe: Não sei, estou com dor de garganta, com dor de cabeça, e com tosse. Acho que estou com gripe.

Dr. Benjamin: Eu tenho que verificar a sua temperatura, e também quero fazer um exame geral. Sente-se nesta cadeira, por favor.

Felipe: O senhor acha que posso viajar amanhã? Tenho que visitar um cliente em outro estado.

Dr. Benjamin: Sinto muito, mas a sua temperatura está muito alta, e a sua garganta está bastante inflamada. Você deve ficar em casa por dois ou três dias e descansar. Você também precisa tomar esses remédios de seis em seis horas. Você também deve tomar muito líquido. Se não melhorar em três dias, volte aqui para um outro exame.

Felipe: Está bem. Vou obedecer às suas recomendações: ficar em casa, descansar, e tomar os remédios. Muito obrigado.

Dr. Benjamin: Não se preocupe, e melhoras!

Dr. Benjamin: *Good afternoon, Mr. Felipe. What's the matter? What's your problem?*

Felipe: *I don't know. I have a sore throat, a headache, and a cough. I think I have the flu.*

Dr. Benjamin: *I have to take your temperature, and I also want to give you a general checkup. Sit here, please.*

Felipe: *Do you think I can travel tomorrow? I have to visit a client in another state.*

Dr. Benjamin: *I'm sorry, but your temperature is too high, and your throat is pretty inflamed. You should stay at home for two or three days and rest. You also need to take this medicine every six hours. You should also drink a lot of liquids. If you're not better in three days, come back for another checkup.*

Felipe: *Okay. I'll do as you say (lit., obey your suggestions): stay at home, rest, and take the medicine. Thank you very much.*

Dr. Benjamin: *Don't worry, and get better soon!*

NUTS & BOLTS 2

Querer *(TO WANT TO)*, TER QUE *(TO HAVE TO)*, AND PRECISAR *(TO NEED TO)*

The verbs **querer** *(to want to)*, **ter que** *(to have to, must)*, and **precisar** *(to need to)* are used in the same way as **dever** and **poder** above. They are followed by infinitives, for example **falar**:

eu quero falar *(I want to speak)*	**nós queremos falar** *(we want to speak)*
você quer falar *(you want to speak)*	**vocês querem falar** *(you want to speak)*
ele/ela quer falar *(he/she wants to speak)*	**eles/elas querem falar** *(they want to speak)*

eu tenho que falar *(I have to speak)*	**nós temos que falar** *(we have to speak)*
você tem que falar *(you have to speak)*	**vocês têm que falar** *(you have to speak)*
ele/ela tem que falar *(he/she has to speak)*	**eles/elas têm que falar** *(they have to speak)*

eu preciso falar *(I need to speak)*	**nós precisamos falar** *(we need to speak)*
você precisa falar *(you need to speak)*	**vocês precisam falar** *(you need to speak)*
ele/ela precisa falar *(he/she needs to speak)*	**eles/elas precisam falar** *(they need to speak)*

Eu quero aprender japonês; eu gosto da cultura japonesa.
I want to learn Japanase; I like the Japanese culture.

Você tem que tomar esse remédio de três em três horas.
You have to take this medicine every three hours.

Eles precisam fazer ginástica.
They need to work out.

PRACTICE 2
Complete with **ter que, precisar,** or **querer.** Follow the example, and try to translate the questions and answers, using context or by looking up unfamiliar words.

Ex. O que vocês têm que fazer hoje? <u>Nós temos que</u> escrever um relatório.

1. Por que você precisa estudar italiano? _____italiano porque vou mudar para Itália.

2. Que horas você quer correr no parque? _____ no parque às 7:00 da manhã.

3. O que ela precisa comprar? _____os jornais.

4. Qual remédio o menino tem que tomar? _____xarope.

5. Quanto dinheiro nós precisamos depositar? _____ $300.00.

6. O que os clientes querem comprar? _____os nossos produtos.

7. O que as professoras têm que fazer? _____escrever os exercícios.

8. Onde vocês querem morar? _____no Brasil.

9. O que você quer beber?_____vinho.

10. Por que eles têm que tomar injeção? _____ injeção porque estão muito doentes.

Culture note

Brazil is essentially a Catholic country, but other forms of religious expression are found there as well, with unique and interesting healing practices. For example, Macumba, Candomblé and Umbanda are based on African religious traditions and were originally brought to Brazil in the 1550s through the slave trade. The term Macumba is now slang for magic and superstition, and it generally has a pejorative meaning. Candomblé has its greatest followers in Bahia, and Umbanda in Rio, although variations of both are present in all parts of Brazil. About two million Brazilians identify themselves as followers of Candomblé or Umbanda. One of the main characteristics of these religions is the importance of mediums. After performing or taking part in rituals involving dancing and singing, mediums "receive," or are possessed by, spiritual guides. The spiritual guides come to earth to counsel, help, and heal the devotees present at places of worship or temples.

A related belief system is Spiritism, which also has a large following in Brazil. Spiritism was established in France, in the nineteenth century, by the French educator Allan Kardec (Hippolyte Léon Denizard Rivail). One of its rituals is the séance, which is also used by Brazilians as a form of counseling and healing, and as a cure for ailments. Spiritist mediums are famous for their healing abilities. Chico Xavier (1910-2002) was one of the most renowned Brazilian mediums, as well as a prolific writer.

You can read more about Macumba, Candomblé, Umbanda, Spiritism, and Chico Xavier on the internet. If you decide to practice your Portuguese by renting *Orfeu Negro* (Black Orpheus), you'll find an arresting portrayal of one of these rituals.

ANSWERS
PRACTICE 1: 1. pode (Can you give the present back?)
2. devem (The children shouldn't run in the street.) **3.** posso (I can't solve the problem.) **4.** pode (She can't hide her face.)
5. deve (The manager should get the report.) **6.** deve (The

student should answer.) **7.** podem (What can they drink?)
8. devo (When should I arrive?) **9.** podemos (We can see the beach.) **10.** devem (What should the students read?)

PRACTICE 2: **1.** Eu preciso estudar (Why do you need to study Italian? I need to study Italian because I'm going to move to Italy.) **2.** Eu quero correr (What time do you want to run in the park? I want to run in the park at 7 A.M.) **3.** Ela precisa comprar (What does she need to buy? She needs to buy the papers.) **4.** Ele tem que tomar (Which medicine does the boy have to take? He has to take cough medicine.) **5.** Vocês precisam depositar (How much money do we need to deposit? You need to deposit $300.00.) **6.** Eles querem comprar (What do the clients want to buy? They want to buy our products.) **7.** Elas têm que escrever (What do the teachers have to do? They have to write the exercises.) **8.** Nós queremos morar (Where do you want to live? We want to live in Brazil.) **9.** Eu quero beber (What do you want to drink? I want to drink wine.) **10.** Eles têm que tomar (Why do they have to have injections? They have to have injections because they are very sick.)

UNIT 4 ESSENTIALS

Este livro tem mais de quatrocentas páginas.
This book has more than 400 pages.

Este remédio é para resfriado?
Is this a cold medicine?

Essa receita médica é a minha?
Is that prescription (you're holding) mine?

Estes aqui são meus e aqueles com você são seus.
These here are mine, and those with you are yours.

Eu gosto disso, mas não gosto daquilo.
I like this, but I don't like that.

Eu não entendo a pergunta.
I don't understand the question.

Nós aprendemos português.
We learn Portuguese.

Você vê aquele homem?
Do you see that man?

Nós estamos com sono.
We're not sleepy.

Vocês estão com fome?
Are you hungry?

Elas estão com vontade de comer pizza.
They feel like eating pizza.

O paciente está com dor de cabeça.
The patient has a headache.

Ele está com dor de barriga.
He has a stomachache.

As crianças estão com tosse.
The children have a cough.

As minhas pernas doem.
My legs hurt.

Como você se sente?
How do you feel?

Não me sinto bem.
I don't feel very well.

Estou mal.
I feel terrible.

UNIT 5
On the phone

Alô? In Unit 5 you'll learn how to make phone calls, including some courtesy expressions that you can use on the phone. This unit also covers the last group of regular verbs, as well as the present continuous tense, so you'll be able to say what you are doing, where you are going, and other things that are happening at the moment you're speaking.

──────────── Lesson 17 (words) ────────────

WORD LIST 1

alô	*hello*
ligar	*to call*
telefonar	*to telephone*
atender	*to answer (the phone)*
desligar	*to hang up*
gravar	*to record*
o telefone/o aparelho de telefone	*telephone*
a linha	*telephone line*
a ligação/a chamada	*phone call*
a secretaria eletrônica	*answering machine*
o ramal	*extension*
o sinal	*signal*
ocupado	*busy*
o recado	*message*
caixa postal	*voice mail*
a conexão	*connection*
e-mail	*e-mail*

o celular/o telefone celular	*cell phone*
o celular/o telefone celular	*internet*
a internet	*internet*
o site	*website*

NUTS & BOLTS 1
REGULAR -IR VERBS

In Unit 3 you learned that regular verbs in Portuguese are divided into three groups, ending in **-ar, -er,** and **-ir.** Now, take a look at the verb **abrir** *(to open)* as an example of an -**ir** verb.

eu abr<u>o</u>	nós abr<u>imos</u>
você abr<u>e</u>	vocês abr<u>em</u>
ele/ela abr<u>e</u>	eles/elas abr<u>em</u>

Here's a list of some other regular verbs ending in **-ir.**

assistir *(to attend, to be present, to watch)*	**insistir** *(to insist)*
discutir *(to discuss/to argue)*	**incluir** *(to include)*
preferir *(to prefer)*	**possuir** *(to own/to possess)*
dividir *(to divide/to share)*	**sentir** *(to feel/to be sorry)*
partir *(to depart/to leave)*	**repetir** *(to repeat)*
decidir *(to decide)*	**sortir** *(to supply, to mix)*

Você prefere chá ou café?
Do you prefer tea or coffee?

Nós partimos para Londres às vinte e uma horas.
We leave for London at 9:00 P.M.

Você discute demais!
You argue too much!

A oferta não inclui o transporte.
The offer doesn't include transportation.

Quantas vezes ela repete a pergunta?
How many times does she repeat the question?

Let's look at a table with all three conjugations side by side, so you can compare the differences and see the similarities.

-ar group	-er group	-ir group
falar (*to speak*)	comer (*to eat*)	assistir (*to watch*)
eu fal<u>o</u>	eu com<u>o</u>	eu assist<u>o</u>
você fal<u>a</u>	você com<u>e</u>	você assist<u>e</u>
ele/ela fal<u>a</u>	ele/ela com<u>e</u>	ele/ela assist<u>e</u>
nós fal<u>amos</u>	nós com<u>emos</u>	nós assist<u>imos</u>
vocês fal<u>am</u>	vocês com<u>em</u>	vocês assist<u>em</u>
eles/elas fal<u>am</u>	eles/elas com<u>em</u>	eles/elas assist<u>em</u>

PRACTICE 1
Use the correct form of the **-ir** verbs in parentheses. Translate the full sentences.

1. Eu não viajo, porque _____ (preferir) ficar em casa.

2. Os gerentes _____ (discutir) os novos planos.

3. As crianças _____ (assistir) mais de quatro horas de TV todos os dias.

4. Que horas _____ (partir) o seu vôo?

5. Nós não _____ (insistir) no desconto.

6. A professora _____ (repetir) a lição.

Now practice all three categories of verbs.

7. Nós _____ (comprar) muitas coisas para a viagem.

8. Vocês _____ (beber) vinho tinto ou branco?

9. Nós _____ (preferir) cerveja, obrigado.

10. Carlos e Márcia _____ (receber) muitos cartões de Natal.

11. Eu _____(acordar) às seis da manhã.

12. Por que você não _____ (dividir) a casa com uma amiga?

13. Aqueles rapazes não _____ (gostar) de estudar muito.

14. A que horas ela _____ (chegar)?

15. Quando ele _____ (encontrar) o gerente do banco?

WORD LIST 2

a reclamação	*complaint*
reclamar	*to complain*
encomendar	*to order (by phone, online, catalog)*
a encomenda	*order (noun)*
o produto	*product*
aguardar	*to wait*
esperar	*to wait/to hope*
anotar	*take note*
a semana	*week*
o mês	*month*
o calendário	*calendar*
ajudar	*to help/to aid/to assist*
a tela	*screen*

a urgência	*urgency*
a mercadoria	*merchandise*
a inauguração	*the opening/inauguration*

NUTS & BOLTS 2
THE VERB IR *(TO GO)* AND CONTRACTIONS WITH A *(TO)*

The irregular verb **ir** means *to go.*

eu vou	nós vamos
você vai	vocês vão
ele/ela vai	eles/elas vão

Eu vou à escola de francês.
I'm going to the French school.

Quando nós vamos?
When are we going?

Elas sempre vão ao aeroporto duas horas antes do vôo.
They always go to the airport two hours before the flight.

Você não vai?
Aren't you going?

Just as in English, the verb **ir** is often followed by the preposition **a** *(to)*. **A** forms contractions with definite articles, much as **de**. Notice the grave accent in the feminine forms.

a + o = ao	a + os = aos
a + a = à	a + as = às

Ele vai à praia de Copacabana.
He's going to Copacabana beach.

Ela vai ao parque.
She's going to the park.

Nós vamos aos jogos de futebol.
We're going to the soccer games.

Eles vão às partes mais pobres da cidade.
They go to the poorest parts of the city.

The grave accent is also used when the preposition **a** is followed by the demonstratives **aquele, aquela,** and **aquilo.**

Por que vocês vão àquela cidade?
Why are you going to that city?

Ele prefere este hotel àquele.
He prefers this hotel to that one.

PRACTICE 2

Complete the following with the correct forms of **ir,** and add **à(s)** or **ao(s).**

1. Eu _____ aeroporto encontrar minha amiga.

2. Os meninos _____ piscina esta tarde.

3. Os turistas não _____ áreas isoladas.

4. Meu marido e eu sempre _____ jardins públicos.

5. Solange não _____ loja de sapatos hoje.

6. Quem _____ festa da Mariana?

7. Por que vocês não _____ Rio de Janeiro?

ANSWERS

PRACTICE 1: 1. prefiro (I don't travel because I prefer to stay at home.) **2.** discutem (The managers discuss the new plans.) **3.** assistem (The children watch more than four hours of TV every day.) **4.** parte (What time does your flight leave?) **5.** insistimos (We don't insist on the discount.) **6.** repete (The teacher repeats the lesson.) **7.** compramos (We buy many things for the trip.) **8.** bebem (Do you drink red or white wine?) **9.** preferimos (We prefer beer, thank you.) **10.** recebem (Carlos and Márcia get many Christmas cards.) **11.** acordo (I wake up at 6:00 A.M.) **12.** divide (Why don't you share a house with a friend?) **13.** gostam (Those young men don't like to study very much.) **14.** chega (What time does she arrive?) **15.** encontra (When does he meet with the bank manager?)

PRACTICE 2: 1. vou ao; **2.** vão à; **3.** vão às; **4.** vamos aos; **5.** vai à; **6.** vai à; **7.** vão ao

––––––––––––––– Lesson 18 (phrases) –––––––––––––––

PHRASE LIST 1

o atendimento eletrônico	*recorded message*
deixar um recado	*to leave a message*
o código de área	*area code*
digitar o número	*to dial the number*
Pois não?/Pois não!	*Yes?/Can I help you?/Of course!*
pois é	*that's true*
a galeria de arte	*art gallery*
na parte esquerda da tela	*on the left hand side of the screen*

do lado direito	*on the right side*
em cima da mesa	*on the table*
em baixo do console	*under the console*
no meio do filme	*in the middle of the film*
ao lado da mesa	*next to the table*
dentro do cofre	*in the safe deposit box*
fora de casa	*outside the house*
atrás da impressora	*behind the printer*
em frente à TV	*in front of the TV*
entre as duas e as três	*between 2:00 and 3:00*

NUTS & BOLTS 1
EM AND OTHER PREPOSITIONS

The preposition **em** means *at, on, in* or *into*. It is sometimes contracted with the definite articles **a, o, as, os** and becomes **na, no, nas, nos**. But with no article, **em** is used alone.

Eu estou no escritório. (em+o)
I'm at the office.

Ela não entra na piscina. (em+a)
She doesn't go into the pool.

Você escreve nos livros? (em+os)
Do you write on the books?

As roupas estão nas malas. (em+as)
The clothes are in the bags.

Ele mora em Belo Horizonte.
He lives in Belo Horizonte.

Em also contracts with **um, uma, uns, umas,** and become **num, numa, nuns, numas.**

Ele mora numa avenida larga. (em+uma)
He lives on a wide avenue.

Ela vive num bairro pobre. (em+um)

She lives in a poor neighborhood.

A pizzaria só entrega numas regiões da cidade. (em+umas)

The pizzeria only delivers to some areas of the city.

Ela come nuns restaurantes vegetarianos. (em+uns)

She eats in some vegetarian restaurants.

You also contract **em** with the demonstratives **este(s), esse(s), esta(s), essa(s), aquele(s), aquela(s) isto, isso, aquilo,** to form **neste(s), nesse(s), nesta(s), nessa(s), naquele(s), naquela(s), nisto, nisso, naquilo.**

O carro está nesta rua ou naquela?

Is the car in this street or in that one?

Por que você não coloca seu celular naquilo?

Why don't you keep your cell in that?

Ele não pode insistir nisso!

He can't insist on that!

Some other common prepositions that show location are: **em cima** *(on, on top of)*, **em baixo** *(under)*, **ao lado** *(next to)*, **no meio** *(between)*, **em frente** *(in front of)*, **fora** *(outside)*, **dentro** *(inside)*, **atrás** *(behind)*, **entre** *(among, between)*.

A revista está em cima da mesa.

The magazine is on the table.

Os sapatos estão em baixo da cama.

The shoes are under the bed.

A impressora está ao lado do computador.

The printer is next to the computer.

O cachorro está no meio da rua.

The dog is in the middle of the street.

Eles estão em frente ao cinema.
They are in front of the movie theater.

Ele mora fora da cidade.
He lives outside the city.

O dinheiro está dentro da bolsa.
The money is in the handbag.

O espelho está pendurado atrás da porta.
The mirror is hanging behind the door.

O sofá está bem entre as duas mesas.
The sofa looks nice between the two tables.

PRACTICE 1

Complete the following sentences with one of the following prepositions: **fora, dentro, em cima, em baixo, entre, ao lado, em frente.**

1. As chaves estão _____ da mesa.

2. O dinheiro está _____ do cofre.

3. O cachorro fica _____ de casa?

4. Ele estaciona o seu carro _____ ao hotel.

5. A colher sempre está _____ da faca.

6. O que há _____ da cama?

7. Ela coloca a flor _____ as páginas do livro.

Complete the following sentences with: **neste, nessa, naquilo, naquelas, naqueles, nisso.**

8. Quem mora _____ apartamento?

9. Você coloca água _____ plantas todos os dias?

10. Você compra sempre _____ loja?

11. Ele prefere o vinho _____ ou _____?

12. Ele viaja _____ países.

PHRASE LIST 2

as estações do ano	*the seasons of the year*
a primavera florida	*the blossoming spring*
o verão úmido	*the humid summer*
o ar fresco de outono	*the fresh fall air*
o inverno frio	*the cold winter*
no fim de semana	*over the weekend, during the weekend*
no final da tarde	*at the end of the afternoon*
antes da data	*before the date*
depois do evento	*after the event*
durante a cerimônia	*during the ceremony*
Que tal amanhã?	*How about tomorrow?*
estamos em dois de abril	*this is April 2nd*
no dia onze de abril	*on April 11th*
em mil novecentos e noventa e sete	*in 1997*
neste século	*in this century*
no final do ano	*at the end of the year*
na semana que vem	*next week*

NUTS & BOLTS 2

DAYS, DATES AND PREPOSITIONS OF TIME

First let's learn the days of the week and the months of the year.

dias da semana *(days of the week)*	quinta-feira *(Thursday)*
segunda-feira *(Monday)*	sexta-feira *(Friday)*
terça-feira *(Tuesday)*	sábado *(Saturday)*
quarta-feira *(Wednesday)*	domingo *(Sunday)*

Note that the days of the week are not capitalized, and that the word **feira** is optional in informal and spoken Portuguese. If you want to say that something happens on a particular day, use **no** *(on the)* for **sábado** and **domingo,** which are masculine, and **na** *(on the)* for the other days, which are feminine.

Eu chego no domingo.
I arrive on Sunday.

Ele telefona na sexta-feira.
He calls on Friday.

When you want to say that something happens in general, for example, *on Mondays,* use **aos** (**sábado** and **domingo**) or **às** (other days):

Eu assisto programas de TV aos sábados, e faço ginástica às segundas e quartas.
I watch TV shows on Saturdays, and work out on Mondays and Wednesdays.

Now let's look at **os meses do ano** *(the months of the year),* which are also not capitalized.

janeiro	abril	julho	outubro
fevereiro	maio	agosto	novembro
março	junho	setembro	dezembro

If you want to say that something happens in a particular month, use the preposition **em:**

No Brasil é verão em janeiro.

It's summer in Brazil in January.

Eles gostam de viajar em setembro.

They like to travel in September.

You learned the names for the seasons in the phrase list: **a primavera** *(spring)*, **o verão** *(summer)*, **o outono** *(fall)*, **o inverno** *(winter)*. If you want to say that something happens in a particular season, use **na** for spring, and **no** for the other seasons.

As praias nunca estão muito cheias na primavera.

The beaches aren't too crowded in spring.

As aulas deles começam no outono.

Their classes start in fall.

Dates in Portuguese are expressed in the order: day, month, and year, with the preposition **de** between. In the written language, dates are written as dd/mm/yyyy. So, **27/11/1956** is November 27, 1956; and **06/08/11** is August 6, 2011.

vinte e seis de outubro de dois mil e oito	*October 26, 2008*
doze de janeiro de mil, novecentos e sessenta e sete	*January 12, 1967*

If you want to say that something happened in a particular year or on a particular date, use the preposition **em**. **Em** is also used with the word **século** *(century)*, although it is contracted with the article:

em dois mil e seis	*in 2006*
em vinte e seis de julho de mil novecentos e oitenta e cinco	*on July 26th, 1985*
no século vinte e um	*in the 21st century*

Finally, some other common prepositions of time are **antes de** *(before)*, **depois de** *(after)*, and **durante** *(during)*. Note that the **de** is contracted with the articles:

A professora chega antes dos alunos.
The teacher arrives before the students.

O avião parte depois das seis.
The plane leaves after 6:00.

Eles não atendem ao telefone durante o jogo de futebol.
They don't answer the phone during the soccer game.

PRACTICE 2
Write the dates:

1. May 25, 1884; October 19, 2005; February 21, 1937

Use the correct preposition:

2. Eu chego depois _____ amanhã.

3. Eles jogam tênis _____ quintas-feiras e _____ sábados.

4. Você chega antes _____ professora?

5. Nós vamos a Paris _____ 2010.

6. As mercadorias chegam _____ abril.

Answer the questions using the cues in parentheses.

7. Quando você vai viajar? (3 de abril)

8. Que dia é o seu aniversário? (5 de dezembro)

9. Qual a data no contrato? (20 de junho de 2005)

10. Quando ele vai para universidade? (outono)

ANSWERS:

PRACTICE 1: 1. em cima; 2. dentro; 3. fora; 4. em frente; 5. ao lado; 6. em baixo; 7. entre; 8. neste; 9. naquelas; 10. nessa; 11. nisso, naquilo; 12. naqueles

PRACTICE 2: 1. vinte e cinco de maio de mil, oitocentos e oitenta e quatro; dezenove de outubro de dois mil e cinco; vinte e um de fevereiro de mil, novecentos e trinta e sete; 2. de; 3. às, aos; 4. da; 5. em; 6. em; 7. Eu vou viajar em três de abril. (I'm going to travel on April 3.); 8. O meu aniversário é em cinco de dezembro. (My birthday is on December 5.); 9. A data no contrato é vinte de junho de dois mil e cinco. (The date on the contract is June 20, 2005.); 10. Ele vai para universidade no outono. (He's going to university in fall.)

—————————— Lesson 19 (sentences) ——————————

SENTENCE LIST 1

Aqui quem fala é o Pedro.	*This is Pedro speaking.*
Um momento, por favor, a linha esta ocupada.	*Please hold, the line is busy.*
De onde fala?	*What number did I call?*
Com quem você gostaria de falar?	*Who would you like to speak to?*
Eu gostaria de falar com a senhora Ana Maria.	*I'd like to speak to Ms. Ana Maria.*
Você pode transferir a ligação?	*Can you transfer the call?*
Você discou para o número errado.	*You've dialed the wrong number.*

Qual é o seu telefone?	*What's your phone number?*
Posso ligar mais tarde?	*Can I call back later?*
Você pode deixar um recado, por favor?	*Can you leave a message, please?*
Qual é o ramal desejado?	*What is the extension you want?*
Nós perdemos a conexão.	*We've lost the connection.*
Vocês têm acesso gratuito para internet?	*Do you have free internet access?*
Você precisa discar zero para falar com a recepção.	*You need to dial zero to talk to reception.*
Esse hotel tem internet rápida?	*Does this hotel have high-speed internet?*
Vocês podem usar internet sem fio aqui?	*Can you use wireless internet here?*
Ele manda mensagens de texto para os amigos.	*He sends text messages to his friends.*
Eu telefono mais tarde.	*I'll call later.*
Vocês ligam para o hotel.	*You call the hotel.*

NUTS & BOLTS 1

THE VERBS vir *(TO COME)*, PEDIR *(TO ASK FOR)*, AND TRAZER *(TO BRING)*

Let's look at a few more common irregular verbs.

vir *(to come)*

eu venho	nós vimos
você vem	vocês vêm
ele/ela vem	eles/elas vêm

pedir *(to request, to order, to ask for)*

eu peço	nós pedimos
você pede	vocês pedem
ele/ela pede	eles/elas pedem

trazer *(to bring)*

eu trago	nós trazemos
você traz	vocês trazem
ele/ela traz	eles/elas trazem

Você traz uma garrafa de vinho e eu trago cerveja para a festa.
You bring a bottle of wine, and I'll bring beer to the party.

Nós não trazemos muito dinheiro à praia.
We don't bring a lot of money to the beach.

Eles pedem um táxi na recepção.
They order a taxi at the reception.

Ângela pede um empréstimo no banco.
Ângela requests a bank loan.

Posso pedir um favor?
Can I ask for a favor?

Quando vocês vêm a nossa casa?
When are you coming to our house?

A menina não vem a pé da escola?
Doesn't the girl walk home from school?

Note that **vir a pé** is *to come on foot;* **vir de carro** is *to come in a car,* and **vir de ônibus, trem, avião** is *to come by bus, train,* or *plane.*

Ele vem de carro ou de ônibus?
Is he taking a car or the bus?

Por que vocês não vêm de trem?
Why don't you take the train here?

PRACTICE 1
Complete the following sentences with the correct form of the verb given in parentheses.

1. O funcionário _____ (vir) ao escritório de carro.

2. Quando eu estou com fome, eu geralmente_____ (pedir) uma pizza.

3. O que Júlia _____(traz) para a academia?

4. Você e seus amigos _____(vir) à festa de natal?

5. Quando nós _____(trazer) os documentos?

6. Eu não _____(vir) aqui sozinha porque tenho medo.

7. Os vizinhos sempre_____(pedir) favores ao porteiro.

8. Eu _____(trazer) um cartão de crédito, mas não dinheiro quando vou às compras.

9. João e Adelaide _____ (pedir) ajuda aos amigos.

10. O que nós _____(pedir) neste restaurante?

SENTENCE LIST 2

Você gostaria de fazer uma excursão?	*Would you like to go on a tour?*
Vocês querem usar a sauna?	*Do you want to use the sauna?*
Não, obrigado. Agora estou ocupado.	*No, thank you. I'm busy now.*
Não, muito obrigado.	*No, thank you. I'd love to,*
Adoraria, mas nesse dia	*but I'm busy that day.*
estou ocupado.	

Sinto muito. Não posso, estou com pressa.	*I'm sorry. I can't, I'm in a hurry.*
Sim, adoraria experimentar um doce.	*Yes, I'd love to try a candy.*
Aceitamos o convite com muito prazer.	*We accept this invitation with pleasure.*
Muito obrigado pelo convite. A que horas devemos chegar?	*Thank you for the invitation. What time should we arrive?*
Agradeço a oferta, mas não podemos ir.	*I thank you for the offer, but we can't make it.*
Vocês gostariam de jantar agora?	*Would you like to have dinner now?*
Ele gostaria de ir ao museu?	*Would he like to go to the museum?*
Ela gostaria de não ser incomodada.	*She would rather not be disturbed.*
Nós não gostaríamos de pagar extra.	*We wouldn't like to pay extra.*
Eu gostaria de fazer uma reclamação.	*I'd like to make a complaint.*

NUTS & BOLTS 2

COURTESY EXPRESSIONS AND GOSTARIA DE *(WOULD LIKE)*

As you know, there are both masculine and feminine forms of *thank you:* **obrigado** and **obrigada**. Some possible responses are: **Não tem de que.** *(Don't mention it.),* **De nada.** *(You're welcome.),* and **Obrigado você.** *(Thank you.)* Both **sinto (muito)** and **desculpe** can be translated as *I'm sorry,* but **sinto** is used before a negative, while **desculpe** is an apology.

Sinto muito, não tenho relógio.

I'm sorry, I don't have a watch.

Eu sinto, mas não posso ir a sua festa.

I'm afraid I can't go to your party.

Desculpe, eu disquei o numero errado.

Sorry, I've dialed the wrong number.

Desculpe o meu atraso.

I'm sorry for my delay.

Não é nada./Não faz mal.

It's nothing.

Não foi nada.

It was nothing.

When you want to say *excuse me,* say **com licença,** as in: **Com licença, onde fica o banheiro?** *(Excuse me, where is the restroom?)*

Some common verbs that express courtesy or politeness are **agradecer** *(to thank),* **desculpar** *(to forgive),* and **sentir** *(to be or feel sorry):*

Eu quero agradecer.

I want to thank you.

Você pode me desculpar?

Can you forgive me?

Nós sentimos muito, mas não vamos.

We're sorry, but we're not coming.

You've already learned the verb **gostar de** *(to like).* You can use its conditional form to make polite requests, just as the English *would like.* We'll come back to conditionals later, but for now take a look at the polite forms of **gostar de,** used to soften a request:

eu gostaria de	nós gostaríamos de
você gostaria de	vocês gostariam de
ele/ela gostaria de	eles/elas gostariam de

Note that there's an accent over the **i** in **gostaríamos**. This causes the stress to fall on that syllable, so you pronounce it **gos-ta-RI-a-mos.**

Você gostaria de um chá ou um café?
Would you like some coffee or some tea?

Nós gostaríamos de chegar às nove da manhã, por favor.
We'd like to arrive at 9:00 A.M., please.

Another polite request verb is **adorar** *(to love),* which forms its conditionals *(would love)* just like **gostaria: adoraria, adoraríamos, adorariam:**

Eu adoraria ir à festa de Ano Novo.
I'd love to go to the New Year's party.

Eles adorariam visitar o seu país.
They'd love to visit your country.

PRACTICE 2
Match the phrase in Column A to its response in Column B, and then give the translation.

Column A	Column B
1. Muito obrigado, Sr. Paulo.	A. Pois não. O que a senhora gostaria?
2. O senhor pode me dizer as horas, por favor?	B. Sim, muito obrigada.
3. Ai! Meu pé!	C. Não faz mal.
4. Com licença, posso entrar?	D. Não tem de quê.

Column A	Column B
5. Desculpe, estou atrasado.	E. Sinto muito, não tenho relógio.
6. A senhora gostaria de uma bebida?	F. Desculpe!

Culture note

An Anglicism is the use of an English word in another language. In both Brazil and Portugal this trend has been making inroads into Portuguese for decades. The main reason for this is that new technologies have come mostly from the United States, and the Portuguese language is sometimes slow to coin new terms for these advancements. As a result, by the time a new technology or device gets a Portuguese name, its English name has already become entrenched, either out of habit or sometimes because words in English are considered more distinctive. Whatever the reason, the incorporation of all these English names and terms happens, some believe, to the detriment of the Portuguese language, giving rise to sentences like: **No Brasil você já pode navegar na *internet* num *cybercafé* que tenha um *hotspot wireless* para ler o seu *e-mail*, para visitar *sites* com *blogs*, ou para fazer *downloads*. Mas cuidado com os *pop-ups* e com os *spams* na *web*!** *(In Brazil you can already surf the web in an internet café that has a wireless hotspot to read your e-mails, or visit sites with blogs or to download stuff. But be careful with the pop-ups or spam on the web!)*

But not all internet-related vocabulary comes from English. Here's a list of common terms, some of which are related to English, and some of which aren't: **internet** *(internet)*, **cibercafé** *(cybercafe)*, **hotspot** *(hotspot/Wi-Fi access area)*, **sem fio** *(wireless)*, **correio eletrônico** *(e-mail)*, **sítio** *(site)*, **blog** *(blog)*, **baixar** *(to download)*, **pop-up** *(pop-up)*, **spam** *(spam)*, **rede** *(web, network)*.

And, in case you think that English is somehow immune to borrowing from other languages, think again. English has been called the "vacuum cleaner" of languages, gobbling up words from languages all over the world without shame or remorse. Of course, Portuguese is one of them:

http://en.wikipedia.org/wiki/List_of_English_words_of_Portuguese_origin

http://en.wikipedia.org/wiki/Lists_of_English_words_of_international_origin

ANSWERS
PRACTICE 1: **1.** vem; **2.** peço; **3.** traz; **4.** vêm; **5.** trazemos; **6.** venho; **7.** pedem; **8.** trago; **9.** pedem; **10.** pedimos

PRACTICE 2: **1.** D. -Thank you very much, Mr. Paulo. -Don't mention it. **2.** E. -Can you please tell me the time? -No, I can't. I don't have a watch. **3.** F. -Ouch! My foot! -Sorry! **4.** A. -Excuse me, can I come in? -Certainly. What would you like? **5.** C. -I'm sorry, I'm late. -It doesn't matter. **6.** B. -Would you like a taxi? -Yes, thank you.

———— Lesson 20 (conversations) ————

CONVERSATION 1
Mensagem Eletrônica: Bem-vindo ao atendimento eletrônico de Digital Comunicações. Caso saiba o ramal desejado digite agora, ou aguarde para falar com um dos nossos agentes.

    Gustavo: Alô Luiza?

    Luiza: Pois não, quem fala?

    Gustavo: Aqui é o Gustavo, tudo bem?

    Luiza: Oi Gustavo, tudo bem. Quanto tempo!

    Gustavo: Pois é! Eu estou ligando para convidá-la para a festa de inauguração da minha galeria de arte.

    Luiza: Que legal. Quando?

    Gustavo: A festa vai ser na quarta-feira que vem, dia vinte e três, às sete e meia da noite. Você vem? Pode trazer alguém com você.

Luiza: Não sei, deixe ver . . . Ah, que pena, não posso. Na quarta que vem estarei viajando a negócios.

Gustavo: Não faz mal. Você gostaria de vir à galeria outro dia? Quando voltar?

Luiza: Adoraria ir. Para quando você quer combinar? Eu estou voltando para Belo Horizonte na sexta-feira, dia vinte e cinco.

Gustavo: Que tal no sábado à tarde, então? Você vem à galeria, e depois a gente pode tomar um café juntos.

Luiza: Combinado. Sábado à tarde, entre três e quatro da tarde eu apareço por lá. Boa sorte na inauguração!

Gustavo: Obrigado, Luiza. Tchau, um abraço.

Luiza: Outro.

Recorded message: *Welcome to Digital Communication's automated answering service. If you know your party's extension, dial it now, or hold the line to speak to one of our representatives.*

Gustavo: *Hello, Luiza?*

Luiza: *Yes, who's this?*

Gustavo: *This is Gustavo, how are you doing?*

Luiza: *Hi, Gustavo. I'm fine. It's been a long time!*

Gustavo: *It sure has! I'm calling to invite you to the opening party of my art gallery.*

Luiza: *That's nice. When?*

Gustavo: *The party will be next Wednesday, the 23rd, at 7:30 in the evening. Can you come? You can bring a friend with you.*

Luiza: *I don't know, let me see . . . Oh, what a pity, I can't. Next Wednesday I'm traveling on business.*

Gustavo: *It doesn't matter. Would you like to come to the gallery some other day? When you return?*

Luiza: *I'd love to go. When do you want to plan it for? I'm coming back to Belo Horizonte on Friday, the 25th.*

> Gustavo: How about Saturday afternoon, then? You come to the gallery, and then we can have some coffee together.
>
> Luiza: It's a date. I'll show up there Saturday afternoon, between 3:00 and 4:00. Good luck at the opening!
>
> Gustavo: Thanks, Luiza. Bye, take care.
>
> Luiza: You too.

NUTS & BOLTS 1
THE PRESENT CONTINUOUS

The present continuous tense describes an ongoing action, like the English *I am reading*. Portuguese forms its present continuous with the verb **estar** + the gerund of the main verb. The gerund is formed by taking off the final **-r** of the infinitive, and adding **-ndo**: **falar–falando** *(to speak–speaking)*, **escrever–escrevendo** *(to write–writing)*, **partir–partindo** *(to leave–leaving)*, **fazer–fazendo** *(to do/make–doing/making)*, **ir–indo** *(to go–going)*. Let's see the conjugation of **estar falando** *(to be speaking)*.

eu estou falando	**nós estamos falando**
você está falando	**vocês estão falando**
ele/ela está falando	**eles/elas estão falando**

Just as in English, you use the present continuous to talk about something that's happening at the moment you're talking, or to express an ongoing trend. Some typical adverbs you can use with the present continuous are: **agora** *(now)*, **agora mesmo** *(right now)*, **neste momento** *(at this moment)*, **actualmente** *(currently–not actually!)*

Eu estou escrevendo agora. O que você está fazendo?

I'm writing now. What are you doing?

Ele está assistindo à TV enquanto ela está falando ao telefone.

He's watching TV while she's talking on the phone.

Atualmente nós estamos ampliando as instalações da nossa fábrica.
Currently we are expanding the facilities in our factory.

Esta semana eles estão trabalhando hora extra.
This week they're putting in overtime.

PRACTICE 1

Complete with the present continuous of the verbs in parentheses.

1. Umas crianças _____ (jogar) bola.

2. Um homem _____ (ler) jornal.

3. Uns cachorros_____ (correr) na grama.

4. Um homem e um menino _____ (alimentar) os pássaros.

5. Os patos _____ (nadar) no lago.

6. Um homem _____ (pintar) um banco.

7. Uns turistas_____ (tirar) fotos.

8. Uma moça _____ (fazer) jogging.

CONVERSATION 2

Recepcionista: Recepção, bom dia.

Sr. Duarte: Bom dia. Eu gostaria de fazer uma reclamação.

Recepcionista: Pois não. Qual é o problema?

Sr. Duarte: Eu sempre fico neste hotel, e nunca tenho problemas. Desta vez, porém, estou tendo problemas com a o ar condicionado, com o chuveiro, e com o acesso à internet.

Recepcionista: Nossa! O senhor pode dizer que tipo de problemas?

Sr. Duarte: O ar condicionado não está funcionando; não está saindo água quente do chuveiro, e não estou conseguindo conexão com a internet.

Recepcionista:	O senhor realmente está tendo muitos problemas. O senhor gostaria de mudar de quarto?
Sr. Duarte:	Sim, gostaria. A senhorita pode pedir para alguém vir ajudar com as malas?
Recepcionista:	Pois não, agora mesmo. Eu realmente sinto muito, e gostaria também de pedir desculpas em nome do nosso hotel.
Sr. Duarte:	Não tem nada. Estou esperando o ajudante.

Receptionist:	Front desk, good morning.
Sr. Duarte:	Good morning. I'd like to make a complaint.
Receptionist:	Certainly. What is the matter?
Sr. Duarte:	I always stay at this hotel, and have never had a problem. This time, though, I'm having problems with the air conditioning, with the shower, and with the internet access.
Receptionist:	My goodness! Could you tell me what kind of problems?
Sr. Duarte:	The air conditioning isn't working; there's no hot water coming out of the shower; and, I'm not managing to get onto the internet.
Receptionist:	You are really having a lot of problems. Would you like to change rooms?
Sr. Duarte:	Yes, I would. Could you please ask someone to come up to help with my bags?
Receptionist:	Of course, immediately. I am really very sorry, and would like to apologize on behalf of our hotel.
Sr. Duarte:	That's all right. I'll be waiting for the bellboy.

NUTS & BOLTS 2
USES OF DEFINITE AND INDEFINITE ARTICLES

Even though both English and Portuguese have definite and indefinite articles, there are some differences in usage. Let's start with the definite articles. Use definite articles with: abstract nouns; nouns used in a general sense; expressions of time; the days of the week and seasons of the year; names of most countries and other geographical names; first names, family names, and titles of people you know or that are close to you; and parts of the body and articles of clothing in place of the possessive form.

A justiça é cega.
Justice is blind.

Os brasileiros são bons jogadores de futebol.
Brazilians are good soccer players.

O samba é famoso em todo o mundo.
Samba is famous all over the world.

Ele deve chegar na próxima semana.
He should arrive next week.

Faltam dez para as cinco horas.
It's ten to five.

Ela vai ao cinema na quinta-feira.
She's going to the movies on Thursday.

Ele prefere viajar no verão.
He prefers to travel in summer.

O Brasil é o maior país da América do Sul.
Brazil is the biggest country in South America.

O Carlos vem aqui mais tarde?
Is Carlos coming by later?

Os Silveira são muito conhecidos no Paraná.
The Silveira family is very well known in Paraná.

Ele lava as mãos.
He washes his hands.

Ela coloca as luvas.
She put on her gloves.

Don't use the definite article with the noun **casa** when it means your home; the names of most cities; dates; and family names, titles, and names of famous and unfamiliar people.

Ele está em casa.
He's at home.

Nós moramos em Tókio.
We live in Tokyo.

A encomenda chega no dia vinte e dois de maio.
The order arrives on May 22.

Antônio Carlos Jobim é músico.
Antônio Carlos Jobim is a musician.

Use the indefinite article with singular nouns to mean *a/an* or *one*, and plural nouns to mean *some*.

Há um homem esperando o senhor.
There's a man waiting for you.

Há umas lojas de pedras preciosas brasileiras no aeroporto.
There are some Brazilian gem shops in the airport.

Don't use the indefinite article before an unqualified noun of occupation or nationality after the verb **ser** *(to be)*. But if that noun is modified, then use the indefinite article. Also remember that the indefinite article is omitted before **cem** *(one hundred)* and **mil** *(one thousand)*.

Ele é engenheiro, e elas são japonesas.
He's an engineer, and they're Japanese.

Ele é um bom engenheiro, ela é uma designer famosa.
He's a good engineer, and she's a well-known designer.

A livraria está encomendando cem livros desse autor.

The bookshop is ordering a hundred books by this author.

PRACTICE 2

Fill in the blanks with one of the options given in parentheses. The correct answer may be nothing, or Ø:

1. _____ Ferreiras vêm à festa? (Os/Ø)

2. Que horas são? Faltam vinte para _____ sete. (as/Ø)

3. Ele mora _____ Grécia. (na/Ø)

4. As folhas caem _____ outono. (no/Ø)

5. _____ meu amigo Pedro está vindo aqui. (O/Ø)

6. O Pedro é _____ arquiteto. (um/Ø)

7. _____ Caetano Veloso é compositor de música brasileira. (O/Ø)

8. Ele prefere _____ Paris. (a/Ø)

Tip!

Look up a hotel where you'd like to stay in Brazil (whether you're planning a trip there or not) on www.ondehospedar.com.br/, www.hotelinsite.com.br/, www.decolar.com/paginas/hoteles/busquedahoteles.asp, or any other site you prefer, and get acquainted with the vocabulary. Then, if you're feeling brave enough, call the hotel to ask a few questions about prices, dates, amenities and things to do. Try to get all the information in Portuguese. This is a great way to practice, because it exposes you to the real language and real speakers.

ANSWERS

PRACTICE 1: 1. estão jogando; **2.** está lendo; **3.** estão correndo; **4.** estão alimentando; **5.** estão nadando; **6.** está pintando; **7.** estão tirando; **8.** está fazendo

PRACTICE 2: 1. Os; **2.** as; **3.** na; **4.** no; **5.** O; **6.** Ø; **7.** Ø; **8.** Ø

UNIT 5 ESSENTIALS

Posso deixar um recado?

Can I leave a message?

Eu telefono mais tarde.

I'll call later.

Você prefere chá ou café?

Do you prefer tea or coffee?

Nós partimos para Londres às vinte e uma horas.

We leave for London at 9:00 P.M.

Eles vão à festa de aniversário?

Are they going to the birthday party?

Nós vamos aos jogos de futebol.

We're going to the soccer games.

O carro está nesta rua ou naquela?

Is the car in this street or in that one?

A revista está em cima da mesa.

The magazine is on the table.

O espelho está pendurado atrás da porta.

The mirror is hanging behind the door.

Amanhã eu não posso, que tal depois de amanhã?

Tomorrow I can't, how about the day after tomorrow?

Eles gostam de viajar em setembro.

They like to travel in September.

Com quem você gostaria de falar?

Who would you like to speak to?

Nós não trazemos muito dinheiro à praia.

We don't bring a lot of money to the beach.

O senhor quer fazer o pedido agora?
Do you want to order now?

Eu estou escrevendo agora. O que você está fazendo?
I'm writing now. What are you doing?

UNIT 6
Around town

In Unit 6 you'll learn how to get around town. That means asking for and giving directions, clarifying information, and using the imperative form of verbs. In Unit 6 you'll also learn object pronouns and many new verbs to use them with: **dar** *(to give)*, **pôr** *(to put)*, and **dizer** *(to say)*, for example. You'll also be introduced to the ordinal numbers *first*, *second*, and so on. **Vá em frente!** *(Full speed ahead!)*

─────────── Lesson 21 (words) ───────────

WORD LIST 1

explicar	*to explain*
seguir	*to follow*
parar	*to stop*
estacionar	*to park*
cruzar	*to cross*
o cruzamento	*the intersection*
atravessar	*to cross, to traverse*
subir	*to go up*
descer	*to go down*
a velocidade	*speed*
a praça	*square, garden*
o jardim	*garden*
a rua	*street*
a avenida	*avenue*
a estrada	*road*
a alameda	*boulevard*
a auto-estrada	*highway*

| a rotatória | *traffic circle, roundabout* |
| a esquina | *corner* |

NOTES

The verb **seguir** *(to follow)* is irregular: **eu sigo, nós seguimos, você segue, vocês seguem, ele/ela segue, eles/elas seguem.**

NUTS & BOLTS 1
ORDINAL NUMBERS

Ordinal numbers are used to show a sequence or order. Here are *first* through *tenth:* **primeiro** (1st), **segundo** (2nd), **terceiro** (3rd), **quarto** (4th), **quinto** (5th), **sexto** (6th), **sétimo** (7th), **oitavo** (8th), **nono** (9th), **décimo** (10th).

For 11th through 19th just add décimo: **décimo primeiro** (11th), **décimo segundo** (12th), **décimo terceiro** (13th), **décimo quarto** (14th), **décimo quinto** (15th), **décimo sexto** (16th), **décimo sétimo** (17th), **décimo oitavo** (18th), **décimo nono** (19th).

Here are the ten places, along with 100th and 1000th: **vigésimo** (20th), **trigésimo** (30th), **quadragésimo** (40th), **qüinquagésimo** (50th), **sexagésimo** (60th), **septuagésimo** (70th), **octogésimo** (80th), **nonagésimo** (90th), **centésimo** (100th), **milésimo** (1000th).

For numbers in between, just add the smaller ordinal: **vigésimo primeiro** (21st), **vigésimo segundo** (22nd), **trigésimo quinto** (35th).

Ordinal numbers are adjectives, so they agree in gender and number. That means that **primeiro** also has the forms **primeira, primeiros,** and **primeiras.** Look at these examples.

Pedro é o primeiro na fila do cinema.

Pedro is the first in line at the movies.

Os dois primeiros meses do ano são os mais quentes.
The first two months of the year are the hottest.

A Rua Augusta é a segunda rua à direita.
Augusta Street is the second street on the right.

Eles estão entre os vigésimos colocados.
They are among the twentieth finalists.

Todas as décimas quartas notas musicais são iguais nesta música.
All the fourteenth musical notes are the same in this piece of music.

Elas estão entre as vigésimas primeiras pessoas a chegar.
They're among the twenty-first people to arrive.

In written Portuguese, the ordinal numbers are abbreviated with a superscript ° for masculine and a superscript ª for feminine.

Ele está no 1° ano da escola.
He's in the 1st year at school.

Ela está na 2ª série.
She's in the 2nd grade.

PRACTICE 1

Write out the ordinal numbers. Then try to translate the full sentences.

1. As 1ª viagens são as melhores.

2. Ele viaja todas as 3ª semanas.

3. Essa é a 10ª vitória consecutiva desse time de futebol.

4. O seu quarto é no 15° andar.

5. O 22° assento é ao lado da saída de emergência.

WORD LIST 2

o veículo	*vehicle*
passar	*to pass (by a building, park, etc.)*
ultrapassar	*to pass (a car on the highway)*
o/a motorista	*driver*
errar	*to make a mistake*
proibido	*forbidden*
o suvenir	*souvenir*
a lembrança	*souvenir*
o elevador	*elevator*
Cuidado.	*Watch out.*
a atenção	*attention*
o metrô	*subway*
o metro	*meter*
o quilômetro	*kilometer*
o bonde	*tram/streetcar*
o prefeito	*mayor*
a prefeitura	*city hall*
o/a guia	*guide (person or book)*
o viaduto	*viaduct*
a igreja	*church*
a sinagoga	*synagogue*
a mesquita	*mosque*

NOTES

In the above word list there are several words that are masculine even though they end in **a**. Similar cases are: **o dia** *(day)*, **o turista** *(tourist)*, and **o guia** *(guide)*. Some professions that end in **-ista,** such as **motorista** *(driver)*, **jornalista** *(journalist)*, **pianista** *(pianist)*, **guitarrista** *(guitarist)*, **violinista** *(violinist)* are used for both genders. But remember: you can always tell the gender of a noun by the article: **O violinista é muito bom.** *(The (male) violinist is very good.)* **Aquela jornalista é famosa.** *(That (female) journalist is famous.)*

THE VERB FICAR *(TO STAY)* AND PHRASES OF LOCATION AND DIRECTION

In Lesson 16 you learned that the verb **ficar** means *to stay* or *to remain*. It's actually a very common verb in Portuguese, with several other meanings. Let's look at them.

to stay, to remain (temporary location)	**Você fica aqui enquanto eu peço informações.**	*You stay here while I ask for information.*
to be located (permanent location)	**O nosso escritório fica na Avenida Paulista.**	*Our office is located on Avenida Paulista.*
to keep, to take, followed by **com** *(with)*	**Eu fico com este livro e você fica com aquele.**	*I'll take this book, and you take that one.*
to become, to get (followed by an adjective)	**Ele fica feliz quando você chega em casa.**	*He gets happy when you get home.*
to keep on, to continue doing something (followed by a verb in the gerund)	**Ele fica falando, mas nós não entendemos nada.**	*He keeps on talking, but we don't understand anything.*

The verbs **ser** *(to be)* and **ficar** *(to be, to stay)* are interchangeable when they imply a permanent location of something or somebody.

Onde fica o parque?
Where's the park?

Onde é a praia?

Where's the beach?

Now let's look at common phrases of location and direction. Note that **cá** and **aqui** *(here)* are interchangeable as are **ali** and **lá** *(there)*.

O meu celular não está aqui.

My cell phone isn't here.

Venha cá, por favor.

Come over here, please.

O estacionamento fica ali, está vendo?

The parking lot is there, do you see it?

Quem fica lá com seus filhos?

Who stays there with your children?

O aeroporto fica perto da cidade?

Is the airport near the city?

O seu hotel não é longe.

Your hotel isn't far.

O cinema fica do outro lado da rua.

The movie theater is across the street.

O correio fica do lado oposto da igreja.

The post office is opposite the church.

Há uma sinagoga a cem metros daqui.

There's a synagogue a hundred meters from here.

Devo virar à esquerda ou à direita?

Should I turn left or right?

Há um posto de gasolina mais adiante.

There's a gas station farther on.

PRACTICE 2

Complete the following dialogue with the following words: **à, fica, a, lado, ali, longe**

> Paula: Com licença, onde (1) _____ o correio? Fica (2) _____ daqui?
>
> Jornaleiro: Não. O correio é (3) _____, do outro (4)_____ da rua. Mas hoje está fechado.
>
> Paula: Onde posso comprar selos?
>
> Jornaleiro: A senhora pode comprá-los na loja de suvenires: (5)_____ dois quarteirões, vire (6) _____ esquerda.

Cool link

With Google Maps, you can check out the place you want to visit in Brazil or Portugal and even see where your hotel will be located. http://maps.google.com/

If you want to challenge yourself in Portuguese, this Yahoo site offers maps, directions, and other useful information for Brazil:

http://br.dir.yahoo.com/Ciencia/Geografia/Cartografia/Mapas/

Another great map resource is: www.lib.utexas.edu/maps/index .html. You can find all sorts of different maps on just about any place on the planet.

ANSWERS

PRACTICE 1: 1. primeiras (First trips are the best.) **2.** terceiras (He travels every third week.) **3.** décima (This is the tenth consecutive victory of this soccer team.) **4.** décimo quinto (Your room is on the fifteenth floor.) **5.** vigésimo segundo (The twenty-second seat is next to the emergency exit.)

PRACTICE 2: 1. fica; **2.** longe; **3.** ali; **4.** lado; **5.** a; **6.** à

PHRASE LIST 1

a faixa de pedestre	*pedestrian crosswalk*
o sinal de trânsito	*traffic sign*
o engarrafamento de carros	*traffic jam*
o tráfego contrário	*oncoming traffic*
a rua contramão	*one-way street*
a rua de mão dupla	*two-way street*
o elevador panorâmico	*panoramic elevator*
a escada rolante	*escalator*
a passarela de pedestre	*pedestrian overpass*
o jardim público	*public garden*
a rua arborizada	*tree-lined street*
o bairro residencial	*residential neighborhood*
o bilhete de ônibus	*bus ticket*
o bilhete de metrô	*subway ticket*
o carro alugado	*rented car*

NUTS & BOLTS 1

THE IMPERATIVE

The imperative is used to give orders, commands, and instructions. It can be affirmative *(Have a seat!)* or negative *(Don't smoke!)*. To form the imperative, start with the **eu** form of the present, remove the final **-o,** and add the following endings, depending on the type of verb, and on whether you're speaking to one person or to a group of people:

	-ar	-er/-ir
singular	-e	-a
plural	-em	-am

Notice that the vowels in these endings are the reverse of the vowels used in the regular conjugation. Here are some examples with three different verbs:

Infinitive	Present	Imperative Sg.	Imperative Pl.	
falar	eu falo	Fale!	Falem!	*Speak!*
beber	eu bebo	Beba!	Bebam!	*Drink!*
vir	eu venho	Venha!	Venham!	*Come!*

Vire à direita e ande três quarteirões.
Turn left and walk three blocks.

Não fume aqui!
Don't smoke here!

Preencham esses formulários, por favor.
Fill in these forms, please.

A few common verbs have irregular imperative forms.

ser: seja, sejam	Seja feliz!	*Be happy!*
estar: esteja, estejam	Estejam à vontade!	*Make yourselves comfortable!*
ir: vá, vão	Não vá lá.	*Don't go there.*
dar: dê, dêem	Dê-me um.	*Give me one.*
querer: queira, queiram	Queiram sentar-se.	*Please sit down.*

There are also spelling changes in some verbs. For example, verbs ending in **-car** and **-gar** change the **c** to **qu** and the **g** to **gu** before the ending **-e** to keep the hard *k* and *g* sounds. Take **explicar** *(to explain)* and **pagar** *(to pay)* as examples.

Explique-me como funciona, por favor.
Explain to me how that works, please.

Pague depois.
Pay later.

To retain the soft *s* sound, verbs ending in **-cer** change the **c** to **ç** before the ending **-a.** Here's an example with **esquecer** *(to forget).*

Não esqueçam o guarda-chuva!
Don't forget your umbrella!

And if a verb ends in the soft **-çar,** there's no need to keep the spelling **ç** before **-e,** since **-ce** is pronounced as a soft *s.* Take **dançar** *(to dance)* as an example.

Dancem perto da piscina.
Dance near the pool.

You can soften commands by using **querer** *(to want)* and **poder** *(can),* or with common courtesy expressions.

Vocês podem vir aqui, por favor?
Can you come here, please?

Você quer repetir o seu nome, por favor?
Would you care to repeat your name, please?

Venha aqui, por gentileza.
Would you be kind enough to come here?

Abram a porta, por favor.
Open the door, please.

Por favor, não façam barulho.

Please don't make any noise.

PRACTICE 1

Give the imperative of the verbs in parentheses. Try to translate the whole sentences.

1. Mariana, _____ (fechar) a porta, por favor.

2. _____ (seguir) em frente por duzentos metros.

3. Crianças, _____ (comer) tudo!

4. Atenção alunos: _____ (começar) a prova.

5. Turistas, não _____ (dar) comida aos pássaros.

6. Não _____ (vir) tarde, _____ (chegar) cedo.

7. _____ (ver) esse programa, é muito bom.

8. Primeiro, _____ (assinar) os seus nomes.

9. Pedro e Silvia, não _____ (fazer) barulho, o seu pai está dormindo!

10. _____ (trazer) um documento e duas fotos para o passaporte.

PHRASE LIST 2

o limite de velocidade	*speed limit*
a cabine de pedágio	*toll booth*
a parada obrigatória	*mandatory stop*
passar o sinal vermelho	*run a red light*
a faixa exclusiva de ônibus	*restricted bus lane*
a parada de ônibus/de táxi	*bus stop/taxi stand*
a calçada estreita	*narrow sidewalk*
o calçadão público	*pedestrian street*
a estrada em obras	*road works*
a ponte elevadiça	*drawbridge*

seguir em frente	*to go straight ahead*
virar à direita	*turn right*
a rua sem saída	*dead end street*
à sua esquerda	*on your left*
a uns dez quarteirões	*about ten blocks ahead*

NUTS & BOLTS 2
OBJECT PRONOUNS

A direct object is a noun or pronoun that in a sense "receives" the action of the verb. In **Mariana compra uma revista** *(Mariana buys a magazine)*, **revista** *(magazine)* is the direct object of **compra** *(buys)*. It is the thing that Mariana buys. An indirect object is a noun or pronoun that benefits in some way from the action of the verb. In **ele manda a carta à Maria** *(he sends the letter to Maria)*, **Maria** is the indirect object of the verb **manda** *(sends)*. (Notice that there is also a direct object, **a carta** *(the letter)*, which is the thing sent.) Just like with subject nouns, you can replace both direct and indirect object nouns with pronouns.

Ele vê a lua. Ele _a_ vê da janela do quarto.

He sees the moon. He sees _it_ from his bedroom window. (direct object)

Ela escreve um e-mail ao amigo. Ela _lhe_ escreve muitos e-mails.

She writes an e-mail to her friend. She writes many e-mails _to him_. (indirect object)

Here are all the direct and indirect object pronouns in Portuguese.

Subject Pronouns	Direct Object Pronouns	Indirect Object Pronouns
eu	**me** *(me)*	**me** *(to me)*
tu	**te** *(you)*	**te** *(to you)*

Subject Pronouns	Direct Object Pronouns	Indirect Object Pronouns
você/ele	**o** *(him/it)*	**lhe** *(to him/it)*
você/ela	**a** *(her/it)*	**lhe** *(to her/it)*
nós	**nos** *(us)*	**nos** *(to us)*
vocês/eles	**os** *(you/them, m.)*	**lhes** *(to you/them, m.)*
vocês/elas	**as** *(you/them, f.)*	**lhes** *(to you/them, f.)*

Notice that **me, te** and **nos** have the same forms for both types of objects. But don't forget that the form **tu** is not commonly used in Brazil, except for some regions such as Porto Alegre and Rio Grande do Sul. It is, however, used in Portugal in informal speech between family members or close friends. Also notice that the pronoun **nós** *(we)* has an accent, but **nos** *(us, to us)* does not. **Nós** is pronounced with an open **o,** as in *off,* and **nos** is pronounced with a closed **o,** as in *rose.*

For the third person forms, notice that the direct object pronouns are the same as the articles: **o, a, os, as.** These forms can refer to people *(him, her, them),* or to inanimate objects *(it, them).* The gender of the noun determines which pronoun to use. So, **a** can mean **Maria** in one context, but **a caneta** *(the pen)* in another.

The third person indirect object pronouns only make a distinction for number, not gender: **lhe** *(to him/to her/to it)* and **lhes** *(to them).* These forms are also used to mean *you/to you,* corresponding to **você** and **vocês,** or **o Senhor/os Senhores** or **a Senhora/as Senhoras** in formal conversation.

In lesson 24 we'll come back to the use and position of direct and indirect object pronouns. For now, just familiarize yourself with their forms.

PRACTICE 2

Give the appropriate direct object pronoun corresponding to the subject pronoun given in parentheses. The blank space indicates where in the sentence each pronoun should be placed. Don't use any prepositions, even if the corresponding English requires one.

1. (eu) O professor _____ ensina. *(The teacher teaches me.)*

2. (o Pedro) Eu _____ espero. *(I wait for him.)*

3. (as moças) O rapaz _____ vê. *(The young man sees them.)*

4. (os rapazes) O motorista_____ leva. *(The driver takes them.)*

5. (você–feminine) Ele _____ chama. *(He calls you.)*

6. (você–masculine) A sua mulher _____procura. *(Your wife is looking for you.)*

7. (os meus amigos) Eu _____ encontro numa festa. *(I invite them to a party.)*

8. (eu e você) O hotel _____ cobra muito caro. *(The hotel charges us a lot.)*

Now use an indirect object pronoun.

9. (eu) Pedro _____convida para um jogo de futebol. *(Pedro invites me to a soccer game.)*

10. (você) O hotel não _____ pede um documento. *(The hotel asks you for ID.)*

11. (eu e você) A vendedora _____ promete um bom desconto. *(The saleswoman promises us a good discount.)*

12. (amiga) Ele _____ dá um presente. *(He gives her a gift.)*

13. (pais) Os filhos _____ levam para a casa da praia. *(They take them to the beach house.)*

14. (amigos) Nós _____ informamos o nosso novo endereço. *(We inform them of our new address.)*

ANSWERS

PRACTICE 1: 1. feche (Mariana, please close the door.) **2.** siga (Go ahead for 200 meters.) **3.** comam (Children, eat everything!) **4.** comecem (Attention students: start the test.) **5.** dêem (Tourists, don't feed the birds.) **6.** venha, chegue (Don't come late; arrive early.) **7.** veja (Watch this show; it's very good.) **8.** assine (First, sign your names.) **9.** façam (Pedro and Silvia, be quiet—your father's sleeping!) **10.** traga (Bring an ID and two photos for the passport.)

PRACTICE 2: 1. me; **2.** o; **3.** as; **4.** os; **5.** a; **6.** o; **7.** os; **8.** nos; **9.** me; **10.** lhe; **11.** nos; **12.** lhe; **13.** lhes; **14.** lhes

--- Lesson 23 (sentences) ---

SENTENCE LIST 1

Cuidado com os carros!	*Watch out for the cars!*
É uma avenida muito movimentada.	*It's a very busy avenue.*
É proibido fumar.	*Smoking is prohibited.*
É permitido estacionar aqui?	*Is it legal to park here?*
Onde posso comprar um cartão de "zona azul"?	*Where can I buy a "park and show" ticket?*
Onde fica a Rua Augusta?	*Where is Augusta Street?*
A Praça da Sé fica perto daqui?	*Is Praça da Sé near here?*
É melhor ir de carro ou a pé?	*Is it better to go by car or to walk?*
Vocês querem pegar o ônibus das dez?	*Do you want to take the 10:00 bus?*
Quanto é o bilhete do metrô?	*How much is the subway ticket?*
Quanto custa a corrida de táxi?	*How much is the taxi ride?*
Posso tomar conta do carro?	*Can I keep an eye on your car?*

Você pode ficar de olho no nosso carro?	*Can you keep an eye on our car?*
É possível chamar um táxi para nós?	*Can you call a taxi for us?*
Qual o jeito mais fácil para chegar lá?	*What's the easiest way to get there?*

NUTS & BOLTS 1

THE VERBS PÔR *(TO PUT)*, SAIR *(TO GO OUT)*, DIZER *(TO SAY)*, AND DAR *(TO GIVE)*

These common verbs are all irregular. Here are their conjugations in the present tense.

pôr *(to put)*

eu ponho	nós pomos
você põe	vocês põem
ele/ela põe	eles/elas põem

sair *(to go out/to leave)*

eu saio	nós saímos
você sai	vocês saem
ele/ela sai	eles/elas saem

dizer *(to say/to tell)*

eu digo	nós dizemos
você diz	vocês dizem
ele/ela diz	eles/elas dizem

dar *(to give)*

eu dou	nós damos
você dá	vocês dão
ele/ela dá	eles/elas dão

Here are some examples of how to use these verbs, including some common idiomatic expressions and commands, which you learned earlier in this unit. Let's start with the verb **pôr** *(to put)*.

Ele não põe o nome na lista.
He doesn't put his name on the list.

Quando vocês põem os casacos?
When do you put your coats on?

Não ponha os pés no sofá!
Don't put your feet on the couch!

Nós estamos pondo nossa casa para vender.
We're putting our house on sale.

Eles põem a mesa para os convidados.
They set the table for the guests.

Next look at some examples with the verb **sair** *(to go out/to leave)*.

Eu não saio de casa à noite.
I don't go out at night./I don't leave the house at night.

A que horas sai o avião para o Rio?
What time does the plane leave for Rio?

Para o cachorro: Saia já daí!
To the dog: get out of there!

Eles estão saindo juntos?
Are they going out together?/Are they seeing each other?

Essa mancha não sai; não sei o que fazer!
This stain does not come out; I don't know what to do!

Não saiam daqui! Esperem-me.
Don't leave here! Wait for me.

Now, look at some examples of how to use the verb **dizer** *(to say/to tell)*.

Nós dizemos o endereço para o motorista.
We tell the driver the address.

Eu não digo mentiras.
I don't tell lies.

Diga-me as horas, por favor.
Tell me the time, please.

Você acha que ele diz coisas interessantes?
Do you think he says interesting things?

O que eles estão dizendo?
What are they saying?

Diga a verdade, você gosta deste vestido?
Tell me the truth, do you like this dress?

Finally, here are examples with the verb **dar** *(to give)*.

Eu dou dinheiro para caridade.
I give money to charity.

Que horas vocês dão comida para o bebê?
What time do you feed the baby?

Eles não dão atenção para crítica negativa.

They pay no attention to negative criticism.

Assim não dá!

That's impossible!/That won't work!

Os planos delas dão certo.

Their plans work out.

A viagem dele dá errado.

His trip works out wrong.

Por favor, dê-me uma chance.

Please give me a chance.

Nós estamos dando-lhes uma oportunidade.

We're giving them an opportunity (a chance).

PRACTICE 1

Complete the sentences using the appropriate form of the verb in parentheses. The verbs may be in the present tense, the present continuous, or the imperative. Then try to translate each complete sentence.

1. De manhã, ela _____ (pôr) a mesa do café e _____ (dizer) bom dia ao marido.

2. Crianças, _____(dizer) a verdade: vocês gostam desse parque?

3. Por que eles não _____(sair) do caminho?

4. Por favor, _____(pôr) mais gelo no meu copo.

5. Pedro e Lúcia estão _____(sair) juntos ou são só amigos?

6. Eu não _____(dizer) a minha idade para as pessoas!

7. A nova escola está _____(dar) certo?

8. Eles não _____(dar) uma nova chance se você _____(diz) mentiras.

9. O nosso avião está ____(sair) atrasado, mas o seu está ____(sair) adiantado.

10. Meu marido e eu ____(dizer) às crianças onde elas podem nos encontrar.

SENTENCE LIST 2

Faça-me um favor.	*Do me a favor.*
Você pode me explicar o caminho?	*Can you give me directions?*
O senhor pode me dar uma informação?	*Can you give me some information?*
A senhora pode nos indicar o melhor caminho para chegar ao Museu do Ipiranga?	*Can you show us the best way to get to the Ipiranga Museum?*
Você pode completar o tanque com álcool, por favor?	*Can you fill it up with ethanol, please?*
Você quer abastecer o automóvel com álcool ou gasolina?	*What kind of fuel do you want in the car—ethanol or gasoline?*
Você pode verificar os pneus?	*Can you check the tires?*
Vocês têm carro flex fuel para alugar?	*Do you rent "flex-fuel" cars?*
Leve-nos ao aeroporto, por favor.	*Take us to the airport, please.*
Deixe-me do outro lado da rua, por favor.	*Drop me off on the other side of the street, please.*
Dou-lhe uma gorjeta?	*Do I give him a tip?*
Telefone-me mais tarde, tá?	*Call me later, okay?*

NUTS & BOLTS 2
USE AND POSITION OF OBJECT PRONOUNS

Direct and indirect object pronouns may either precede or follow the verb in Portuguese. Their position varies depending on the region, the type of verb, whether the language is spoken or written, and on other factors. There are some general tendencies that we can look at more closely now. For example, if a sentence begins with a noun or pronoun subject, Brazilians tend to place the pronoun before the verb, and the Portuguese tend to place it after the verb, linked with a hyphen:

O carro? Ele o comprou. (Brazil)
The car? He bought it.

O carro? Ele comprou-o. (Portugal)
The car? He bought it.

Guias nos informam sobre o país. (Brazil)
Guides inform us about the country.

Guias informam-nos sobre o país. (Portugal)
Guides inform us about the country.

The same generalization is true if an object pronoun is used with an infinitive.

É preciso lhes avisar. (Brazil)
It's necessary to advise them.

É preciso avisar-lhes. (Portugal)
It's necessary to advise them.

Object pronouns usually follow the verb, and are attached to it with a hyphen, after command forms and gerunds.

Diga-lhe a verdade.
Tell him the truth.

Abra-o.
Open it.

Estou escrevendo-lhes.
I'm writing to (all of) you.

Estamos comprando-a.
We're buying it.

They also follow the verb in sentences that would otherwise begin with the object pronoun, in other words, in sentences where the subject is dropped.

Levo-os depois.
I'll take them later.

Telefono-lhes mais tarde.
I'll call them later.

There are also cases where the object pronouns come before the verb, such as in negative sentences:

Não me acorde cedo.
Don't wake me up early.

Ele nunca o bebe.
He never drinks it.

Nada nos perturba.
Nothing disturbs us.

Ela jamais os convidou.
She never invited them.

Object pronouns also generally come before the verb in questions with question words and with conjunctions such as **que** *(that)*, **como** *(how)*, **porque** *(because)*, and so on.

Quem lhe diz isso?

Who's telling you that?

Eu vou porque me pediram.

I'm going because they asked me.

They also come before the verb with certain adverbs such as **ainda** *(still)*, **tudo** *(everything)*, **todos/todas** *(every)*, **sempre** *(always)*, **também** *(also/too)*, **talvez** *(maybe)*, **pouco** *(little)*, **bastante** *(plenty/enough)*, and **muito** *(a lot)*.

Vera também nos visita.

Vera also visits us.

Sempre lhes escrevo.

I always write to them.

Nós já o vimos muitas vezes.

We've already seen it many times.

There's a special point to be made about the direct object pronouns **o, a, os,** and **as.** If they're used after a verb form that ends in the consonants **-r** (as in infinitives), **-s,** or **-z,** then that consonant is dropped, and the object pronoun becomes **lo, los, la,** and **las.**

Ela quer comprá-los.

She wants to buy them.

Amamo-lo como um filho.

We love him like a son.

Eu fi-lo sem ajuda!

I did it without help!

In these cases, **-ar** and **-er** verbs take a written accent (**á** and **ê**, respectively), and **-uir** verbs end in **-í**, except for **-guir** verbs, which end in **-gui**.

Quer esperá-lo?
Do you want to wait for him?

Precisamos vê-la.
We need to see her.

Você consegue abri-los?
Can you open them?

É fácil construí-la?
Is it easy to build it?

Eles querem segui-lo.
They want to follow him.

Another such alteration occurs when a verb ends in **-m**, **-ão**, or **õe**. The pronouns **o**, **os**, **a**, and **as** become, **no**, **nos**, **na**, and **nas**.

Eles acordam-no.
They wake him up.

Ela põe-na.
She puts it on.

But these combinations are avoided in conversation by placing the pronoun before the verb.

Eles o acordam.
They wake him up.

Ela a põe.
She puts it on.

PRACTICE 2

Answer the following questions using a direct or indirect object pronoun that refers back to the underlined objects in the question.

1. Ele sempre diz <u>mentiras</u>? Sim, ele sempre _____diz.

2. Pedro convida <u>eu e você</u> à festa? Sim, Pedro _____ convida.

3. Você dá as informações <u>aos turistas</u>? Sim, _____ dou as informações.

4. As crianças põem <u>os dedos</u> na boca. Sim, elas _____põem na boca.

5. Ele diz a verdade <u>a você</u>? Sim, ele _____disse a verdade.

6. Nós damos o cheque <u>à recepcionista</u>? Sim, vocês _____ dão o cheque.

7. Os estudantes telefonam <u>as suas famílias</u>? Sim, eles _____ telefonam.

8. Os turistas trazem <u>os mapas</u>? Não, eles não _____ trazem.

Culture note

Flex-fuel cars, cars that run on either ethanol (made from sugarcane) or gasoline or both, mixed in any proportion, have been on the Brazilian market since 2003. These dual-fuel cars account for more than 77% of Brazilian vehicles, and that proportion has been growing at a steady pace. Seven out of every ten cars sold are flex-fuel cars, and more than half of the 30,000 service stations in the country are equipped to supply cars with ethanol as well as gasoline.

Brazil began its alternative fuel program more than twenty years ago after the oil crisis of the 1970s. It now has the cheapest ethanol in the world thanks, in part, to the genetically engineered sucrose-rich sugarcane crop. The benefits aren't just environmental, either. Not only is alcohol less polluting than gasoline, it's also cheaper for the consumer than gasoline. No wonder Brazil has sold more than 2 million of these cars.

ANSWERS

PRACTICE 1: 1. põe, diz (In the morning she sets the table and says good morning to her husband.) **2.** digam (Children, tell me the truth: do you like this park?) **3.** saem (Why don't they get out of the way?) **4.** ponha (Please put more ice in my glass.) **5.** saem (Are Pedro and Lúcia going out or are they only friends?) **6.** digo (I never tell people my age!) **7.** dando (Is the new school working out?) **8.** dão, diz (They will not give you a new chance if you tell lies.) **9.** saindo, saindo (Our plane's leaving late, but your plane's leaving early.) **10.** dizemos (My husband and I always tell the children where they can find us.)

PRACTICE 2: 1. as; **2.** nos; **3.** lhes; **4.** os; **5.** me; **6.** lhe; **7.** lhes; **8.** os

--- Lesson 24 (conversations) ---

CONVERSATION 1

Listen in while Robert asks the receptionist at the front desk of his hotel for some information.

Receptionista:	Bom dia, Senhor Robert. Posso ajudá-lo?
Senhor Robert:	Bom dia. Sim, eu preciso de algumas informações. Primeiro, eu gostaria de saber qual o jeito mais fácil para ir a Praça da República.
Receptionista:	Bem, o senhor quer ir de táxi?
Senhor Robert:	É possível caminhar?
Receptionista:	Sim, não é longe. Eu lhe explico o caminho. Saia do hotel, vire à direita e siga a rua até o segundo semáforo, então vire à esquerda. Cuidado ao atravessar a rua porque ela é muito movimentada.
Senhor Robert:	Sim, obrigado. E depois?
Receptionista:	Depois, vá até a próxima esquina e a Praça de República fica bem ali no cruzamento. Não

tem como errar, é uma praça muito grande e arborizada. O senhor deseja mais alguma informação?

Senhor Robert: Sim. Por favor, diga-me onde posso comprar algumas lembranças para os meus filhos.

Receptionista: Pois não. O senhor pode comprar suvenires típicos desta região na loja de suvenires no mezanino, ou pode comprá-los no shopping que fica a uns dez quarteirões daqui.

Senhor Robert: Não, não posso ir ao shopping, estou sem tempo. Onde fica a loja de suvenires do hotel?

Receptionista: É fácil. Volte às escadas rolantes e suba um andar até o mezanino. Ou pegue o elevador, aperte o M. É a terceira ou quarta loja à sua direita.

Senhor Robert: Muito obrigado e tenha um bom dia.

Receptionist: Good morning, Mr. Robert. Can I help you?

Senhor Robert: Good morning. Yes, I need some information. First, I'd like to know the best way to get to Praça da República.

Receptionist: Well, do you want to take a cab?

Senhor Robert: Can I walk?

Receptionist: Yes, it isn't far. I'll give you directions. When you leave the hotel, turn right, and go straight until you get to the second traffic light, then turn left. Be careful when you cross the street because it's a very busy road.

Senhor Robert: Thank you. And then?

Receptionist: After that, walk to the next corner, Praça da República is right there at the intersection. You can't miss it; it's a very large square full of trees. Would you like to know anything else?

Senhor Robert: Yes. Please tell me where I can buy some souvenirs for my children.

Receptionist: Of course. You can buy souvenirs typical of this region at the souvenir shop on the mezzanine, or you can buy them at the shopping mall located about ten blocks from here.

Senhor Robert: No, I don't have time to go to the mall. Where's the hotel souvenir shop?

Receptionist: It's easy. Go back to the escalator and go up one floor to the mezzanine. Or take the elevator, press M. It's the third or fourth store on your right.

Senhor Robert: Thank you very much; have a nice day.

NUTS & BOLTS 1
THE PREPOSITION PARA

The preposition **para** has a few main uses. It can be used before an infinitive to indicate purpose. In these cases it can be translated as *in order to, to,* or *so*. It can also indicate a recipient, like the English *for*. It can also indicate a destination. And when used with **estar,** it can mean *to be about to do something.*

Isso é para comer ou para beber?
Is this to drink or to eat?

Para chegar ao parque, vire a primeira à direita.
To get to the park, take the first right.

Ele entra nas pontas dos pés para não acordá-la.
He comes into the room on tiptoe in order not to wake her up.

Faça um favor para o professor.
Do a favor for the teacher.

Eu posso fazer um bolo para o seu aniversário.
I can make a cake for your birthday.

Ele vai para Paris no vôo das sete horas.
He's going to Paris on the 7 o'clock flight.

Nós estamos viajando para nossa casa de praia.
We're traveling to our beach house.

Agora não podemos. Estamos para viajar.
We can't now. We're about to travel.

PRACTICE 1

Choose the expression in column B that completes column A. Translate your answers.

1. Esse remédio é para	A. não ter problemas.
2. Ele não tem tempo para	B. chegar à igreja.
3. Faça silêncio para	C. não perturbá-la.
4. Encha os pneus do carro para	D. tomar de três em três horas.
5. Ande dois quarteirões para	E. estudar ou trabalhar.

CONVERSATION 2

Listen in while Anne asks the assistant at a São Paulo airport car rental agency the best way to get to her hotel.

Assistente: Isso é tudo. Não esqueça de trazer o carro com o tanque cheio porque é mais econômico para a senhora. A senhora precisa de mais alguma coisa?

Anne: Sim. Qual o melhor caminho para chegar ao Hotel Fasano?

Assistente: Olhe neste mapa. Nós estamos aqui e o seu hotel é aqui, vê? Você conhece o Parque do Ibirapuera?

Anne: Sim, conheço.

Assistente: O seu hotel fica próximo. A senhora deve pegar essa avenida larga bem em frente ao aeroporto que se chama Avenida Rubem Berta. A senhora vai em frente, uns três quilômetros, até passar o parque do Ibirapuera. Quando chegar numa rotatória, fique à sua direita, e vire na segunda rua. Essa rua se chama Brigadeiro

Luís Antônio. Vá em frente por uns cem ou duzentos metros, e vire à esquerda na Rua Estados Unidos. A rua do seu hotel é essa, veja.

Anne: Posso levar o mapa?

Assistente: Claro que pode levá-lo.

Anne: Então, por favor, marque o caminho para mim.

Assistente: Claro, aqui está. Mais alguma coisa?

Anne: Sim, por favor. Onde fica o posto de gasolina mais próximo daqui?

Assistente: Na sua volta, a senhora pode encher o tanque em qualquer posto ao longo desta avenida. Olhe, bem ali em frente há um, está vendo?

Anne: Bem, muito obrigada.

Assitente: Boa estada em São Paulo.

Assistant: That's all. Don't forget to bring the car back with a full tank because it's cheaper for you. Is there anything else I can do for you?

Anne: Yes. What's the easiest way to get to the Fasano Hotel?

Assistant: Take a look at this map. We're here, and your hotel is here, see? Have you ever heard of the Ibirapuera Park?

Anne: Yes, I have.

Assistant: Your hotel is close to it. You should get on the big street that's right outside the airport called Avenida Rubem Berta. Go straight ahead for about three kilometers until you go by the Ibirapuera Park. When you get to a traffic circle, stay to your right, and turn onto the second street. This street is called Brigadeiro Luís Antônio. Go straight for about two or three hundred meters, then turn left onto Rua Estados Unidos. Your hotel is on this street, take a look here.

Anne: Can I have the map?

Assistant: Of course you can take it.

Anne: Then can you please mark down the directions.

Assistant: Sure, here it is. Anything else?

Anne: Yes, please. Where's the nearest gas station?

Assistant:	When you return the car, you can fill it up at any service station along this avenue. Look, there's one right there, opposite the store. Do you see it?
Anne:	Well, thank you.
Assistant:	Have a good stay in São Paulo.

NOTES

In Portuguese there's a difference between the verbs **saber** *(to know)* and **conhecer** *(to know, to meet)*. **Conhecer** means to know a place, or to know or to meet someone. **Eu conheço o Brasil.** *(I know Brazil.)* **Elas não conhecem o ator do filme.** *(They don't know the actor in the movie.)* **Vocês já conhecem os meus pais?** *(Do you already know/Have you already met my parent?)* Sometimes **conhecer** has the same meaning as the English *to have been to (a place)*. **Você conhece a floresta amazônica?** *(Have you been to the Amazon forest?)*

On the other hand, **saber** is an irregular verb meaning to have intellectual knowledge of something, to know a fact. Its forms are **sei, sabe, sabemos,** and **sabem. Eu não sei o seu nome.** *(I don't know your name.)* **Você sabe que horas são?** *(Do you know what time it is?)* **Ela sabe falar francês.** *(She knows how to speak French.)* The imperative forms are **saiba** and **saibam. Saiba o preço antes de comprar.** *(Know the price before you buy it.)*

NUTS & BOLTS 2
PERSONAL INFINITIVES

Personal infinitives are infinitives that are conjugated to make it clear who the action of the verb relates to. To link these constructions to similar constructions in English, *to write* is a general infinitive, but *for me to write* is personal; you know who's doing the writing. The difference in Portuguese is that the infinitive is actually conjugated; it takes endings (in the plural, at least) to agree with the subject, which is indicated with the regular subject pronouns. Personal infinitives are usually introduced with the preposition **para.** Let's look at **levar** *(to take)* as an example.

para eu levar *(for me to take)*	para nós levarmos *(for us to take)*
para você levar *(for you to take)*	para vocês levarem *(for you to take)*
para ele/ela levar *(for him/her to take)*	para eles/elas levarem *(for them/you to take)*

Take a look at how these constructions are used, and how you could translate them into English:

Dê-me uma caneta para eu escrever meu endereço.
Give me a pen so I can write down my address/for me to write down my address.

Esse mapa é para nós levarmos?
Is this map for us to take?

Cuidado para você não chegar atrasada.
Be sure not to arrive late.

É muito cedo para nós comermos?
Is it too early for us to eat?

Ele avisa para vocês andarem atrás do guia.
He advises you to walk behind the guide.

PRACTICE 2
Complete the following sentences using the correct form of the infinitive. Use the translation to help you.

1. Ele pede para não _____ (nadar) à noite. *(He asks us to not swim at night.)*

2. É para _____ (esperar) aqui for a ou lá dentro? *(Should they wait inside or outside?)*

3. Estamos prontos para _____ (viajar). *(We're ready to travel.)*

4. É necessário _____ (trocar) de avião? *(Do we need to change planes?)*

5. Precisamos _____ (ir) ao banco? *(Do we need to go to the bank?)*

ANSWERS

PRACTICE 1: 1. A (You should take this medicine every three hours.) **2.** E (He has no time to work or study.) **3.** C (Be quiet so you don't disturb her.) **4.** A (Put air in the tires so you don't have any problems.) **5.** B (Walk two blocks to get to the church.)

PRACTICE 2: 1. nadarmos; **2.** esperarem; **3.** viajarmos; **4.** trocarmos; **5.** ir

UNIT 6 ESSENTIALS

A Rua Augusta é a segunda rua à direita.
Augusta Street is the second street on the right.

Desculpe, mas eu não lembro o seu nome.
Sorry, but I can't remember your name.

O nosso escritório fica na Avenida Paulista.
Our office is located on Avenida Paulista.

O aeroporto fica perto da cidade?
Is the airport near the city?

Há um posto de gasolina mais adiante.
There's a gas station farther on.

Vire à direita e ande três quarteirões.
Turn left and walk three blocks.

Preencham esses formulários, por favor.
Fill out these forms, please.

Vocês podem vir aqui, por favor?
Can you come here, please?

Ela lhe escreve muitos e-mails.
She writes many e-mails to him.

É permitido estacionar aqui?
Is it legal to park here?

Quanto custa a corrida de táxi?
How much is the taxi ride?

A que horas sai o avião para o Rio?
What time does the plane leave for Rio?

Reserve o hotel com antecedência para não ter problemas.
Make hotel reservations beforehand so you don't have problems.

Você pode me explicar o caminho?
Can you give me directions?

Você conhece a floresta amazônica?
Have you been to the Amazon forest?

Unit 7
Shopping

Vamos às compras! (Let's go shopping!) In this unit you'll go shopping for clothing and groceries. You'll also learn how to use the comparative (more) and the superlative (most), as well as constructions that let you make things smaller or bigger. Unit 6 also covers a new verb tense, the immediate future, as well as other useful grammatical constructions.

─────── Lesson 25 (words) ───────

WORD LIST 1

a loja	store
a livraria	bookstore
a biblioteca	library
o jornaleiro	newsstand
a boutique	boutique
o vendedor/a vendedora	salesperson
a liquidação	sale (on sale)
a barbearia	barber shop
o desconto	discount
a roupa	clothes
a saia	skirt
o vestido	dress
a camisa	shirt
a blusa	blouse
as meias	socks
os sapatos	shoes
as sandálias	sandals
o terno	suit

a gravata	*tie*
o chapéu	*hat*
as luvas	*gloves*
a carteira	*wallet*
a bolsa	*handbag*
a jaqueta	*jacket*
o cinto	*belt*
estampado	*patterned (with prints)*
liso	*solid (colors)*
branco	*white*
preto	*black*
amarelo	*yellow*
vermelho	*red*
azul	*blue*
verde	*green*
laranja	*orange*
marrom	*brown*
cinza	*gray*
cor-de-rosa	*pink*

NOTES

The adjectives **branco, preto, amarelo,** and **vermelho** are completely regular, so, for example, you have the forms **preto, preta, pretos,** and **pretas.** A few colors have a single form in the singular, and a single form in the plural: **azul–azuis, verde–verdes,** and **marrom–marrons.** Finally, **cor-de-rosa, cinza** and **alaranjado** are completely invariant, meaning that those forms are used for both genders and numbers.

NUTS & BOLTS 1
COMPARATIVES

A comparative is the form of an adjective that compares one thing to something else. In Portuguese, use **mais** + adjective +

(do) que to mean *-er/more than* and **menos** + adjective + **(do) que** to mean *less than*. The use of **do** is optional.

O Rio Amazonas é mais comprido (do) que o Rio Mississipi.
The Amazon River is longer than the Mississippi River.

Viajar de avião é mais caro (do) que viajar de ônibus.
Traveling by plane is more expensive than traveling by bus.

O Rio Mississipi é menos comprido (do) que o Rio Amazonas.
The Mississippi River is less long than the Amazon River.

Just as in English, there are some common Portuguese adjectives with irregular comparatives: **bom—melhor** *(good—better)*, **mau/ruim—pior** *(bad—worse)*, **grande—maior** *(big—bigger)*, **pequeno—menor** *(small—smaller)*, **pouco—menos** *(few/little—fewer/less)*. Notice that with the exception of **menos,** all of these adjectives have just two forms, the singulars for both genders as given above, and the plurals for both genders, which end in **-es. Menos** is actually an adverb, so it doesn't agree with the thing it describes.

Meu carro é melhor do que o seu.
My car is better than yours.

As escolas da região sul são melhores do que as escolas da região norte.
The schools in the southern region are better than the ones in the northern region.

O trânsito hoje está pior do que o normal.
Traffic today is worse than usual.

A Bahia é maior do que o Rio.
Bahia is bigger than Rio.

Os prédios do centro são maiores do que os prédios da periferia.
The buildings in the center are bigger than the ones on the city outskirts.

O Mar Mediterrâneo é menor do que o Mar do Caribe.
The Mediterranean Sea is smaller than the Caribbean Sea.

O carro a álcool usa mais combustível do que o carro a gasolina?
Do ethanol-powered cars use more fuel than gas-powered cars?

You can also compare two things that are similar using **tão** + adjective + **quanto** *(as* + adjective + *as)*.

A musica brasileira é tão boa quanto a música americana.
Brazilian music is as good as American music.

As praias do Paraná não são tão belas quanto às do Rio de Janeiro.
The beaches in Paraná are not as pretty as the beaches in Rio de Janeiro.

You can compare two nouns with **tanto . . . quanto**. This is like the English *as much/many . . . as*. Just make sure that **tanto** (but not **quanto**!) agrees with the noun it modifies.

Nós temos tantos pontos quanto vocês.
We have as many points as you.

Este copo tem tanta água quanto aquele.
This glass has as much water as that one.

PRACTICE 1
Use the adjectives in parentheses to make comparative sentences. Translate your answers.

1. Um vinho brasileiro é _____ um vinho francês. (barato)

2. A viagem de ônibus é _____ a viagem de avião. (cansativa)

3. Os hipermercados não são sempre _____ os pequenos mercados. (bom)

4. Hoje eu estou me sentindo _____ ontem. (mal)

5. O Airbus A380 é muito _____ o Jumbo 747. (grande)

6. O Fusca não é muito _____ o Golf. (grande)

Now complete the sentences below with **tão** + adjective + **quanto**.

7. O nosso país é _____ o seu. (belo)

8. As nossas empresas são _____ as estrangeiras. (boa)

9. O Rio é _____ São Paulo? (grande)

10. O sotaque carioca não é _____ o paulista para entender. (fácil)

Now practice with nouns. Complete the sentences with **tanto** + noun + **quanto**.

11. Ele sabe _____ matemática _____ ela.

12. O meu filho pratica _____ esporte _____ os outros meninos.

WORD LIST 2

o desodorante	*deodorant*
a maquiagem	*makeup*
a padaria	*bakery*
o açougue	*butcher*
a adega	*liquor store*
o supermercado	*supermarket*
a mercearia	*grocery store*
o pão	*bread*
a manteiga	*butter*
o leite	*milk*
o vegetal	*vegetable*
o legume	*legume*
a fruta	*fruit*
o laticínio	*dairy*

o iogurte	*yogurt*
a carne	*meat*
o peixe	*fish*
o frango	*chicken*
o sal	*salt*
a pimenta	*pepper*
a comida	*food*
a bebida	*beverages*
pechinchar	*to bargain*

NUTS & BOLTS 2
SUPERLATIVES

In Portuguese, use the definite article + **mais** + adjective to mean *-est/the most,* and the definite article + **menos** + adjective for *the least.*

O Rio Nilo é o mais comprido do mundo.
The Nile River is the longest (river) in the world.

As praias do Rio são as mais famosas do Brasil.
The beaches in Rio are the most famous in Brazil.

As cidades do norte são as menos desenvolvidas do país.
The cities in the north are the least developed in the country.

For adjectives with irregular comparatives, just add the article, as in **o/a melhor** *(the best),* **o/a pior** *(the worst),* and so on.

O Dr. Silva é o melhor professor da universidade.
Dr. Silva is the best teacher in the university.

O trânsito de São Paulo é sempre o pior do Brasil.
Traffic in São Paulo is always the worst in Brazil.

As cidades industriais são as piores para a saúde.
Industrial cities are the worst for your health.

O Amazonas é o maior estado do Brasil.

Amazonas is the biggest state in Brazil.

Sergipe é o menor estado brasileiro.

Sergipe is the smallest Brazilian state.

There's also a form of the superlative called the absolute superlative, which can be translated as *very* . . . , *extremely* . . . , *incredibly* . . . , and so on. To form it, take off the final vowel on the adjective, and add the suffix **-íssimo**.

Esse carro é caríssimo.

This car is extremely expensive.

A paisagem aqui é belíssima.

The view here is very pretty.

There are a few spelling changes to keep in mind with the absolute superlative. First, if an adjective ends in a hard **c-**, change the **c-** to **qu-** and then add **-íssimo**, as in **branco–branquíssimo**. Also note these spellings: **facilíssimo, dificílimo, felicíssimo**. Also note that **bom** and **mau/ruim** have irregular absolute superlatives: **ótimo** and **péssimo**.

A neve na montanha é branquíssima.

The snow in the mountains is incredibly white.

Esquiar é facilíssimo.

Skiing is very easy.

Aprender a escrever chinês deve ser dificílimo.

Learning to write in Chinese must be extremely difficult.

Eu estou felicíssimo com o resultado.

I'm super happy with the result.

As férias estão ótimas, mas o tempo hoje está péssimo!

Vacations are great, but the weather today is terrible!

PRACTICE 2

Give the superlative form of the adjective in parentheses, and translate each sentence.

1. O apartamento dele é _____(barato) do bairro.

2. Esses ingressos são _____(caro) do teatro.

3. Aquela empresa dá _____(boas) festas da cidade.

4. Esses são _____(maus) lugares do estádio.

5. Os veículos utilitários são _____(grandes) modelos no mercado.

Now complete the following with: **péssimo, pertíssimo, altíssimas, ótimas, moderníssima.**

6. A arquitetura daquele shopping center é _____.

7. Eu não vou trabalhar hoje porque estou me sentindo _____.

8. As modelos na passarela são _____.

9. As liquidações desta loja são _____.

10. O meu apartamento fica _____do meu trabalho.

Culture note

Feiras livres are open-air/street markets that are an essential part of the everyday lives of the people of both Brazil and Portugal. In Brazil, the **feiras livres** started out in colonial Rio de Janeiro in the late 1700s, in the port area. Local fishermen set up stands to sell the catch of the day. They've come a long way since those days, and now they supply the public with everything from local seafood to imported fish and shellfish to all varieties of meats, from every imaginable kind of fruit and vegetable, tropical and otherwise, to an incredible assortment of flowers and plants, from pots and pans to clothing and services such as shining shoes and re-caning of wicker furniture. A stroll through one of these markets is an incredible journey among the variety of immigrant populations in Brazil. You'll hear a veritable Babel of accents, especially in the markets of the south and southeast. There you'll see first-, second, and third-generation Japanese, the dominant green-belt farmers, alongside people of German and Italian descent, and migrants from the north and northeast advertising their wares at the top of their lungs, and crafting witty come-ons to lure passersby. While you walk around, and there may be a lot of walking involved since these markets can stretch over several blocks, you can sip some **caldo de cana** (*sugarcane juice*), made fresh from long green sugarcanes in presses that can resemble Rube Goldberg contraptions. This is the same sugarcane that makes ethanol and **cachaça,** the local rum. Have fun, be careful of pickpockets, and be sure to **pechinchar** (*bargain)!* The following link will help you find open-air street markets if you're visiting Rio or Portugal.

www.rio.rj.gov.br/clf/feiras/

www.portugaltravelguide.com/pt/lx/shop.htm

ANSWERS

PRACTICE 1: 1. mais barato (do) que (A Brazilian wine is cheaper than a French wine.) **2.** mais cansativa (do) que (A trip by bus is more tiring than a trip by plane.) **3.** melhores (do) que (Hypermakets aren't always better than small markets.) **4.** pior (do) que (Today I feel worse than yesterday.) **5.** maior (do) que (The A380 Airbus is much bigger than the 747 Jumbo.) **6.** menor (do) que (The VW Beetle isn't much smaller than the VW Golf.) **7.** tão belo quanto (Our country is as beautiful as yours.) **8.** tão boas quanto (Our companies are as good as foreign companies.) **9.** tão grande quanto (Is Rio as big as São Paulo?) **10.** tão fácil quanto (The carioca accent is not as easy to understand as the paulista accent.) **11.** tanta, quanto (He knows as much math as she does.) **12.** tanto, quanto (My son plays as many sports as the other boys.)

PRACTICE 2: 1. o mais barato (His apartment is the cheapest in the neighborhood.) **2.** os mais caros (These are the most expensive tickets in the theater.) **3.** as melhores (That company throws the best parties in the city.) **4.** os piores (These are the worst seats in the stadium.) **5.** os maiores (SUVs are the biggest cars on the market.) **6.** moderníssima (The architecture of that shopping mall is very modern). **7.** péssimo (I'm not going to work today because I'm feeling terrible.) **8.** altíssimas (The models on the catwalk are very tall.) **9.** ótimas (The sales in this store are great.) **10.** pertíssimo (My home is very close to the office.)

―――――――― Lesson 26 (phrases) ――――――――

PHRASE LIST 1

os pijamas listrados	striped pajamas
a roupa esportiva de lycra	lycra sportswear/casual wear
o traje de passeio	formal outfit/evening wear
os sapatos de salto alto pretos	black high-heel shoes
o cheque pré-datado	predated check
comprar à vista	to pay cash
comprar a prazo	to pay in installments
o cartão de crédito	credit card
o cartão de débito	debit card
as prestações sem juros	interest-free installments
a loja de departamentos	department store
a seção de brinquedos	toy department
a caixa registradora	cash register
o trocador de roupas	fitting room
a revendedora de automóveis	car dealership
a loja de antigüidades	antique shop
o corredor do supermercado	supermarket aisle
o cabide de roupas	clothes hanger

NUTS & BOLTS 1
DIMINUTIVES AND AUGMENTATIVES

A diminutive is formed by adding **-inho** or **-inha** to the base word, after its final vowel is dropped. For example, from **escola** *(school)* you can form **escolinha** *(little school),* and from **bonito** *(pretty)* you can form **bonitinho** *(cute).* Diminutives are commonly used to add a sense of smallness or cuteness. They also show affection and can be used in nicknames.

Eu quero um pedacinho de bolo.
I want a small piece of cake.

Que gatinho bonitinho.
What a cute kitten.

Esse é o meu filhinho.
This is my little boy (son).

O Sr. Roberto é o pai do Betinho.
Mr. Roberto is Betinho's/Bobby's father. (Betinho is the diminutive of Roberto.)

Diminutives can also be used to add emphasis, or even to show irony or to give a pejorative sense.

O meu escritório fica pertinho de casa.
My office is really near my house.

Que livrinho ruim!
What an awful (little) book!

The regular diminutive ending is **-inho/a,** but if the base word ends in a stressed vowel, two vowels, a nasal vowel, or an **-l,** add a **-z-** before the diminutive ending.

café (coffee)	cafezinho (coffee, little cup of coffee)
papel (paper)	papelzinho (small slip of paper)
pai (dad)	paizinho (daddy)
boa (good)	boazinha (sort of good, not so good)
mãe (mom)	mãezinha (mommy)
pão (bread)	pãozinho (bread roll)

Augmentatives, which are less common than diminutives, are used to indicate largeness or quantity. To form the augmentatives, drop any final vowel and add -**ão** in the singular, and -**ões** in the plural for masculine nouns. For feminine nouns, drop any final vowel and add -**ona** in the singular, and -**onas** in the plural.

O jacaré tem um bocão.
The alligator has a big mouth.

Olha que tijelão de comida!
Look at the enormous dish of food!

Pegue aquele almofadão para você se sentar.
Get that big cushion to sit on.

PRACTICE 1
Replace the italicized words with a diminutive or augmentative.

1. Ele mora *muito perto* daqui.

2. A faxineira sempre deixa a casa *muito arrumada*.

3. Na feira você pode comprar frutas *muito baratas*.

4. Você quer tomar um *tradicional café brasileiro?*

5. O meu *pequeno gato* é *muito bonito*.

6. Ele tem um *pequeno carro,* mas pensa que é um *grande piloto* de Formula Um.

7. Eles moram numa *casa muito grande.*

8. Aquele animal tem uma *cabeça muito grande* e um *corpo muito pequeno.*

PHRASE LIST 2

o fio dental	*dental floss*
o condicionador de cabelos	*hair conditioner*
o creme hidratante	*moisturizer*
a escova de dentes verde e branca	*green and white toothbrush*
a escova de cabelos	*hairbrush*
o protetor solar	*sunscreen*
a entrega em domicílio	*home delivery*
a pronta entrega	*ready-to-wear*
a seção de congelados	*frozen food section*
a embalagem a vácuo	*vacuum packed*
embrulhar para presente	*to gift wrap*
pagar na saída	*to pay on the way out*
marcar hora	*make an appointment*
o salão de beleza	*beauty parlor, hairdresser*
fazer as unhas, fazer as mãos	*to get a manicure*
fazer os pés	*to get a pedicure*
perfumaria	*beauty product store*

NUTS & BOLTS 2
POSITION OF ADJECTIVES

Remember that most Portuguese adjectives usually come after the noun they modify. But there are some adjectives in Portuguese that have a different meaning depending on their position. When used after the noun they modify, they have a literal meaning, and before the noun they have a figurative meaning. Compare these pairs of examples.

Ele é um homem grande./Ele é um grande homem.
He's a big man./He's a great man.

Maria é minha amiga velha./Maria é minha velha amiga.
Maria is my old (elderly) friend./Maria is an old friend of mine.

Esse equipamento é caro./Meu caro amigo . . .
This equipment is expensive./My dear friend . . .

PRACTICE 2
Match the Portuguese sentence in column A to its translation in column B.

Column A	Column B
1. A nossa diretora é uma grande mulher.	A. I'm visiting the school of the good old neighborhood.
2. A nossa diretora é uma mulher grande.	B. José has various ideas for the project.
3. Eu visito a escola do velho bairro.	C. Our director is a great woman.
4. Eu visito a escola do bairro velho.	D. Our director is a big woman.
5. José tem idéias diferentes para o projeto.	E. I'm visiting the school in the old neighborhood.
6. José tem diferentes idéias para o projeto.	F. Maria has cherished books.
7. Maria tem livros caros.	G. Maria has pricey books.
8. Maria tem caros livros.	H. José has unique ideas for the project.

ANSWERS

PRACTICE 1: 1. pertinho (He lives really nearby.)
2. arrumadinha (The cleaning woman always leaves the house really tidy.) **3.** baratinhas (At the open-air/street market, you can buy really cheap fruit.) **4.** cafezinho (Would you like to have the traditional Brazilian coffee?) **5.** gatinho, bonitinho (My small cat is very cute.) **6.** carrinho, pilotão (He has a small economy car, but he thinks he's a Formula One pilot.) **7.** casona (They live in a very big house.) **8.** cabeção, corpinho (That animal has a really big head and a very little body.)

PRACTICE 2: 1. C; **2.** D; **3.** A; **4.** E; **5.** B; **6.** H; **7.** F; **8.** G

───────── Lesson 27 (sentences) ─────────

SENTENCE LIST 1

Onde podemos encontrar tênis de corrida?	*Where can I find running shoes?*
A senhora pode me ajudar?	*Can you help me?*
Você gostaria de experimentá-lo?	*Would you like to try it on?*
Onde fica o provador?	*Where's the fitting room?*
Estou só olhando, obrigada.	*I'm just looking, thank you.*
Eu vou pensar e volto mais tarde.	*I'll think about it, and I'll come back later.*
Posso me olhar naquele espelho?	*Can I look at myself in that mirror?*
O senhor quer que entregue?	*Would you like to have it delivered?*
Qual é o seu tamanho?	*What's your size?*
Vocês não têm um número maior?	*Don't you have a larger size?*
Eu gostaria de um tamanho menor em outra cor.	*I'd like a smaller size in a different color.*

Essa malha de lã vem em que cores?	*What colors does this sweater come in?*
Você acha que essa blusa azul combina mais com a saia florida ou com a saia lisa?	*Do you think the blue blouse goes better with the floral skirt or the solid one?*
Essa roupa está na última moda!	*This outfit is the latest fashion!*
Esse estilo já saiu de moda.	*This style is out of fashion.*
Eu não consigo achar a seção de eletrônicos.	*I can't manage to find the electronics department.*
Elas conseguem chegar na hora?	*Will they manage to arrive on time?*

NUTS & BOLTS 1
REFLEXIVE VERBS (1)

A reflexive verb is a verb that shows that the subject performs the action on himself or herself. Reflexive verbs in Portuguese are conjugated like non-reflexive verbs, but they always appear with a reflexive pronoun, equivalent to *myself, yourself, ourselves,* etc. Reflexive infinitives include the verb, joined to the reflexive pronoun **se** *(oneself)* with a hyphen: **vestir-se** *(to dress oneself, to get dressed),* **ver-se** *(to see oneself),* **cortar-se** *(to cut oneself),* and so on. Here's the full conjugation of **vestir-se,** along with the other reflexive pronouns. Notice that **me** *(myself)* and **nos** *(ourselves)* are the only other two commonly used reflexive pronouns. The other forms all use **se.**

eu me visto	nós nos vestimos
você se veste	vocês se vestem
ele/ela se veste	eles/elas se vestem

Cuidado! Assim, você se corta.
Be careful! You'll cut yourself like that.

Eu me lavo de manhã.
I wash myself in the morning.

Ele se serve de café.
He serves himself coffee.

Nós nos chamamos "Os Incríveis."
We call ourselves "The Incredibles."

Vocês se vêem no rio?
Do you see yourselves in the river?

Elas não se divertem na festa.
They don't enjoy themselves at the party.

Note that the reflexive pronouns usually come before the verb. But if the subject is dropped so that the reflexive pronoun would be at the beginning of the sentence, then the reflexive follows the verb, and is joined to it with a hyphen. This is similar to the situation with object pronouns.

Cortei-me com a faca.
I cut myself with the knife.

Olhei-me no espelho do vestiário.
I looked at myself in the locker-room mirror.

Reflexive verbs can also have a reciprocal sense, translated into English as *each other* or *one another*. Obviously, in these cases the subjects must be plural, just as in English:

Nós não nos conhecemos ainda.
We haven't met each other yet.

Eles se telefonam todas as noites.
They call each other every night.

Vocês se vêem todas as férias?
Do you see each other every vacation?

Os empregados se cumprimentam.
The employees greet one another.

PRACTICE 1
Complete the following sentences with a reflexive/reciprocal pronoun, and with the appropriate form of the regular verbs given in parentheses.

1. As amigas _____ (gostar). *(The friends like each other.)*

2. Eles _____ (amar) muito. *(They love each other very much.)*

3. Os gatinhos _____ (lamber). *(The kittens are licking one another.)*

4. Eu _____ (beliscar) quando penso que estou sonhando. *(I pinch myself when I think I'm dreaming.)*

5. Eu e meus amigos não _____ (ofender). *(My friends and I don't offend one another.)*

6. Ele não _____ (enganar) com os preços. *(He doesn't fool himself with the prices.)*

7. Vocês gostariam de_____ (servir)? *(Would you like to serve yourselves?)*

8. Você pode _____ (lavar) naquele banheiro. *(You can wash yourself in that bathroom.)*

SENTENCE LIST 2

Que gracinha de óculos de leitura!	*What a cute little pair of reading glasses!*
Essa é uma das grandes marcas nacionais.	*This is one of the great national brands.*
Quanto custa esse abrigo esportivo?	*How much is this track suit?*
Quanto é o quilo de salmão?	*How much is the kilo of salmon?*

Vocês têm mercadorias em liquidação?	*Do you have merchandise on sale?*
A livraria da esquina está em liquidação.	*The corner bookshop is having a sale.*
Essa é a melhor papelaria da redondeza.	*This is the best stationery store around.*
Aquela marca é a mais famosa do Brasil.	*That's the most famous brand in Brazil.*
Pegue uma ficha e pague na saída, por favor.	*Get the receipt, and pay on your way out, please.*
Esse caixa esta livre?	*Is this register open?*
Posso trocar esse casaco?	*Can I exchange this coat?*
Vou ficar com esse vestido de noite azul e branco.	*I'll take the blue and white evening dress.*
Não dá para entregar amanhã?	*Can't you deliver it tomorrow?*
Dá para fazer um descontinho?	*Can you give me a discount?*
Vamos fazer um desconto porque a senhora é freguesa.	*I'll give you a discount because you're a regular customer.*
Vocês já são clientes?	*Are you already our clients?*

NUTS & BOLTS 2
REFLEXIVE VERBS (2)

Let's turn back to reflexive verbs. Many Portuguese reflexive verbs translate into English as reflexive verbs, using a *-self* pronoun, such as **vestir-se** *(to dress oneself)*. But many verbs that are reflexive in Portuguese are not in English, at least not without a forced or unnatural translation: **sentar-se** *(to sit down, to seat oneself)*, **deitar-se** *(to lie down, to lay oneself down)*, **sentir-se** *(to feel)*, **esquecer-se** *(to forget)*, **preocupar-se** *(to worry)*.

Eu não me sinto bem.
I don't feel well.

Ela se senta no sofá.
She sits on the sofá.

Eu me chamo Lisa.
My name is Lisa.

Ele se veste depois do banho.
He gets dressed after his bath.

Elas se levantam às sete.
They get up at 7:00 A.M.

A empresa não quer se envolver.
The company doesn't want to get involved.

Ela se penteia antes de sair.
She combs (her hair) before she leaves.

As pessoas estão se divertindo na festa?
Are people having fun at the party?

Você se lembra do nome daquele homem?
Do you remember that man's name?

Nós nos decidimos sobre a casa.
We've made up our minds about the house.

Eles se demoram a chegar.
They take a long time to arrive.

Por favor, dirija-se ao portão de embarque.
Please go to the departure gate.

PRACTICE 2

Complete the following sentences with a form of: **vestir-se, divertir-se, sentir-se, dirigir-se, despedir-se, levantar-se, decidir-se, pentear-se, demorar-se, lembrar-se.** See if you can translate your answers.

1. Ela sempre precisa _____ quando lava a cabeça.

2. Ele vai para casa porque não está _____ bem. Ele está resfriado.

3. Eles _____ à recepção para pedir mais informações.

4. É hora de nós _____. A festa está acabando.

5. Por que você não está _____ ? Você não gosta da festa?

6. Quando eu _____ tarde, chego atrasada para o trabalho.

7. Se vocês _____, perdem o começo do filme.

8. Qual vestido você prefere? Você precisa _____ porque a loja vai fechar.

9. As senhoras estão _____. Por favor, não entre no quarto.

10. O diretor não _____ do que promete aos funcionários.

ANSWERS

PRACTICE 1: 1. se gostam; **2.** se amam; **3.** se lambem; **4.** me belisco; **5.** nos ofendemos; **6.** se engana; **7.** se servirem; **8.** se lavar

PRACTICE 2: 1. se pentear (She needs to comb her hair when she washes it.) **2.** se sentindo (He's going home because he's not feeling well.) **3.** se dirigem (They go to the reception to get more information.) **4.** nos despedirmos (It's time to say good-bye. The party is ending.) **5.** se divertindo (Why aren't you having a good time? Don't you like the party?) **6.** me levanto (When I get up late, I arrive late for work.) **7.** se demoram (If you take long to arrive, you'll miss the beginning of the movie.) **8.** se decidir (Which dress do you prefer? You have to decide because the shop is going to close.) **9.** se vestindo (The women are getting dressed; please don't go into the room.) **10.** se lembra (The director can't remember what he promises the employees.)

CONVERSATION 1

Listen in as Vera and Bianca shop at a supermarket for a delicious dinner.

Vera: O que vamos comprar para o jantar? Você tem uma lista?

Bianca: Não tenho. Vamos ver o que está mais fresco.

Vera: Olhe, o peixe, me parece, está fresquíssimo! Vamos levar um quilo e meio deste atum aqui?

Bianca: Vamos. E o que vamos servir com o peixe?

Vera: Que tal: batatas e uma salada?

Bianca: Perfeito! Onde fica mesmo a seção de verduras? Vamos até lá ver o que eles têm.

Vera: Puxa, veja quanta variedade! Vai ser difícil escolher!

Bianca: Acho que devemos levar um ou dois pés de alface e meio quilo destes tomates pequeninos para uma salada. E que tal essas ervilhas ao invés das batatas. Ervilhas engordam menos!

Vera: Boa idéia. Agora só falta comprarmos uma sobremesa. A seção de congelados é por aqui.

Bianca: Já sei: vamos comprar sorvete de baunilha com cobertura de chocolate.

Vera: Hummm que delícia!

Vera: What are we going to buy for dinner? Do you have a list?

Bianca: No, I don't. But let's see what's the freshest.

Vera: Look, the fish seems to be very fresh! Let's take a kilo and a half of the tuna.

Bianca: Let's. And, what are we going to serve with the fish?

Vera: What about potatoes and a salad?

Bianca: Perfect! Where's the vegetable section again? Let's see what they have.

Vera: Wow, look at the wide selection! It's going to be difficult to choose!

Bianca: I think we should take some lettuce and half a kilo of these small tomatoes for a salad. And how about these peas instead of the potatoes? Peas are less fattening!

Vera: Good idea. Now we only need to buy something for desert. The frozen food section is this way.

Bianca: I have a good idea: let's buy vanilla ice cream with chocolate topping.

Vera: Yummy, delicious!

NUTS & BOLTS 1
THE IMMEDIATE FUTURE

The immediate future is used to express an action in the near future. It's formed with **ir** *(to go)* followed by the main verb in the infinitive.

eu vou comprar *(I'm going to buy)*	**nós vamos comprar** *(we're going to buy)*
você vai comprar *(you're going to buy)*	**vocês vão comprar** *(you're going to buy)*
ele/ela vai comprar *(he/she is going to buy)*	**eles/elas vão comprar** *(they're going to buy)*

Eu vou acordar cedo amanhã.

I'm going to wake up early tomorrow.

Para onde eles vão viajar no próximo mês?

Where are they going to travel to next month?

Vocês acham que as garotas vão chegar na semana que vem?

Do you think the girls are going to arrive next week?

O seu carro só vai ficar pronto daqui a um mês.
Your car is only going to be ready after a month.

O professor vai nos dar uma prova no dia seguinte à revisão.
The teacher is going to give us a test on the day after the review.

One thing to keep in mind is that the verbs **ir** *(to go)* and **vir** *(to come)* are not used in this construction. Instead, just use the simple present tense.

Você vai à festa no fim de semana?
Are you going to go to the party this weekend?

Eles vêm a minha festa do sábado.
They're going to come to my party on Saturday.

PRACTICE 1
Use the words given to make complete sentences.

1. Suzana/estacionar/o carro

2. O senhor/pedir/um café

3. Eu e meus filhos/nadar/no mar

4. Os alunos/passar/o exame

5. Os jogadores/ganhar/o jogo

6. O país/não/importar/o petróleo

CONVERSATION 2
Listen to Cristiana talking to the salesperson at an electronics store trying to help her exchange a birthday present.

Cristiana: Boa tarde, eu gostaria de trocar essa máquina fotográfica digital.
Vendedor: Pois não, qual o problema?
Cristiana: Bem, ela não tem as funções que eu quero, ela não tem zoom.

Vendedor: A senhora se lembra quando a comprou?

Cristiana: Foi um presente de aniversário. Eu não tenho a nota fiscal. Tem problema?

Vendedor: Não, não tem importância, a máquina está na caixa. Vou mostrar outros modelos para a senhora. Olhe essa máquina: ela tem mais recursos do que o seu modelo, mas é um pouco mais cara.

Cristiana: Nossa! É cara demais.

Vendedor: É verdade, essa é a mais cara que oferecemos. Vou pegar um modelo mais em conta. Veja essa.

Cristiana: Não, ainda é cara demais. O senhor não tem uma um pouquinho mais barata? Posso trocá-la pela mesma marca que a minha, mas com zoom?

Vendedor: Claro, vou providenciar a troca.

Cristiana: Obrigada.

Cristiana: Good afternoon, I'd like to exchange this digital camera.

Vendedor: Certainly, what's wrong with it?

Cristiana: Well, it doesn't have the features I want—it doesn't have zoom.

Vendedor: Do you remember when you purchased it?

Cristiana: It's a birthday gift. I don't have the receipt. Is that a problem?

Vendedor: No, it doesn't matter; the camera is in the box. I'll show you some other models. Look at this camera. It has more resources than your camera, but it's more expensive.

Cristiana: Wow! It's too expensive.

Vendedor: In fact, it's the most expensive camera we have. I'll get a less expensive model.

Cristiana: No, it's still too expensive. Don't you have something a bit cheaper? Can I just exchange it for the same brand as mine, but with the zoom?

> *Vendedor:* Of course, I'll take care of that.
> *Cristiana:* Thank you.

NOTES

To say *too* as in *too much*, use **demais** after the adjective: **Esse vestido está apertado demais.** *(This dress is too tight.)* **A casa está grande demais.** *(The house is too big.)*

NUTS & BOLTS 2
THE PREPOSITION POR

You can use the preposition **por** to mean *by, along, through,* or *throughout.* It can mean *for,* either in the sense of *benefiting someone* or *in exchange for.* It can also be used with durations of time, as well as in the sense of *per* in English.

Esse ônibus passa por Ipanema?
Does this bus go by Ipanema?

Eu gosto de andar por ruas silenciosas.
I like to walk along quiet streets.

Passe por aquela porta.
Go through that door.

Eu faço isso por você.
I do this for you.

Eles compram as mercadorias por um preço ótimo.
They buy the merchandise for a great price.

Vamos ficar aqui por um mês.
We're going to stay here for a month.

A loja vai ficar aberta por mais duas horas.
The store is going to stay open for two more hours.

Eu pago cinqüenta reais por hora, duas vezes por semana.
I pay fifty real per hour, twice a week.

The preposition **por** is contracted with the articles **o, a, os,** and **as** to form **pelo, pela, pelos,** and **pelas** respectively.

Quanto você quer pelo cinto de couro?
How much do you want for the leather belt?

Ele repete as instruções pela terceira vez.
He repeats the instructions for the third time.

Eu gosto de passear pelos parques públicos.
I like to take walks through public parks.

Nós passamos pelas praias mais populares da costa.
We went along the most popular beaches on the coast.

There are also a lot of idiomatic phrases you'll come across with **por.**

Pelo menos eu não cheguei em último lugar.
At least I didn't arrive in last place.

Eu não estou doente. Pelo contrário, nunca me senti melhor!
I'm not sick. On the contrary, I've never felt better!

Pelo jeito, vai chover.
From what I can tell, it's going to rain. (It's probably . . .)

Pelo amor de Deus, pare com esse barulho!
For God's sake, stop that noise!

PRACTICE 2
Complete the following sentences with the preposition **por** or its contractions. Try to translate your answers.

1. Eu estou viajando _____ Rio Amazonas.

2. Os turistas passeiam _____dunas em Fortaleza.

3. Não quero cerveja, _____ contrário, só tomo bebidas não alcoólicas.

4. Nós precisamos de, _____menos, uma hora para nos arrumarmos.

5. Você vai votar neste candidato _____ mesmas razões que eu.

6. Ele não está comendo nada. _____ jeito ele não gosta de carne.

7. Quanto é quinze _____cento da conta?

8. Elas estão passando _____um período muito difícil.

9. Essas lembranças são feitas _____ uma tribo indígena da região.

10. Eles vão nos esperar _____mais uma hora.

11. _____menos você não precisa acordar cedo.

12. O motorista vai _____ ruas mais turísticas.

ANSWERS

PRACTICE 1: 1. Suzana vai estacionar o carro. **2.** O senhor vai pedir um café. **3.** Eu e meus filhos vamos nadar no mar. **4.** Os alunos vão passar o exame. **5.** Os jogadores vão ganhar o jogo. **6.** O país não vai importar o petróleo.

PRACTICE 2: 1. pelo (I'm traveling through the Amazon River.) **2.** pelas (The tourists walk along the dunes in Fortaleza.) **3.** pelo (I don't want beer; on the contrary, I only drink nonalcoholic beverages.) **4.** pelo (We need, at least, one hour to get ready.) **5.** pelas (You're going to vote for this candidate for the same reasons I am.) **6.** Pelo (He isn't eating anything. He probably doesn't like meat.) **7.** por (How much is 15% of the bill?) **8.** por (They're going through a very difficult period.) **9.** por (These souvenirs are made by a native tribe from this region.) **10.** por (They're going to wait for us for another hour.) **11.** Pelo (At least you don't have to wake up early.) **12.** pelas (The driver takes the most touristy streets.)

UNIT 7 ESSENTIALS

Eu assisti um lindo filme em preto e branco.

I watched a beautiful black and white movie.

A minha cor favorita é vermelho.

My favorite color is red.

Viajar de avião é mais caro do que viajar de ônibus.

Traveling by plane is more expensive than traveling by bus.

As escolas da região sul são melhores do que as escolas da região norte.

The schools in the southern area are better than the ones in the northern area.

As praias do Paraná não são tão belas quanto as do Rio de Janeiro.

The beaches in Paraná are not as pretty as the beaches in Rio de Janeiro.

O Rio Nilo é o mais longo do mundo.

The Nile River is the longest river in the world.

A paisagem aqui é belíssima.

The view here is very pretty.

O meu escritório fica pertinho de casa.

My office is right near my house.

Ele é um grande homem.

He's a great man.

Eu gosto de passear pelos parques públicos.

I like to take walks through public parks.

Eu não consigo achar a seção de eletrônicos.

I can't find the electronics department.

Nós não nos conhecemos ainda.

We haven't met each other yet.

Vocês têm mercadorias em liquidação?

Do you have merchandise on sale?

Para onde eles vão viajar no próximo mês?

Where are they going to travel to next month?

Unit 8
In a restaurant

In Unit 8 you'll learn vocabulary and expressions you can use to talk about food, menus, and restaurants. You'll also learn how to talk about actions in the past, and how to use adverbs and quantity expressions like *some*, *much*, and *many*. **Bom apetite!**

────────────────── Lesson 29 (words) ──────────────────

WORD LIST 1

o cardápio/o menu	*menu*
o guardanapo	*napkin*
os talheres	*flatware*
a faca	*knife*
a colher	*spoon*
o garfo	*fork*
o vinagre	*vinegar*
o óleo	*oil*
o tempero	*spices*
a salsinha	*parsley*
a cebola	*onion*
o alho	*garlic*
a torrada	*toast*
a geléia	*jam*
o mel	*honey*
o almoço	*lunch*
o lanche	*snack*
o jantar	*dinner*
a farofa	*side dish based on manioc flour*

NUTS & BOLTS 1
PRONOUNS USED AFTER PREPOSITIONS

You've already learned a few types of pronouns: subject pronouns (lesson 2), object pronouns (lesson 23), and reflexive pronouns (lesson 27). Now let's focus on pronouns used after prepositions such as **para, por, de, com,** and so on.

mim *(me)*	**nós** *(us)*
você *(you)*	**vocês** *(you)*
ele/ela *(him/her)*	**eles/elas** *(them)*

Notice that they're the same as subject pronouns, except for **mim.**

Dê a chave para mim.
Give the key to me.

Não esperem por mim.
Don't wait for me.

Vamos trabalhar com você.
We're going to work with you.

Você consegue fazer isso para ela?
Are you able to do this for her?

O porteiro chama um táxi para nós.
The doorman calls a taxi for us.

Suzana quer jantar com eles.
Suzana wants to have dinner with them.

There are two special forms that are used after the preposition **com** *(with)*. The pronouns **mim** *(me)* and **nos** *(us)* contract with **com,** forming **comigo** and **conosco.**

Ele só pode falar comigo depois das onze.
He can only talk to me after 11:00.

Vocês vão viajar conosco?
Are you traveling with us?

You can express an indirect object either as an indirect object pronoun, or as the object of a preposition, but the pronouns will be different in these two constructions.

Ele lhe deu o livro.
He gave you the book.

Ele deu o livro a você.
He gave the book to you.

PRACTICE 1
Answer with the correct form of the pronoun in parentheses. Try to translate the answers.

1. Com quem vocês vão ao parque? (elas)

2. De quem Cristina se lembra? (nós)

3. Para quem faço o cheque? (ele)

4. Com quem ele vai sair? (eu)

5. Com quem Mário vai jantar? (nós)

6. Por quem eles estão esperando? (elas)

7. De quem elas estão falando? (eu)

8. Para quem é esse presente? (você)

WORD LIST 2

a salada	*salad*
a entrada	*appetizer*
a sobremesa	*dessert*

o coquetel	*cocktail*
o aperitivo	*aperitif*
a refeição	*meal*
o pastel	*an appetizer pastry similar to a fried samosa*
o refrigerante	*soft drink*
a limonada	*lemonade*
o pudim	*pudding*
o sorvete	*ice cream*
o gelo	*ice*
o couvert	*pre-dinner appetizers served at restaurants*
a porção	*portion*
a gorjeta	*tip, gratuity*
o acompanhamento	*side dish*
o molho	*sauce*

NUTS & BOLTS 2
THE IMPERSONAL SE

The impersonal pronoun **se** is used in Portuguese when the subject is unknown or unidentified. The verb in these constructions is always in the third person singular form. You can translate the impersonal **se** as general statements with *people, they, one, you,* and so on. Note that **se** can come before the verb, as long as it's not the first word in the sentence. If **se** comes after the verb, it is linked to the verb with a hyphen.

Como se chega ao parque?

How does one get to the park?

Onde se compra selos?

Where can you buy stamps?

Na Bahia come-se muito bem.

In Bahia people eat very well.

Diz-se que tempo é dinheiro.
They say time is money.

Não se sabe o que aconteceu.
They don't know what happened./It's not known what happened.

Se can also be used in third person passive sentences, when the subject is unknown or unimportant. A passive sentence is formed when the object of an active sentence is "promoted" to subject— for example, in the pair *John writes letters* (active) and *letters are written* (passive). In Portuguese passive **se** sentences, the verb is still in the third person, but it can be singular or plural depending on the number of the grammatical subject.

Não se fala inglês aqui.
English is not spoken here.

Reservam-se mesas até às oito horas.
Tables are reserved until 8:00.

You'll see the impersonal **se** form in want ads or classifieds, such as: **Precisa-se de cozinheiro.** *(Cook wanted.)* **Vende-se uma casa.** *(House for sale.)* **Alugam-se apartamentos.** *(Apartments for rent.)*

PRACTICE 2
Choose a verb from the following list to complete the sentences with the impersonal **se.** Use the appropriate form of the verb, singular or plural, and then translate your answers.

fumar, precisar, vender, escrever, alugar, aprender, beber, falar

1. _____-se garçom com experiência.

2. _____-se muita cerveja neste país?

3. A guerra terminou! Não se _____ em outra coisa nos jornais.

4. Para quem se _____ para fazer uma reclamação?

5. _____-se antiguidades aqui?

6. _____-se muito viajando para outros países.

7. _____-se casas e apartamentos para temporada de verão.

8. Neste estabelecimento não se _____.

ANSWERS

PRACTICE 1: 1. Vamos ao parque com elas. (We're going to the park with them.) **2.** Cristina se lembra de nós. (Cristina remembers us.) **3.** Faça o cheque para ele. (Make the check out to him.) **4.** Ele vai sair comigo. (He's going out with me.) **5.** Mário vai jantar conosco. (Mário is going to have dinner with us.) **6.** Eles estão esperando por elas. (They're waiting for them.) **7.** Elas estão falando de mim. (They're talking about me.) **8.** Esse presente é para você. (This present is for you.)

PRACTICE 2: 1. Precisa (Waiter with experience wanted.) **2.** Bebe (Do people drink a lot of beer in this country?) **3.** fala (The war is over! That's all they talk about in the news.) **4.** escreve (Who do you write to in order to make a complaint?) **5.** Vendem (Are antiques sold here?) **6.** Aprende (One learns a lot by traveling to other countries.) **7.** Alugam (Summer vacation houses and apartments are rented.) **8.** fuma (This is a nonsmoking establishment.)

———————— Lesson 30 (phrases) ————————

PHRASE LIST 1

a carne bem passada	*well-done meat*
o bife mal passado	*rare steak*
o churrasco ao ponto	*medium-rare barbecue*
muito apimentado	*very hot (spicy)*
o prato principal	*main dish*
o azeite (de oliva)	*olive oil*
o rodízio de carnes	*skewered meats brought to you throughout the meal*

a churrascaria gaúcha	*Brazilian-style steak house*
o arroz com feijão	*rice and beans*
o suco de laranja	*orange juice*
a água com gás	*carbonated water*
a água mineral sem gás	*still mineral water*
o purê de batatas	*mashed potatoes*
o frango assado	*roast chicken*
o ensopado de camarão	*shrimp stew*
o peru recheado	*stuffed turkey*
o peixe grelhado	*grilled fish*
a torta de palmito	*heart-of-palm pie*
o bolo de chocolate	*chocolate cake*

NOTES

Churrascarias are Brazilian barbecue houses that originated in Rio Grande do Sul, the southernmost state of Brazil. They are usually very large restaurants, where waiters serve large, sword-like skewers with prime cuts of sizzling hot barbecued meats, pieces of which they then slice off straight onto your plate. **Churrascarias** are also known as **rodízios de carne** *(rotations of meat)* because of the all-you-can-eat aspect of the meal. They are famous for their buffet-style salad bars, offering a rich variety of salads and appetizers. They charge a fixed price per person.

NUTS & BOLTS 1
ADVERBS

Adverbs are words that answer questions such as *how, why, when,* or *to what degree.* In English, a typical adverbial ending is *-ly,* which corresponds to **-mente** in Portuguese. You can form adverbs by taking the feminine form of an adjective, and adding the ending **-mente.** If the adjective ends in **-e** or a consonant, add **-mente** to that:

rápido *(quick)*	rápida + mente	rapidamente *(quickly)*
eficiente *(efficient)*	eficiente + mente	eficientemente *(efficiently)*
fácil *(easy)*	fácil + mente	facilmente *(easily)*

Ele espera os seus amigos pacientemente.
He waits for his friends patiently.

Nós caminhamos lentamente.
We walk slowly.

A aluna responde claramente.
The student answers clearly.

There are also lots of common adverbs that tell you how something is done, but they don't follow this regular -**mente** pattern.

Ele escreve mal.
He writes badly.

Ela cozinha bem.
She cooks well.

Eles vão sair depressa.
They're going to arrive fast.

A chuva chega de repente.
The rain arrives suddenly.

Some useful adverbs of time are: **hoje** *(today)*, **ontem** *(yesterday)*, **amanhã** *(tomorrow)*, **cedo** *(early)*, **às vezes/de vez em quando** *(sometimes)*, **freqüentemente** *(frequently)*, **raramente** *(rarely)*, **sempre** *(always)*, and **nunca** *(never)*.

Eu acordo cedo.

I wake up early.

Elas vão chegar amanhã.

They arrive tomorrow.

Eu raramente vou ao teatro.

I rarely go to the theater.

And then there are adverbs that express probability, intensity, and quantity.

Vocês provavelmente não vão dormir.

You probably aren't going to sleep.

Ele possivelmente não sabe o endereço.

He possibly doesn't know the address.

Você vem comigo? Talvez.

Are you coming with me? Maybe.

Aquele carro quase bateu no nosso!

That car almost crashed into ours!

O vôo dele ainda não chegou.

His plane hasn't arrived yet.

Eu gosto tanto de flores.

I like flowers so much.

Ela come apenas peixe.

She only eats fish.

Crianças comem pouco.

Children eat little.

Meu amigo está tão sozinho.

My friend is so alone.

Essa loja cobra menos, e essa loja cobra mais.

That store charges less, and that store charges more.

Nós dançamos muito.
We dance a lot.

Ele trabalha muito pouco.
He works very little.

PRACTICE 1
Choose an adverb from the following list to complete the sentences: **exclusivamente** *(exclusively)*, **ultimamente** *(lately)*, **separadamente** *(separately)*, **imediatamente** *(immediately)*, **raramente** *(rarely)*, **eficientemente** *(efficiently)*, **diariamente** *(daily)*, **completamente** *(completely)*

1. A loja vende esses casacos _____ aqui.

2. Eu não sei onde estou. Estou_____ perdido.

3. _____ me sinto tão cansada, acho que estou doente.

4. As crianças não vão ficar no quarto com os pais. Eles vão dormir_____.

5. Eu o chamo e ele vem_____.

6. Nós _____vamos à opera porque é muito caro.

7. Ela trabalha muito_____, ele vai receber um aumento.

8. Ele faz ginástica todos os dias. Ele faz ginástica _____.

PHRASE LIST 2

pedir a conta	*to ask for the check*
chamar o garçom	*to call the waiter*
fazer uma reserva	*to make a reservation*
reservar uma mesa para quatro	*to reserve a table for a party of four*
deixar uma gorjeta	*to leave a tip*
serviço incluído	*service included*
lavar a louça	*to wash the dishes*
enxugar os pratos	*to dry the plates*

pôr a mesa	_to set the table_
a área reservada para fumantes	_smoking area_
a xícara e o pires	_the cup and saucer_
o prato de sopa	_the soup bowl_
o especial do dia	_the special_
parecer bom	_to look (seem) good_
prato feito (PF)	_popular style restaurants where you are served a complete meal in a single dish._
o restaurante por quilo	_a restaurant that charges by weight_

NUTS & BOLTS 2
THE PRETERITE OF ESTAR _(TO BE)_

So far we've mostly been talking about actions that happen in the present, either in general or as a progressive action taking place right now. We've also seen a construction with **ir** that corresponds to the English immediate future with _going to._ Now let's look at the preterite tense, which is used to express a past fact or action that is completely finished. The preterite corresponds to the English simple past _(talked, went, did,_ etc.) Let's start with the preterite of the verb **estar** _(to be)._

eu estive _(I was)_	**nós estivemos** _(we were)_
você esteve _(you were)_	**vocês estiveram** _(all of you were)_
ele/ela esteve _(he/she was)_	**eles/elas estiveram** _(they were)_

Since the preterite is used to express past actions, you'll often see it used with time expressions such as: **ontem** _(yesterday),_ **ontem de manhã** _(yesterday morning),_ **ontem à tarde** _(yesterday afternoon),_ **ontem à noite** _(last night),_ **a noite passada** _(last night),_ **a semana passada** _(last week),_ **uma semana atrás** _(one week ago),_ **o mês pas-**

sado *(last month)*, **dois meses atrás** *(two months ago)*, **o ano passado** *(last year)*, **há vários anos atrás** *(several years ago)*.

Ontem estive muito ocupado.
I was very busy yesterday.

Nós não estivemos de férias no mês passado.
We weren't on vacation last month.

João e Carmem estiveram em nossa casa ontem à noite.
João and Carmem were at our home last night.

Vocês estiveram em Madrid no verão passado?
Were you in Madrid last summer?

Quanto tempo você esteve no seu último emprego?
How long were you at your last job?

Eu não estive em casa todo o dia ontem.
I wasn't at home all day yesterday.

Você esteve no restaurante do Bruno no sábado passado?
Were you at Bruno's restaurant last Saturday?

PRACTICE 2
Complete the sentences with the verb **estar** in the preterite, and then translate.

1. Ele_____ no Japão durante a Segunda Guerra Mundial.

2. O ônibus _____aqui até às três da tarde.

3. Que horas vocês _____ aqui ontem?

4. Quanto tempo elas _____ no hotel?

5. Eu nunca _____ naquele restaurante.

6. Onde as crianças _____ todo esse tempo?

7. Carmem _____ desempregada até o ano passado.

8. Você já _____ numa churrascaria?

9. Pedro _____ no Canadá em 2006.

10. Os estudantes _____ na passeata do ano passado.

Culture note

Feijoada, pronounced fay-zhoo-AH-dah, is unarguably Brazil's national dish. It's composed of a hearty stew made with beans **(feijão),** and various kinds of beef and pork. The stew is but one of the components of this immensely popular dish: white rice, **farofa** *(roasted manioc flour)*, fried manioc, **couve** *(thinly sliced collard greens, sometimes prepared with bacon)*, and sliced orange are an essential part of a typical **feijoada.** All of this is better washed down with the traditional Brazilian drink **caipirinha,** made with **cachaça** *(sugarcane rum)*, lime, sugar, and ice. Because it takes so long to prepare (and to digest!) restaurants in general serve **feijoada** only for lunch, and only on Wednesdays and Saturdays. The stew is sometimes served buffet style. First it's all cooked together, and then each meat is served separately so you can choose the kinds you like the most, skipping the parts you don't care for, which traditionally includes parts like pigs' feet, ears, and tails! Sometimes, it's just served in a terra-cotta bowl.

Folk history has it that **feijoada** was created by African slaves, who were not allowed to eat the good parts of the beef and pork butchered for their masters' houses. They would then preserve the leftover meat in salt and later cook it with beans, then serve it with rice and manioc flour. Over time, poor families began to prepare this dish, and then it eventually migrated to all social classes to become the national dish of Brazil. Now it's offered from the humblest roadside diners all the way to 5-star hotel restaurants, where patrons think nothing of plopping down as much as $50.00 a head for this savory dish.

ANSWERS
PRACTICE 1: 1. exclusivamente; **2.** completamente;
3. Ultimamente; **4.** separadamente; **5.** imediatamente;
6. raramente; **7.** eficientemente; **8.** diariamente

PRACTICE 2 : 1. esteve (He was in Japan during WWII.)
2. esteve (The bus was here until 3:00 P.M.) **3.** estiveram (What time were you here yesterday?) **4.** estiveram (How long were they at the hotel?) **5.** estive (I was never at that restaurant.)
6. estiveram (Where were the children all this time?) **7.** esteve (Carmem was unemployed until last year.) **8.** esteve (Were you ever at a Brazilian barbecue restaurant?) **9.** esteve (Pedro was in Canada in 2006.) **10.** estiveram (The students were at the demonstration last year.)

─────────── Lesson 31 (sentences) ───────────

SENTENCE LIST 1

Precisa-se de cozinheira com experiência.	*Experienced cook wanted.*
Vendem-se livros e discos usados.	*Used books and records for sale.*
Eu telefonei para o restaurante ontem à noite.	*I called the restaurant last night.*
Ele só nos avisou antes de ontem.	*He only advised us the day before yesterday.*
Você jantou fora na semana passada?	*Did you go out for dinner last week?*
Ela deixou o carro com o manobrista.	*She left her car with the valet.*
Ele quer um pouco de pão com manteiga.	*He wants a bit of bread and butter.*
Ela gostou do café com bastante açúcar.	*She liked the coffee with a lot of sugar.*
As crianças não tomaram a limonada sem açúcar.	*The children didn't drink the lemonade without sugar.*
Essa salada tem pouco sal, precisamos de um saleiro.	*This salad doesn't have enough salt; we need the salt shaker.*

A menina comeu pouca verdura e muita batatinha frita.	*The girl ate few vegetables and a lot of french fries.*
Vocês gostariam de um pouco mais de doce de leite?	*Would you like a little more caramel candy (dulce de leche)?*
Eu preparei uma sopa bem apimentada.	*I prepared some very spicy soup.*
O restaurante não cobrou o serviço.	*The restaurant didn't charge for service.*

NUTS & BOLTS 1

The preterite of regular -ar verbs

You've already learned the preterite of **estar,** along with some time expressions that are used to talk about the past. Now let's look at the preterite conjugation of regular -**ar** verbs, for example **falar** *(to speak).*

eu falei *(I spoke)*	**nós falamos** *(we spoke)*
você falou *(you spoke)*	**vocês falaram** *(all of you spoke)*
ele/ela falou *(he/she spoke)*	**eles/elas falaram** *(they spoke)*

As you can see, the preterite of -**ar** verbs is formed by adding to the verb stem the endings -**ei** and -**ou** in the singular, and -**amos** and -**aram** in the plural. Here are some examples with other verbs.

Eu trabalhei das oito da manhã até às oito da noite.

I worked from 8:00 A.M. to 8:00 P.M.

Você estudou para o exame ontem?

Did you study for the exam yesterday?

Mário almoçou com uma amiga no sábado passado.

Mário had lunch with a friend last Saturday.

A recepcionista não avisou o gerente que você telefonou ontem à tarde.

The receptionist didn't advise the manager that you called yesterday afternoon.

No ano passado nós não viajamos para o exterior.

Last year we didn't travel abroad.

Onde vocês jantaram no domingo passado?

Where did you have dinner last Sunday?

Os artistas pintaram esses quadros um século atrás.

The artists painted these pictures last century.

Elas chegaram!

They arrived!

PRACTICE 1

Complete the sentences with the preterite of the verbs in parentheses, and translate.

1. Eu _____ (morar) na Bahia de 1990 até 2000.

2. Pedro _____ (praticar) esportes na universidade mas agora não pratica mais.

3. Ela _____ (nadar) muito rapidamente e _____ (ganhar) a competição.

4. Onde vocês se _____ (encontrar) ontem?

5. O que vocês _____ (comprar) na feira de artesanatos?

6. Primeiro nós nos _____ (separar) dois anos atrás, depois nós nos _____ (divorciar).

7. Os médicos _____ (curar) a minha doença.

8. Você já _____ (procurar) as chaves no bolso do seu casaco?

9. Quem _____ (cozinhar) essa deliciosa refeição?

10. O cozinheiro não _____ (preparar) o jantar sozinho, eu o _____ (ajudar).

SENTENCE LIST 2

A comida acabou de chegar.	*The food has just arrived.*
Eu acabei de tomar uma decisão.	*I've just made up my mind.*
Olhe quem acabou de chegar!	*Look who's just arrived!*
Vocês já chamaram o garçom?	*Have you already called the waiter?*
Quanto você deixou de gorjeta?	*How much tip did you leave?*
Eles provavelmente não vão ficar para o jantar.	*They probably won't stay for dinner.*
Os meus filhos raramente almoçam em casa.	*My children rarely have lunch at home.*
Vocês gostariam de um pouco mais de doce de leite?	*Would you like a little more caramel?*
Esse bolo é para o seu aniversário. Parabéns!	*This cake is for your birthday. Happy Birthday!*
Adivinhe quem vem ao restaurante conosco!	*Guess who's coming to the restaurant with us!*
Eles reservaram a mesa para mim.	*They reserved the table for me.*

NUTS & BOLTS 2
THE IMMEDIATE PAST WITH ACABAR DE

The verb **acabar** means *to finish*, but when it's followed by **de** and another verb in the infinitive, it can be translated as *to have just (done something)*. **Acabar** can be conjugated both in the simple present or preterite to have this meaning.

Eu acabei de mudar de casa.

I have just moved.

Ele acaba de telefonar.

He has just called.

Ele acabou de me telefonar.
He has just called me.

Nós acabamos de comprar um carro.
We have just bought a car.

Vocês acabaram de levantar?
Have you just gotten up?

Olhe quem acabou de chegar!
Look who has just arrived!

O avião acabou de partir.
The plane has just left.

PRACTICE 2
Complete the sentences with **acabar de** and the verb in parentheses.

1. (fechar) A empresa dele _____ um ótimo negócio.

2. (ganhar) O menino _____ o presente e já o quebrou.

3. (ser) Eu _____ promovido! Vamos comemorar.

4. (telefonar) Você não _____? O que você quer?

5. (comprar) Os meus sócios e eu _____ mais um restaurante.

6. (apagar) Os bombeiros _____ o fogo.

7. (viajar) As minhas primas _____ para África.

8. (comer) As crianças _____ e já estão com fome.

9. (ganhar) Eu _____ na loteria!

10. (chegar) O novo modelo do carro _____.

ANSWERS
PRACTICE 1: 1. morei (I lived in Bahia from 1990 to 2000.)
2. praticou (Pedro practiced sports in university but now he
doesn't anymore.) **3.** nadou, ganhou (She swam very quickly

and won the competition.) **4.** encontraram (Where did you meet yesterday?) **5.** compraram (What did you buy at the handicrafts fair?) **6.** separamos, divorciamos (First we separated two years ago, and then we got divorced.) **7.** curaram (The doctors cured my illness.) **8.** procurou (Did you already look for the keys in your coat pocket?) **9.** cozinhou (Who cooked this delicious meal?) **10.** preparou, ajudei (The cook didn't prepare dinner by himself; I helped him.)

PRACTICE 2: 1. acabou de fechar (His company has just closed a great deal.) **2.** acabou de ganhar (The boy has just gotten the gift and has already broken it.) **3.** acabei de ser (I've just been promoted! Let's celebrate.) **4.** acabou de telefonar (Haven't you just called? What do you want?) **5.** acabamos de comprar (My partners and I have just bought another restaurant.) **6.** acabaram de apagar (The fire fighters have just put out the fire.) **7.** acabaram de viajar (My cousins have just traveled to Africa.) **8.** acabaram de comer (The children have just eaten and they're hungry again.) **9.** acabei de ganhar (I've just won the lottery!) **10.** acabou de chegar. (The new model of the car has just arrived.)

———————— Lesson 32 (conversations) ————————

CONVERSATION 1
Listen in while Felipe talks to a waiter at a Brazilian fish restaurant.

Garçom: **Boa noite. O senhor já olhou o cardápio?**
Felipe: **Olhei sim, mas o que o senhor recomenda?**
Garçom: **As especialidades da casa são peixes e frutos do mar. Hoje nós temos badejo à baiana e caldeirada de frutos do mar à moda do chefe.**
Felipe: **Eu não entendi uma coisa: o que é "pirão de peixe"?**
Garçom: **Pois não, eu lhe explico. Pirão de peixe é um tipo de molho bem grosso, feito com pedaços**

de peixe e temperos, é um ótimo acompanhamento para peixes grelhados.

Felipe: Então vamos lá. Eu gostaria de pedir uma salada completa para começar, e depois o filé de robalo grelhado. O que acompanha o peixe?

Garçom: Pirão e arroz branco. O que o senhor gostaria de beber?

Felipe: Uma caipirinha.

Garçom: O senhor está pronto para a sobremesa? Temos doces brasileiros, frutas da estação, e sorvetes.

Felipe: Eu vou experimentar o creme de papaia, e depois um cafezinho.

Garçom: Aqui está a conta.

Felipe: Obrigado, o serviço está incluído?

Garçom: Sim senhor. Incluímos dez por cento na conta.

Waiter: *Good evening. Have you looked at the menu?*

Felipe: *Yes, what do you recommend?*

Waiter: *The house specialties are fish and seafood. Today we have a sea bass Bahian style and seafood stew à la Chef.*

Felipe: *I didn't understand what "pirão de peixe" is.*

Waiter: *Let me explain. Pirão de peixe is a kind of gravy made with parts of the fish and spices; it goes very well with grilled fish.*

Felipe: *All right then, I'd like to order a mixed salad to start and then the grilled snook. What comes with the fish?*

Waiter: *Pirão and white rice. What would you like to drink?*

Felipe: *A caipirinha.*

Waiter: *Are you ready for dessert? We have typical Brazilian sweets, seasonal fruit, and ice cream.*

Felipe: *I'll try the cream of papaya, and then coffee.*

Waiter: *Here's the check.*

Felipe: *Is the service included?*

Waiter: *Yes, sir. We include a ten percent service charge.*

NUTS & BOLTS 1
THE PRETERITE OF REGULAR -ER VERBS

Now let's turn to the conjugation of regular -er verbs in the preterite, for example **escrever** *(to write)*.

eu escrevi *(I wrote)*	**nós escrevemos** *(we wrote)*
você escreveu *(you wrote)*	**vocês escreveram** *(all of you wrote)*
ele/ela escreveu *(he/she wrote)*	**eles/elas escreveram** *(they wrote)*

Eu vivi em Paris de dois mil até dois mil e três.
I lived in Paris from 2000 to 2003.

Você bebeu água de coco na praia ontem?
Did you drink coconut water at the beach yesterday?

No fim do ano passado, Mariana recebeu o prêmio de melhor aluna.
Last year Mariana received the student of the year award.

Nós não vendemos o carro no domingo.
We didn't sell the car on Sunday.

Quando a polícia prendeu o ladrão?
When did the police arrest the thief?

Eu comi demais!
I ate too much!

O poeta morreu em mil novecentos e oitenta e sete.
The poet died in 1987.

PRACTICE 1
Complete the sentences with the verb in parentheses in the preterite, and translate.

1. Muitos escritores americanos _____ (viver) na França no século passado.

2. O atleta não _____ (correr) a Maratona de Nova York em 2007.

3. Ontem de manhã Cristina _____ (receber) flores do seu namorado.

4. Quantos cartões postais vocês _____ (escrever) nas férias passadas?

5. Ontem no parque, um cachorro _____ (morder) uma criança.

6. Nós não _____ (entender) o que ele disse. Você _____ (entender)?

7. Segunda-feira passada eu _____ (resolver) fazer uma dieta.

8. Quando o ladrão entrou em casa, nós não _____ (perceber).

9. Quando eu _____ (devolver) o carro, não _____ (perceber) que o tanque estava vazio.

10. No último semestre, Paulo não _____ (aprender) inglês na escola.

CONVERSATION 2

Listen in while Roberto describes his dinner experience at a **churrascaria** to his friend Cristiano.

Roberto: Ontem à noite, minha mulher e eu jantamos no novo rodízio de carnes perto da Lagoa.

Cristiano: É mesmo? O que você achou do lugar?

Roberto: Eu achei a carne muito bem preparada, mas não gostei do serviço.

Cristiano: O que vocês comeram?

Roberto: Primeiro nós escolhemos uns pratos do buffet. Eles tinham, além de saladas e outros pratos frios, uma grande variedade de comida japonesa, como sushi e sashimi, tudo bem arranjado sobre gelo picado. Havia também pratos quentes, como macarrão e bobó de camarão.

Cristiano: Nossa! Que fartura! E vocês conseguiram comer carne depois desse monte de entradas?

Roberto: Bem, não experimentamos tudo: só um pouco de salada e uns pedaços de queijo parmesão. Depois chegou a carne, e comemos fatias de lingüiça, picanha, lombo de porco, frango e até peixe!

Cristiano: Parece muito bom. O que vocês beberam?

Roberto: Nós pedimos chope estupidamente gelado, claro. Mas, as carnes chegaram à mesa muito lentamente, e a sobremesa demorou um tempão. Assim que acabamos o cafezinho pedimos a conta, mas ela só chegou depois de meia hora!

Cristiano: Você falou com o gerente?

Roberto: Não, não falei porque quando esperava a conta, olhei pela janela, e vi do lado de fora, uma placa que dizia: "Precisa-se urgentemente de garçons!"

Roberto: Last night my wife and I had dinner at the new Brazilian steak house near Lagoa.

Cristiano: Really? What did you think of the place?

Roberto: I thought the meat was very well prepared, but I didn't like the service.

Cristiano: What did you eat?

Roberto: First we chose some dishes from the salad bar, which had, apart from salads and other kinds of cold dishes, a large variety of Japanese food, such as sushi and sashimi, all very finely arranged over crushed ice. There were also hot dishes, like pasta and Bahian style shrimp stew.

Cristiano: Wow! That's a lot of food! And you managed to eat meat after all those appetizers?

Roberto: Well, we didn't try everything: just a bit of salad and a few pieces of parmesan cheese. Then the meat arrived, and we ate slices of sausage, top sirloin, pork loin, chicken, and even fish!

Cristiano: It all sounds great. What did you drink?

Roberto: We had incredibly cold draft beer, of course. But, the meats got to the table too slowly, and dessert took a long time to arrive. As soon as we finished the meal we asked for the check, but it didn't get there until after half an hour!

Cristiano: Did you speak to the manager?

Roberto: No, I didn't because while I was waiting for the check, I looked out the window, and saw a sign that read: "Waiters needed urgently!"

NOTES

Chope is a kind of draft beer very popular in Brazil, where the cognoscenti spend endless hours debating the ideal temperature, thickness and height of the **colarinho** *(foam, lit., small collar)*. Another key factor for a top quality **chope** is the length of the tube that links the keg to the tap, known as **serpentina**.

NUTS & BOLTS 2
THE PRETERITE OF TER AND PODER

Ter *(to have)* and **poder** *(can/to be able to)* have irregular preterite conjugations.

ter *(to have)*

eu tive	**nós tivemos**
você teve	**vocês tiveram**
ele/ela teve	**eles/elas tiveram**

Eles tiveram cinco filhos.
They had five children.

Você teve que ir ao escritório no domingo?
You had to go to the office on Sunday?

Eu nunca tive um carro igual a esse!
I never had a car like this.

Nós não tivemos tempo para descansar.
We didn't have time to rest.

poder *(can/to be able to)*

eu pude	nós pudemos
você pôde	vocês puderam
ele/ela pôde	eles/elas puderam

Eu pude fazer a reserva para jantar.
I was able to make the reservation for dinner.

Clara não pôde vir à praia, ela está doente.
Clara couldn't come to the beach; she's sick.

Eles puderam assistir à aula ontem?
Were they able to come to class yesterday?

Nós não pudemos comprar mais porque o dinheiro acabou!
We couldn't buy more because we ran out of money.

PRACTICE 2
Complete the sentences with the preterite of the verbs in parentheses and translate.

1. Sexta-feira passada eu _____ (poder) ver o eclipse da lua.

2. A loja não _____ (poder) entregar as compras ontem.

3. Nós estacionamos o carro onde _____ (poder).

4. Vocês _____ (poder) ir para casa depois da chuva?

5. As fãs não _____ (poder) ver o roqueiro.

6. Eu não _____ (ter) medo do jacaré na selva.

7. Ela sempre _____ (ter) talento para música.

8. O meu amigo e eu não _____ (ter) sorte com o nosso hotel.

9. Por que vocês não _____ (ter) que pagar os impostos no ano passado?

10. Ontem você _____ (ter) que buscar as crianças na escola?

ANSWERS

PRACTICE 1: 1. viveram (Many American writers lived in France last century.) **2.** correu (The athlete didn't run the New York Marathon in 2007.) **3.** recebeu (Yesterday morning Cristina got flowers from her boyfriend.) **4.** escreveram (How many postcards did you write last vacation?) **5.** mordeu (Yesterday at the park a dog bit a child.) **6.** entendemos, entendeu (We didn't understand what he said. Did you understand?) **7.** resolvi (Last Monday I decided to go on a diet.) **8.** percebemos (We didn't notice when the thief broke into our house.) **9.** devolvi, percebi (When I returned the car, I didn't notice the tank was empty.) **10.** aprendeu (Last semester Paulo didn't learn English at school.)

PRACTICE 2: 1. pude (Last Friday I was able to see the lunar eclipse.) **2.** pôde (The store couldn't deliver the merchandise yesterday.) **3.** pudemos (We parked the car where we could.) **4.** puderam (Were you able to go home after the rain?) **5.** puderam (The fans weren't able to see the rock star.) **6.** tive (I wasn't afraid of the alligator in the jungle.) **7.** teve (She always had musical talent.) **8.** tivemos (My friends and I had no luck with our hotel.) **9.** tiveram (Why didn't you have to pay taxes last year?) **10.** teve (Did you have to pick the kids up at school yesterday?)

UNIT 8 ESSENTIALS
Não esperem por mim.

Don't wait for me.

Com quem Mário vai jantar?
Who is Mário having dinner with?

Onde se compra selos?
Where can you buy stamps?

Alugam-se apartamentos.
Apartments for rent.

Nós caminhamos lentamente.
We walk slowly.

A chuva chega de repente.
The rain arrives suddenly.

Você vem comigo? Talvez.
Are you coming with me? Maybe.

Vocês estiveram em Madrid no verão passado?
Were you in Madrid last summer?

Eu trabalhei das oito da manhã até às oito da noite.
I worked from 8:00 A.M. to 8:00 P.M.

Eu acabei de tomar uma decisão.
I have just made up my mind.

Eu vivi em Paris de dois mil até dois mil e três.
I lived in Paris from 2000 to 2003.

Nós não tivemos tempo para descansar.
We didn't have time to rest.

Clara não pôde vir à praia, ela está doente.
Clara couldn't come to the beach; she's sick.

Segunda-feira passada eu resolvi fazer uma dieta.
Last Monday I decided to go on a diet.

Nós não entendemos o que ele disse. Você entendeu?
We didn't understand what he said. Did you understand?

Unit 9
Work and school

In Unit 9 you'll learn vocabulary and expressions to talk about work and school. You'll also continue to focus on the preterite, and you'll be introduced to another past tense construction as well. Unit 9 also covers indefinite pronouns like *everyone*, *someone*, and *anyone*. So, **ao trabalho!** *(to work!)*

———————— Lesson 33 (words) ————————

WORD LIST 1

a escola	*school*
a matéria	*subject (school)*
matemática	*math*
história	*history*
literatura	*literature*
ciência	*science*
química	*chemistry*
biologia	*biology*
física	*physics*
o vestibular	*college entrance exam*
o curso	*course*
a faculdade	*college*
a universidade	*university*
a formatura	*graduation*
o bacharelado	*bachelor's degree*
o mestrado	*master's degree*
o doutorado	*doctorate*
o diploma	*diploma/certificate*

a reitoria	*dean's office*
o reitor	*dean*
a secretaria	*registrar*
a diretoria	*principal's office*
o campus/os campi	*campus/campuses*
a biblioteca	*library*

NUTS & BOLTS 1
THE PRETERITE OF SER AND IR

The verbs **ser** *(to be)* and **ir** *(to go)* have the same form in the preterite.

eu fui *(I was/went)*	nós fomos *(we were/went)*
você foi *(you were/went)*	vocês foram *(you were/went)*
ele/ela foi *(he/she/it was/went)*	eles/elas foram *(they were/went)*

The context will of course make the distinction in meaning.

Pedro foi o primeiro da sua turma.
Pedro was the first in his class.

O passeio não foi divertido.
The stroll wasn't fun.

Vocês foram professores universitários?
Were you university professors?

Eu fui estagiário até conseguir uma vaga fixa.
I was an intern until I got a permanent position.

Isso foi demais!
That was too much! (That was fun!)

Eles foram à escola.
They went to school.

Você foi à aula à tarde?
Did you go to class in the afternoon?

O ônibus foi embora na hora marcada.
The bus left at the scheduled time.

Por que Maria não foi à praia com você?
Why didn't Maria go to the beach with you?

PRACTICE 1
Translate the following.

1. Quem foi à festa de formatura?

2. Cristina foi a minha melhor amiga.

3. Por que você não foi de trem?

4. Nós fomos noivos durante dois anos antes de nos casarmos.

5. Eu fui gerente por dois anos e depois fui promovida.

Now complete the following sentences with the verb given in parentheses.

6. Quem _____ (ser) seu professor no primeiro ano?

7. Você _____ (ser) muito duro com as crianças.

8. Por que eles _____ (ir) a pé?

9. Elas _____ (ir) ao parque ontem?

10. Eu não _____(ir) a escola porque _____ (ser) atropelado por um carro!

WORD LIST 2

| o emprego | *job* |
| o trabalho | *work* |

o operário	*factory worker*
o empregado	*employee*
o funcionário	*office worker*
o salário	*salary*
o empregador	*employer*
a divisória	*partition*
o cubículo	*cubicle*
o departamento	*department*
a divisão	*division*
a reunião	*meeting*
a companhia	*company*
a empresa	*firm*
o projeto	*project*
o relatório	*report*
o sucesso	*success*
o crescimento	*growth*
a falência	*bankruptcy*

NUTS & BOLTS 2
THE PRETERITE OF REGULAR -IR VERBS

You've already seen the preterite of regular verbs ending in **-ar** and **-er**. Now let's look at the ones ending in **-ir,** using the verb **partir** *(to leave)* as a model.

eu parti	nós partimos
você partiu	vocês partiram
ele/ela partiu	eles/elas partiram

Ele construiu a empresa do nada.
He built the company from scratch.

O cheque cobriu todas as despesas?
Did the check cover all the expenses?

Mariana subiu ao quarto andar atrás de você.
Mariana went up to the fourth floor looking for you.

Por que vocês não assistiram ao documentário?
Why didn't you watch the documentary?

Eles não discutiram o aumento de salário.
They didn't discuss the salary increase.

Eu preferi ficar em casa ontem.
I preferred to stay at home yesterday.

Nós não dividimos os lucros.
We didn't share the profits.

Quando a companhia decidiu recrutar mais operários?
When did the company decide to recruit more workers?

Eu não insisti no assunto.
I didn't insist on the matter.

Ela se sentiu mal no meio da reunião.
She felt sick in the middle of the meeting.

Você repetiu, mas eu ainda não entendi.
You repeated it, but I still haven't understood.

PRACTICE 2
Give the preterite of the verbs in parentheses, and translate the full sentences.

1. Nós _____ (dormir) a noite toda e agora estamos descansados.

2. O jornalista não _____ (cobrir) a história porque não a achou importante.

3. Por que vocês _____ (discutir) com o diretor?

4. A que horas o avião _____ (partir)?

5. A minha família e eu _____ (subir) na vida graças ao trabalho duro.

6. O que eles _____ (conseguir) resolver com o chefe?

7. Vocês _____ (dividir) os lucros, mas não podem dividir os prejuízos.

8. Eu não _____ (incluir) os impostos.

9. Você _____ (assistir) o novo programa das oito?

10. Ela _____ (possuir) a empresa até mil novecentos e noventa.

ANSWERS

PRACTICE 1: 1. Who went to the graduation? **2.** Cristina was my best friend. **3.** Why didn't you go by train? **4.** We were engaged for two years before we got married. **5.** I was a manager for two years and then I was promoted. **6.** foi; **7.** foi; **8.** foram; **9.** foram; **10.** fui, fui

PRACTICE 2: 1. dormimos (We slept all night and now we're rested.) **2.** cobriu (The reporter didn't cover the story because he didn't find it interesting.) **3.** discutiram (Why did you argue with the director?) **4.** partiu (What time did the plane leave?) **5.** subimos (My family and I succeeded in life thanks to hard work.) **6.** conseguiram (What did they manage to solve with the boss?) **7.** dividiram (You shared the profits, but you can't share the losses.) **8.** incluí (I didn't include the taxes.) **9.** assistiu (Did you watch the new 8 o'clock program?) **10.** possuiu (She owned the company until 1990.)

—————————— Lesson 34 (phrases) ——————————

PHRASE LIST 1

o ensino fundamental	*grade school (from first to ninth grade)*
o ensino médio	*high school*
o ensino superior	*undergraduate study*

passar de ano	*to be promoted (in school)*
repetir de ano	*to fail (in school)*
formar-se em administração de empresas	*to major in business administration*
fazer pós-graduação	*to go to graduate school*
o melhor da classe	*the best student in the class*
a escola politécnica	*engineering school*
a faculdade de direito	*law school*
a bolsa de estudos	*scholarship*
o laboratório de pesquisas	*research laboratory*
o curso de extensão	*extension course*
o certificado de conclusão	*certificate*

NUTS & BOLTS 1
IRREGULAR VERBS IN THE PRETERITE

Let's look at a few more essential verbs that are irregular in the preterite.

dar *(to give)*

eu dei	nós demos
você deu	vocês deram
ele/ela deu	eles/elas deram

dizer *(to say)*

eu disse	nós dissemos
você disse	vocês disseram
ele/ela disse	eles/elas disseram

fazer *(to do/to make)*

eu fiz	nós fizemos
você fez	vocês fizeram
ele/ela fez	eles/elas fizeram

querer *(to want)*

eu quis	nós quisemos
você quis	vocês quiseram
ele/ela quis	eles/elas quiseram

saber *(to know/to learn about)*

eu soube	nós soubemos
você soube	vocês souberam
ele/ela soube	eles/elas souberam

ver *(to see)*

eu vi	nós vimos
você viu	vocês viram
ele/ela viu	eles/elas viram

vir *(to come)*

eu vim	nós viemos
você veio	vocês vieram
ele/ela veio	eles/elas vieram

Also note that the preterite of **haver,** with the present form **há** *(there is, there are)* is **houve** *(there was, there were).*

Eu dei uma gorjeta para o garçom.
I gave the waiter a tip.

Nós não demos o que eles pediram.
We didn't give them what they asked for.

Vocês disseram a verdade?
Did you tell the truth?

Ela não disse onde posso encontrá-la?
She didn't say where to find her?

O que ele fez na faculdade?
What did he study at college?

Vocês não fizeram a lição de casa.
You didn't do your homework.

Eu quis o mesmo que ela.
I wanted the same as she did.

Por que ela não quis vir ao parque?
Why didn't she want to come to the park?

Nós não soubemos do resultado até ontem.
We didn't know the result until yesterday.

Você soube o que aconteceu com ela?
Did you find out what happened to her?

Por que não houve aula?

Why wasn't there a lesson?

Ele veio à aula, mas elas não vieram.

He came to class, but they didn't come.

Vocês viram as fotos no jornal? Eu não as vi.

Did you see the pictures in the paper? I didn't see them.

PRACTICE 1

Complete the following with the preterite of the verb in parentheses, and translate.

1. Desculpe, eu não _____ (poder) ir a sua festa.

2. Cristina _____ (ter) uma cirurgia no ano passado.

3. Nós não _____ (querer) vender a casa por aquele preço.

4. O que eles _____ (dizer)? Eu não entendi.

5. Vocês _____ (saber) do acidente?

6. Eu _____ (ter) que procurar outro emprego depois que _____ (ser) despedido.

7. Nós não _____ (ser) feliz naquela casa, por isso mudamos.

8. Em que praia vocês _____ (ir) ontem?

9. Onde ele _____ (estar) de maio a junho?

10. Eles _____ (fazer) somente o necessário e depois _____ (ir) para casa.

11. Não _____ (haver) tempo de lhe avisar.

12. Os carros _____ (estar) à venda for dois anos.

13. Ele não _____ (vir) com a namorada.

14. O que você _____ (ver) quando _____ (ir) lá embaixo?

PHRASE LIST 2

o departamento de recursos humanos	*human resources department*
o anúncio de emprego	*help wanted ad*
a fase de expansão	*expansion phase*
os relatórios financeiros semestrais	*half year earnings reports*
o mercado de trabalho	*job market*
o mercado de ações	*stock market*
a pesquisa de mercado	*market research*
o analista financeiro	*financial analyst*
o programa de treinamento	*training program*
a viagem de negócios	*business trip*
o imposto de renda	*income tax*
a empresa multinacional	*multinational company*
a entrevista de emprego	*job interview*
a empresária bem-sucedida	*successful businesswoman*
ter negócio próprio	*have your own business*
o desafio da carreira	*career challenge*
ser despedido	*be fired/be laid off*

NUTS & BOLTS 2
INDEFINITES (I)

Indefinite pronouns can be used to replace a noun, so they stand on their own. Some indefinite pronouns are invariable, but some change form depending on the gender and number of the noun they're replacing. Here are some affirmative indefinite pronouns.

algo	*something*
algum/alguma/alguns/algumas	*some, any*
alguém	*someone, somebody*

um/uma/uns/umas	*one, ones*
outro/outra/outros/outras	*another (one), other (one)*
todo/toda/todos/todas	*everyone, everybody*
todos, todo o mundo	*everyone, everybody*
tudo	*everything*
qualquer *(sg.)*/**quaisquer** *(pl.)*	*anything, whatever*
cada	*each*

Há alguém no escritório agora?
Is there anyone in the office now?

Nós compramos um, igual ao seu.
We bought one like yours.

Você quer uma azul ou verde?
Do you want a blue one or a green one?

Você vai comprar tudo?
Are you going to buy everything?

Ele quer algo para comer.
He wants something to eat.

Cada um vem acompanhado com brinde.
Each one comes with a gift.

Indefinite adjectives are like any adjectives; they agree with the noun they modify in gender and number. The exceptions are **qualquer/quaisquer** *(any, whichever)*, which agree only for number, and **cada** *(each)*, which is invariable. Don't forget that the question word **quanto** *(how much, how many)* functions just like an indefinite adjective.

algum/alguma/alguns/algumas	*some, any*
outro/outra/outros/outras	*another, other*
todo/toda/todos/todas	*all, every*
muito/muita/muitos/muitas	*many, much*
pouco/pouca/poucos/poucas	*little, few*
vários/várias	*various*
qualquer *(sg.)/***quaisquer** *(pl.)*	*any, whichever*
cada	*each*
quanto/quanta/quantos/quantas	*how much, how many*

Você tem algum amigo nessa escola?
Do you have any friend in this school?

Elas procuram algumas informações.
They're looking for some information.

Ele pediu outro café.
He ordered another coffee.

Elas foram a outras praias.
They went to other beaches.

Eu estudei toda a matéria.
I studied the whole subject.

Ele viu todos os documentos.
He saw all the documents.

Telefone para mim qualquer dia.
Call me any day.

Eu vou responder a quaisquer perguntas.

I'll answer any questions.

Cada pessoa tem uma vaga.

Each person has a position.

PRACTICE 2

Choose an indefinite from the following list to complete the sentences: **tudo, toda, todos, cada, alguém, algumas, algum, qualquer, outros, outra, uns, uma.** Translate.

1. Você quer estes sapatos ou quer _____?

2. _____ veio aqui para consertar a máquina de lavar?

3. Há um lugar a mesa para _____ convidado: dez convidados e dez lugares.

4. _____ empresas não têm ações na bolsa de valores.

5. Eu gostei da sua bebida. Você pode comprar _____ igual a sua para mim?

6. Você pode escolher _____dia porque não estou ocupado.

7. Vocês conhecem _____ professor particular de inglês?

8. Eles chamaram _____ os passageiros para embarcar.

9. O bebê comeu _____! Ótimo!

10. A primeira candidata já chegou e a _____ está na recepção.

11. Eu pedi _____ para você porque sei que você vai gostar.

12. Ela faz curso de francês _____ quarta-feira à tarde.

ANSWERS

PRACTICE 1: 1. pude (Sorry, I couldn't go to your party.)
2. teve (Cristina had a surgery last year.) **3.** quisemos (We didn't want to sell the house for that price.) **4.** disseram (What did they say? I didn't understand.) **5.** souberam (Did you know about the accident?) **6.** tive, fui (I had to look for another job after I was fired.) **7.** fomos (We weren't happy in that house so we moved.) **8.** foram (What beach did you go to yesterday?) **9.** esteve (Where was he from May to June?) **10.** fizeram, foram (They did only what was necessary and then they went home.) **11.** houve (There wasn't time to let him know.) **12.** estiveram (The cars were for sale for two years.) **13.** veio (He didn't come with his girlfriend.) **14.** viu, foi (What did you see when you went downstairs?)

PRACTICE 2: 1. outros (Do you want these shoes or do you want other ones?) **2.** Alguém (Did anyone come here to fix the washing machine?) **3.** cada (There's a place at the table for each guest: ten guests and ten places.) **4.** Algumas (Some companies don't have stocks in the stock exchange market.) **5.** uma (I liked your drink. Can you buy me one just like yours?) **6.** qualquer (You can choose any day because I'm not busy.) **7.** algum (Do you know any private English teacher?) **8.** todos (They called all the passengers to board the plane.) **9.** tudo (The baby ate everything! Great!) **10.** outra (The first candidate has already arrived and the other one is in the reception [area].) **11.** uns (I ordered some for you because I know you're going to love them.) **12.** toda. (She has French lessons every Wednesday afternoon.)

--------- Lesson 35 (sentences) ---------

SENTENCE LIST 1

Eu fiz um mestrado na Universidade Estadual.

I got a master's at the State University.

Maria fez um estágio no banco.

Maria did an internship at the bank.

Pedro veio para São Paulo para estudar.	*Pedro came to São Paulo to study.*
Ele enfrentou muitos desafios.	*He faced many challenges.*
Nós trouxemos os relatórios.	*We brought the reports.*
A empresa teve dificuldades financeiras.	*The company had financial difficulties.*
Houve uma greve dos funcionários.	*There was an employee strike.*
O meu chefe não me deu o aumento que pedi.	*My boss didn't give me the raise I asked for.*
Os gerentes disseram que concordam com a medida.	*The managers said they agree with the measure.*
O seu curriculum vitae é muito bom.	*Your résumé is very good.*
Mauro recebeu uma promoção.	*Mauro got a promotion.*
A companhia está em fase de expansão.	*The company is in an expansion phase.*

NUTS & BOLTS 1
THE IMPERFECT OF SER AND ESTAR

You've learned that you use the preterite to express a past fact or action that is completely finished. In this way, the Portuguese preterite corresponds to the English simple past with *-ed* or *did*. Now let's look at another way to talk about the past with the imperfect tense. You use the imperfect to talk about past actions or states that occur over a period of time. The imperfect sometimes corresponds to the English habitual past with *used to,* as in *I used to play with dolls,* or with *would,* as in *I would study day and night when I was in college.* It is also used to describe things in the past, and to talk about a past continuous action, corresponding to the English past progressive with *was/were + ing,* as in *I was speaking on the phone.* We'll contrast the imperfect and the preterite in a later lesson, but for now let's look at how it's used with the verbs **ser** and **estar**.

ser

eu era	nós éramos
você era	vocês eram
ele/ela era	eles/elas eram

estar

eu estava	nós estávamos
você estava	vocês estavam
ele/ela estava	eles/elas estavam

Now study these examples with the imperfect tense of **ser** and **estar**. Note that a typical past time expression for this tense is **antigamente** *(in the past, formerly)*.

Eu era o melhor da classe.
I was the best in the class.

Pedro não era bom em matemática.
Pedro wasn't good in math.

Antigamente éramos vizinhos.
In the past we were neighbors.

Vocês eram os melhores atletas da escola.
You were the best athletes in school.

Por que você estava cansada ontem à noite?
Why were you tired last night?

Ela estava numa reunião quando você telefonou.

She was in a meeting when you called.

Nós estávamos em Paris quando a guerra começou.

We were in Paris when the war started.

Onde eles estavam nas férias passadas?

Where were they last on vacation?

PRACTICE 1

Complete the dialogue between a teacher and some of his students with **ser** or **estar** in the imperfect. The translation is given below to help you.

Professor: Antigamente os alunos 1_____ (ser) mais bem comportados. Eles 2_____ (ser) agradáveis e 3_____ (estar) sempre alegres. Eu e meus colegas 4 _____ (estar) sempre atentos aos ensinamentos dos professores.

Aluno 1: Mas professor, o senhor 5 _____ (ser) assim, porque não 6_____ (estar) sempre cansado.

Aluna 2: Ele está certo. Antigamente, vocês não 7 _____ (ser) obrigados a fazer tantas atividades extracurriculares.

Professor: É verdade, a vida 8_____ (ser) mais tranqüila. Os alunos 9_____ (estar) em casa a tarde toda para fazer lição e brincar. Mas isso tudo 10_____ (ser) antigamente, e hoje é hoje, então vamos prestar mais atenção!

Teacher: *In the past students were better behaved. They were more agreeable and were always happy. My classmates and I were always attentive to the teachers' lessons.*

Student 1: *But teacher, you were like that because you weren't always tired.*

Student 2: *He's right. In the past, you weren't obligated to have so many extracurricular activities.*

> *Teacher:* *That's true, life was more leisurely. Students were at home all afternoon to do their homework and play. But this was all in the past, and today is today, so let's pay attention!*

SENTENCE LIST 2

Eu me formei em engenharia.	*I majored in engineering.*
Onde você fez faculdade?	*Where did you go to university?*
Ele estava na biblioteca quando você telefonou.	*He was in the library when you called.*
Nós trabalhávamos de dia e estudávamos à noite.	*We worked during the day and studied at night.*
Mariana não fazia as pesquisas porque não tinha tempo.	*Mariana didn't do the research because she didn't have time.*
Ela precisava trabalhar para pagar as mensalidades da escola.	*She needed to work to pay the tuition.*
Quando começam as matrículas?	*When does enrollment start?*
Eu me matriculei no curso de literatura.	*I enrolled in the literature course.*
Ele ganhou uma bolsa de estudos.	*He got a scholarship.*
Vocês estudaram para os exames semestrais?	*Did you study for the final exams?*
Você conhece algum professor particular de química?	*Do you know a private chemistry tutor?*
O curso de estatística é bimestral.	*The statistics class is bimonthly.*

Some adjectives describing frequency are: **semanal** *(weekly)*, **quinzenal** *(every two weeks)*, **mensal** *(monthly)*, **bimestral** *(bimonthly)*, **semestral** *(once a semester)*, and **anual** *(yearly)*.

NUTS & BOLTS 2
THE IMPERFECT OF REGULAR VERBS

Look at the following models for conjugating regular verbs ending in **-ar, -er,** and **-ir** in the imperfect. As you can see, the imperfect conjugations of **-er** and **-ir** verbs are the same.

-ar (falar)

eu falava	nós falávamos
você falava	vocês falavam
ele/ela falava	eles/elas falavam

-er (escrever)

eu escrevia	nós escrevíamos
você escrevia	vocês escreviam
ele/ela escrevia	eles/elas escreviam

-ir (assistir)

eu assistia	nós assistíamos
você assistia	vocês assistiam
ele/ela assistia	eles/elas assistiam

Quando era criança eu não gostava de queijo.
When I was a child I used to not like cheese.

246   UNIT 9: Work and school

Antigamente você não comprava pela internet.

In the past you didn't buy things over the internet.

Nós jogávamos futebol todos os fins de semana quando éramos estudantes.

We would play soccer every weekend when we were students.

Vocês aprendiam tudo sem computador?

You used to learn everything without computers?

Os meus avôs não entendiam música rock.

My grandparents didn't understand rock music.

No meu tempo as crianças não comiam tanta besteira.

In my day children didn't use to eat so much junk.

Eles se divorciaram porque discutiam muito.

They got divorced because they argued too much.

Quando era solteiro eu preferia sair todos os sábados.

When I was single I preferred to go out every Saturday.

It's also worth noting that there are only three irregular verbs in the imperfect tense aside from **ser** *(to be)*.

pôr *(to put, to place)*

eu punha	nós púnhamos
você punha	vocês punham
ele/ela punha	eles/elas punham

ter *(to have)*

eu tinha	nós tínhamos
você tinha	vocês tinham
ele/ela tinha	eles/elas tinham

vir *(to come)*

eu vinha	nós vínhamos
você vinha	vocês vinham
ele/ela vinha	eles/elas vinham

PRACTICE 2
Complete the sentences with the imperfect of the verb given in parentheses, and translate.

1. Antigamente as coisas não _____ (custar) tanto.

2. Até o ano dois mil, as pessoas _____ (fumar) em bares e restaurantes.

3. Por que ele sempre _____ (concordar) com os amigos?

4. Mariana nunca _____ (chegar) atrasada quando era solteira.

5. As empresas não _____ (atender) o público tão bem quanto agora.

6. Nós _____ (andar) mais a pé antigamente.

7. As editoras _____ (vender) mais enciclopédias e dicionários no passado.

8. As moças não _____ (viver) com os namorados na época dos meus avôs.

9. Eu _____ (beber) muito mais do que agora.

10. Antes de ter filhos, nós _____ (dormir) melhor.

11. Os trens _____ (partir) sempre no horário.

12. Pedro nunca _____ (sair) à noite quando era estudante.

ANSWERS
PRACTICE 1: 1. eram; **2.** eram; **3.** estavam; **4.** estávamos; **5.** era; **6.** estava; **7.** eram; **8.** era; **9.** estavam; **10.** era

PRACTICE 2: 1. custavam (In the past things didn't cost as much.) **2.** fumavam (Until 2000, people used to smoke in bars and restaurants.) **3.** concordava (Why would he always agree with his friends?) **4.** chegava (Mariana didn't use to arrive late when she was single.) **5.** atendiam (Companies didn't use to serve the public as well as they do now.) **6.** andávamos (We would walk more in the past.) **7.** vendiam (Publishing companies used to sell more encyclopedias and dictionaries in the past.) **8.** viviam (Young women didn't use to live with their boyfriends in my grandparents' time.) **9.** bebia (I used to drink more than now.) **10.** dormíamos (Before we had children, we slept better.) **11.** partiam (Trains used to leave on time.) **12.** saía (Pedro wouldn't go out at night when he was a student.)

─────────── Lesson 36 (conversations) ───────────

CONVERSATION 1
Listen in while Bianca is being interviewed for a job by D. Paula.

D. Paula: Boa tarde, por favor, queira sentar-se.
Bianca: Obrigada. Aqui está o meu curriculum vitae.
D. Paula: Obrigada, mas primeiro, conte-me um pouco sobre você.
Bianca: Bem, eu morei em Blumenau, Santa Catarina até completar a escola média, e então me mudei para São Paulo onde cursei economia na Universidade de São Paulo. Depois disso eu fiz um MBA na Fundação Getúlio Vargas.
D. Paula: E você já trabalhou em alguma empresa?
Bianca: Sim, eu fiz um estágio no Banco do Brasil logo depois do mestrado.
D. Paula: O que você fazia no banco?
Bianca: Eu era estagiária no departamento de comércio exterior. Eu trabalhei lá por seis meses.
D. Paula: O que você mais gostava do seu trabalho?

Bianca: Eu gostava de me comunicar com pessoas de todo o mundo.

D. Paula: E a última pergunta: qual foi o maior desafio que você enfrentou até o momento?

Bianca: Sem dúvida, o meu maior desafio foi vir sozinha para essa cidade tão grande. Eu não sabia nem cozinhar nem pagar contas. Quando morava com meus pais eu só estudava e fazia esportes, não precisava me preocupar com nada. Depois que vim para cá tudo mudou muito rapidamente, mas me adaptei bem.

D. Paula: Gostei muito das suas respostas. Nós vamos mandar um e-mail para avisar sobre os resultados.

D. Paula: *Good afternoon, please have a seat.*

Bianca: *Thank you. Here's my résumé.*

D. Paula: *Thank you, but first tell me a little about yourself.*

Bianca: *Well, I lived in Blumenau in Santa Catarina until I finished high school, and then I moved to São Paulo, where I studied economics at the University of São Paulo. After that I did an MBA at Fundação Getúlio Vargas.*

D. Paula: *Have you ever worked for a company?*

Bianca: *Yes, I did an internship at the Bank of Brazil right after graduate school.*

D. Paula: *What did you do at the bank?*

Bianca: *I was an intern in the foreign trade department. I worked there for six months.*

D. Paula: *What did you like best about your job?*

Bianca: *I liked communicating with people from all over the world.*

D. Paula: *And now the last question. What was the greatest challenge you've faced up to now?*

Bianca: *My greatest challenge, without a doubt, was to come alone to such a big city. I didn't know how to cook or how to pay bills. When I lived with my parents, I only*

> studied and played sports; I didn't have to worry about
> anything. After I came here, everything changed very
> quickly. But I've adapted well.
>
> D. Paula: I liked your answers. We will send you an e-mail to let
> you know about the results.

NOTE

The construction **nem . . . nem** corresponds to the English *neither
. . . nor* or *not either . . . or.* You can use it to join nouns, verbs, or
other like phrases. **Eles não queriam nem café nem chá.** *(They
wanted neither coffee nor tea.)* **Ele não está nem na loja nem na
praia.** *(He's neither in the store nor at the beach.)* **Ele não é nem criativo nem interessante.** *(He's neither creative nor interesting.)*

NUTS & BOLTS 1

THE PAST CONTINUOUS WITH ESTAR

To talk about actions that were happening in the past over a period of time, use the imperfect of the verb **estar** *(to be)* + the gerund.

Eu estava telefonando para você.

I was calling you.

As mulheres estavam trabalhando.

The women were working.

O time estava jogando, e os torcedores estavam cantando.

The team was playing, and the supporters were singing.

You can join two simultaneous past actions with **enquanto**
(while). Or, if a continuous past action was interrupted by another
action, you can join the two with **quando** *(when).* The interrupting action will be in the preterite.

Ele estava cozinhando enquanto ela estava olhando as crianças.

He was cooking while she was watching the children.

Eu estava assistindo a TV enquanto você estava dormindo.
I was watching TV while you were sleeping.

Ele estava jantando quando ela chegou.
He was having dinner when she arrived.

O chefe estava falando quando ele interrompeu.
The boss was talking when he interrupted.

Pedro estava estudando quando as luzes se apagaram.
Pedro was studying when the lights went out.

PRACTICE 1

Complete the sentences below using the past continuous of the first verb in parentheses and then decide whether the second verb should be the past continuous or preterite.

1. Eu _____ (andar) enquanto você _____ (descansar).

2. Pedro _____ (escrever) ao mesmo tempo em que ele _____ (falar) ao telefone.

3. As crianças _____ (dormir) enquanto nós _____ (embrulhar) os presentes de natal.

4. O que vocês _____ (fazer) quando a chuva _____ (começar)?

5. Ela não _____ (dirigir) devagar quando o acidente _____ (acontecer).

6. Eu _____ (ter) problemas com meu carro quando a polícia _____ (aparecer).

7. Qual filme ele _____ (ver) enquanto você _____ (fazer) compras?

8. Nós _____ (ir) para a sua casa quando o nosso carro _____ (quebrar).

9. O gerente _____ (ler) as propostas quando o diretor _____ (pedir) para falar com ele.

10. Algumas pessoas _____ (viajar) a negócios enquanto outras pessoas _____ (se divertir).

CONVERSATION 2

Listen in on a conversation between a grandfather, Seu Vicente, and his ten-year-old grandson, Pedrinho.

Pedrinho: Vovô, a mamãe me disse que quando você era criança, você não tinha computador. Como você fazia as suas pesquisas para a escola e depois para a faculdade?

Seu Vicente: Era simples, Pedrinho, eu usava a enciclopédia.

Pedrinho: Mas quando você tinha que pesquisar em mais de uma fonte?

Seu Vicente: Isso era fácil: eu ia à biblioteca e procurava o tema em vários livros.

Pedrinho: Mas e os livros estavam atualizados?

Seu Vicente: Bem, não estavam tão atualizados como as enciclopédias que você tem hoje na internet, mas cada ano as editoras publicavam o "Livro do Ano" para atualizar os dados.

Pedrinho: Não sei não, isso parece muito trabalho! E depois você tinha que copiar tudo a mão?

Seu Vicente: Claro, Pedrinho. Eu e os meus colegas fazíamos um rascunho, e depois passávamos tudo a limpo, geralmente usando a máquina de escrever.

Pedrinho: E o que acontecia quando você errava algo enquanto batia a máquina?

Seu Vicente: Isso era difícil porque naquela época não tínhamos nem o corretivo líquido, nem a tecla de deletar com temos agora. Tínhamos que apagar com a borracha ou começar tudo de novo. Uma vez eu demorei três dias para passar a limpo um trabalho de história.

Pedrinho: Ai, vovô, que vida dura que você tinha!

Pedrinho:	Grandpa, Mom said that when you were a kid, you didn't have a computer. How did you use to do the research for your school, and later college, papers?
Seu Vicente:	It was simple, Pedrinho, I used an encyclopedia.
Pedrinho:	But, how about when you had to research more than one source?
Seu Vicente:	That was easy: I'd go to the library and look up the topic in several books.
Pedrinho:	But were the books updated?
Seu Vicente:	Well, they weren't as updated as the encyclopedias you have today on the internet, but every year the publishers issued the "Book of the Year" to update the data.
Pedrinho:	I don't know, that sounds like a lot of work! And then you had to copy everything by hand?
Seu Vicente:	Of course, Pedrinho. My classmates and I would write a rough draft, and then we would do the final draft, generally using a typewriter.
Pedrinho:	And what happened when you made a mistake while typing?
Seu Vicente:	That was difficult, because at that time we had neither correction fluid nor the delete key as we do now. We had to use an eraser or start it all over again. Once I took three days to copy a history paper.
Pedrinho:	Oh, Grandpa, what a tough life you had!

NUTS & BOLTS 2
The preterite and the imperfect

Both the preterite and the imperfect are used to talk about the past, but they convey different nuances about the action in the past. Let's take a look at both tenses now, comparing what they convey about a past action. The preterite is used to talk about an action or state that happened at a specific time in the past. It typically conveys a one-time action that happened at a point on a timeline of the past.

Eu conheci o seu marido no verão passado.

I met your husband last summer.

Ele não quis fazer os trabalhos para o dia seguinte.
He didn't want to do the homework for the next day.

The preterite also suggests that an action or state happened at a point in the past, but is now over. In this sense, it conveys a sense of completion, even if the point of completion is not overtly mentioned in a sentence.

Nós estudamos na casa dela ontem.
We studied at her house yesterday.

Ele fumou dez cigarros na festa.
He smoked ten cigarettes at the party.

Eu trabalhei nesta empresa até dois mil e cinco.
I worked for this company until 2005.

On the other hand, the imperfect conveys a sense that an action happened over an imprecise stretch of time in the past. On a timeline, it would be represented as a line rather than a point. This type of action or state often corresponds to background facts or descriptions, or to emotional attitudes.

Eu conhecia o seu marido.
I already knew your husband.

Ele não queria fazer os trabalhos de casa.
He didn't want to do his homework.

A cidade era grande e tinha muitos museus.
The city was big and had many museums.

Eram nove horas e ainda estava claro.
It was 9:00 and there was still light.

Since it represents a span of time rather than a point, the imperfect is used to express a past continuous action.

Eles estavam rindo e nós estávamos chorando.

They were laughing and we were crying.

It is also used to express past habits. This is often expressed in English with *used to* or *would,* but it can also be expressed with the simple past. The important thing to keep in mind is not how to translate a particular tense, but rather what is being expressed about the action or state.

Nós sempre estudávamos na casa dela.

We always studied at her house./We would always study at her house.

Ele fumava um maço de cigarros por dia.

He used to smoke a pack of cigarettes a day.

Ele sempre acordava cedo e dava comida para o gato.

He would always wake up early and feed the cat./He always woke up early and fed the cat.

PRACTICE 2

Complete the following sentences with the preterite or imperfect of the verbs in parentheses. Translate the full sentences.

1. Meu avô _____ (ser) piloto na Segunda Guerra Mundial.

2. Eu _____ (estar) esperando você chegar.

3. Nós _____ (ir) à Itália no ano passado.

4. O carteiro _____ (vir) mais cedo hoje do que de costume.

5. Minha mãe sempre _____ (fazer) bolo de chocolate aos domingos.

6. Quando eu era criança eu não _____ (comer) salada.

7. Vocês _____ (estudar) para a prova ontem?

8. Ontem eu _____ (discutir) com meu chefe e depois me _____ (arrepender).

9. _____ (ser) dez horas quando ela finalmente _____ (acordar).

10. As roupas dela _____ (ser) caras, ela _____ (andar) com elegância.

11. Eu _____ (estar) indo para casa quando o diretor me _____ (chamar).

12. Toda manhã ele _____ (fazer) as mesmas coisas; _____ (acordar) na mesma hora, _____ (tomar) café na mesma padaria, e _____ (pegar) o mesmo ônibus.

Culture note

Portuguese is the official language of Angola, Brazil, Cape Verde, Guinea-Bissau, Mozambique, Portugal, and Sao Tome and Principe, as well as the co-official language, along with Chinese, in Macau, and with Tetum in East Timor. The Portuguese introduced their language to these countries during their period of exploration and colonization. The reach of the Portuguese in the past has made the Portuguese language today the fifth major language in the world in terms of number of native speakers. There are over 200 million native speakers of Portuguese worldwide. The majority of these speakers are found in Brazil, where Portuguese is spoken by over 188 million people, making it the most widely spoken language on the South American continent.

As you're doubtlessly aware, there are certain differences between the variety of Portuguese spoken in Brazil, and the one spoken in Portugal. The varieties spoken in other parts of the world are also unique. In many ways these differences are similar to the differences between American and British English, or American English and the English spoken in New Zealand, for example. There are differences in pronunciation, such as the quality of **d, r,** final **s,** and so on. There are also differences in spelling, as in Brazilian **fato** and **a primavera** and the Portuguese **facto** and **a Primavera.** There are also certain grammatical differences, such as the use of **tu** and its verb forms by Portuguese where Brazilians would use **você,** and the use of certain contractions in Portugal like **mo** (**me** + **o,** *it to me*) or **lhos** (**lhes** + **os,** *them to them*). There are also differences in vocabulary, along the lines of *pants* vs. *trousers,* *truck* vs. *lorry*, or *apartment* vs. *flat*. Some examples you might come across include the following.

Brazil	*Portugal*	
a fila	a bicha	*line (of people)*
o banheiro	o quarto de banho	*bathroom*
o creme de leite	a nata	*cream*
a geladeira	o frigorífico	*refrigerator*
o óleo diesel	o gasóleo	*diesel fuel*
o pedestre	o peão	*pedestrian*

If you're interested in learning about the history and variety of Portuguese and are planning a trip to São Paulo, a good place to visit is the Museum of the Portuguese Language, founded in March of 2006. It's no accident that the museum is located in São Paulo, which, with over 11 million inhabitants, is after all the city with the largest number of Portuguese speakers. You can check out the museum at this website: www.museudalinguaportuguesa.org.br/museu/

ANSWERS
PRACTICE 1: 1. estava andando, estava descansando (I was walking while you were resting.) **2.** estava escrevendo, estava falando (Pedro was writing at the same time as he was talking on the phone.) **3.** estavam dormindo, estávamos embrulhando (The children were sleeping while we were wrapping the Christmas gifts.) **4.** estavam fazendo, começou (What were you doing when the rain started?) **5.** estava dirigindo, aconteceu (She wasn't driving slowly when the accident happened.) **6.** estava tendo, apareceu (I was having problems with my car when the police arrived.) **7.** viu, estava fazendo (Which film did he watch while you were shopping?) **8.** estávamos indo, quebrou (We were going to your house when our car broke down.) **9.** estava lendo, pediu (The manager was reading the proposals when the director asked to speak with him.) **10.** estavam viajando, estavam se divertindo (Some people were traveling for business while others were having fun.)

PRACTICE 2: **1.** era (My grandfather was a pilot in WWII.)
2. estava (I was waiting for you to arrive.) **3.** fomos (We went to
Italy last year.) **4.** veio (The letter carrier came earlier today than
usual.) **5.** fazia (My mother always made chocolate cake on
Sundays.) **6.** comia (When I was a child I didn't eat salad.)
7. estudaram (Did you study for the test yesterday?) **8.** discuti,
arrependi (Yesterday I argued with my boss and later regretted
it.) **9.** Eram, acordou (It was 10:00 when she finally woke up.)
10. eram, andava (Her clothes were expensive and she walked
with elegance.) **11.** estava, chamou (I was on my way home
when the director called me.) **12.** fazia, acordava, tomava,
pegava (Every morning he did the same things: he would wake
up at the same time, he would have breakfast at the same
bakery, and he would take the same bus.)

UNIT 9 ESSENTIALS

Eu fui à faculdade.

I went to college.

Ele fui o chefe do departamento por dois anos.

He was the head of the department for two years.

Eles pediram para ver o meu curriculum vitae.

They asked to see my résumé.

**A companhia dividiu os lucros, mas não os prejuízos, com os
funcionários.**

The company shared the profits but not the losses with their employees.

Ela fez toda a lição de casa.

She did all her homework.

Vocês souberam do acidente com o avião?

Did you learn about the plane accident?

**Telefone para mim qualquer dia, eu não estou ocupado no
momento.**

Call me any day; I'm not busy at the moment.

Ele procurou algumas informações nos relatórios da empresa.
He looked for some information in the company's reports.

Nós estávamos na mesma classe na universidade.
We were in the same class in university.

No meu tempo as crianças não comiam tanta besteira.
In my day, children didn't eat as much junk.

Quando era solteiro eu preferia sair todos os sábados.
When I was single, I went out every Saturday.

Eu era estagiária no departamento de comércio exterior quando eu fui transferida.
I was an intern in the department of foreign trade when I was transferred.

Qual foi o maior desafio que você enfrentou até o momento?
What was the greatest challenge you've faced up to now?

Vocês não compraram nem ações nem títulos?
You bought neither stocks nor bonds?

Eu não estava assistindo a TV enquanto você estava dormindo; eu estava ouvindo o rádio.
I wasn't watching TV while you were sleeping; I was listening to the radio.

UNIT 10
Sports and leisure

In Unit 10 you'll learn vocabulary and expressions to talk about sports and leisure, including several useful idiomatic expressions. **Que divertido!** *(What fun!)* You'll also learn how to link sentences with relative pronouns, like the English *which, who,* and *that.* You'll be introduced to new verb tenses to talk about the future and hypothetical conditions. Finally, you'll learn about the subjunctive, which you can use to talk about possibilities, probabilities, wishes, and doubts.

—————————— Lesson 37 (words) ——————————

WORD LIST 1

a vitória	*victory*
a derrota	*defeat*
o empate	*draw (tie)*
a rede	*net*
a raquete	*racket*
o capacete	*helmet*
o treinador	*coach*
o atleta	*athlete*
o árbitro	*referee*
a natação	*swimming*
a ginástica	*workout*
o esqui	*skiing*
a academia	*gym*
o estádio	*stadium*
o ginásio	*gymnasium*
a arquibancada	*bleachers*

| o ataque | attack (offense) |
| a defesa | defense |

NUTS & BOLTS 1
INDEFINITES (2)

In Unit 9 you learned how to use some of the indefinite pronouns and adjectives with a positive meaning, such as **algum** *(some)*, **todo** *(every)*, and **cada** *(each)*. Now let's study the negative indefinites.

nenhum/nenhuma	*none/not any*
ninguém	*no one/nobody/not anyone/not anybody*
nada	*nothing*

Eu não fui à festa porque ninguém me convidou.
I didn't go to the party because nobody invited me.

Ele procurou um apartamento barato, mas não achou nenhum.
He looked for a cheap apartment but couldn't find any.

Nenhuma cantora é tão boa quanto ela.
No other singer is as good as she.

Nós não queremos nada.
We don't want anything./We want nothing.

Ele não gosta de nada.
He doesn't like anything./He likes nothing.

Note that although the indefinite pronoun is negative, you also use the main verb in the negative. So "double negatives" are perfectly fine in Portuguese. Another point to make is that word order is very important when using indefinite pronouns. Look at these examples.

Eu tive alguma dificuldade.

I had some difficulty.

Eu não tive nenhuma dificuldade.

I had no difficulty.

Eu não tive dificuldade alguma.

I didn't have any difficulty.

Notice that in the second example, the negative indefinite comes before the noun **dificuldade,** but in the last example, the positive indefinite follows it. Look at some other examples.

Ele não quis nenhuma coisa.

He wanted nothing.

Ele não quis coisa alguma.

He didn't want anything.

Vocês não tiveram nenhuma chance.

You had no chance.

Vocês não tiveram chance alguma.

You didn't stand any chance.

PRACTICE 1
Complete with the following: **nenhum, nenhuma, nada, ninguém, nada.** Then translate.

1. Ele não quis escolher _____ roupa.

2. Quando ela chegou a casa, não encontrou _____; ela estava sozinha.

3. Eu não quero comer _____; estou sem fome.

4. Nós não conseguimos fazer reservas em _____ hotel; estavam todos cheios.

5. _____vai impedir a nossa vitória.

Now transform the sentences by using a positive indefinite, as shown in the example. Translate your answers.

Ex: As crianças não precisam de nenhum brinquedo.

As crianças não precisam de brinquedo algum. *(The children don't need any toys.)*

6. Ele não pediu nenhuma ajuda.

7. O repórter ainda não conseguiu nenhuma notícia.

8. Os atletas não deram nenhuma entrevista.

9. Eles não são sócios de nenhum clube.

10. A China não tem nenhum filme na competição.

WORD LIST 2

o balé	*ballet*
o teatro	*theater*
a boate	*nightclub*
o telão	*big screen*
a telenovela	*soap opera*
o forró	*a genre of music from Brazil's northeast*
o fado	*a genre of music from Portugal*
o documentário	*documentary*
o piquenique	*picnic*
a exibição	*exhibition*
o intervalo	*intermission*
as férias	*vacations*
o feriado	*holiday*
a diversão	*amusement*
o ingresso	*ticket*
a imprensa	*press*
a mídia	*media*

NUTS & BOLTS 2
IDIOMATIC EXPRESSIONS

Every language has its assortment of idiomatic expressions, which are very common expressions whose meanings simply have to be memorized because you can't necessarily understand them as the sum of their parts. Here are some very common idiomatic expressions in Portuguese:

não adianta + infinitive	*"there's no use . . ."/"there's no point . . ."*
Ele não quer sair, não adianta insistir.	*He doesn't want to go out; there's no point in insisting.*
Não adianta correr, já perdemos o vôo.	*It's no use running; we've missed the flight.*
deixar de + infinitive	*"quit"/"give up"*
Ela deixou de fumar três meses atrás.	*She quit smoking three months ago.*
não deixar de + infinitive	*"don't miss . . ."/"be sure to . . ."*
Não deixe de assistir a nova peça no Teatro Municipal.	*Don't miss the new play at the Municipal Theater.*
Não deixe de ir ao jogo.	*Be sure to go to the game.*
procurar + infinitive	*"try to . . ."/"make an attempt to . . ."*
Os jogadores sempre procuram melhorar o desempenho.	*The players always try to improve their performance.*
Ele procura estudar à noite porque é mais silencioso.	*He tries to study at night because it's quieter.*
viver + gerund	*"always doing . . ."*
Você vive chegando atrasado.	*You're always arriving late.*
Ela vive inventando desculpas.	*She's always making up excuses.*

PRACTICE 2
Translate the following.

1. Ela está cansada de dia porque vive saindo à noite.

2. O desempenho dele está pior porque deixou de ir ao treinos.

3. O museu de arte moderna é incrível, vocês não devem deixar de visitá-lo.

4. Ele quase repetiu o ano e agora procura estudar dia e noite.

5. O elevador está quebrado, não adianta apertar o botão.

6. Desculpe o atraso, vou procurar chegar na hora de agora em diante.

7. Não adianta telefonar para ele. Ele deixou o celular em casa.

8. Meninos e meninas: Não deixem de estudar os capítulos três e quarto para a prova de amanhã.

9. Por que você deixou de praticar tênis? Você é tão bom!

10. Eles vivem brigando, mas na verdade se amam muito.

Culture note

So far you've seen how the more than two million Africans who were brought to Brazil as slaves contributed to the national culture and traditions of the country. First, in Unit 4, you learned how the practices of **Macumba** and **Cambomblé** still affect religion and medicine in Brazil; and later, in Unit 8, how the slaves' culinary creation of **feijoada** became the all-time favorite Brazilian meal. Now let's look at **capoeira**, a form of martial arts, which is another creation of the Afro-Brazilian slaves that has long influenced physical fitness, dance, and music in Brazil. **Capoeira** was originally created to disguise combat between male slaves. The fighters didn't want to be punished by their masters, so they started adopting rituals in fighting to make it look more like a game. The rituals performed by the fighters then, and still used today, include an array of kicks, sweeps, and dance-like movements, completed in circle (roda) formed by observers. Some of these observers perform rhythmic music, accompanied by musical instruments (berimbau, cuíca, tamborim) and song.

When slaves rebelled or escaped, the lethal fighting skills honed through capoeira became a weapon against their masters. But even when Brazil abolished slavery in 1888, capoeira continued to be practiced and developed on the streets of Brazil. At that time it was associated with professional criminals and disorderly conduct. In 1890 capoeira was forbidden by law, and its practitioners were penalized with two to six months of prison.

Nevertheless, it continued to gain followers, new fight movements, new rituals, songs, and music. Then, finally, in 1932, Mestre (the title used by the master practitioner) Bimba managed to take capoeira out of the streets by opening the first capoeira academy in Salvador, Bahia. Now capoeira is practiced throughout Brazil by men and women of all social classes who appreciate physical fitness, music, and dance. You can also find capoeira academies in major cities around the world.

ANSWERS
PRACTICE 1: 1. nenhuma (He didn't want to pick out any clothes.) 2. ninguém (When she got home she didn't find anybody; she was alone.) 3. nada (I don't want to eat anything; I'm not hungry.) 4. nenhum (We weren't able to make reservations in any hotels; they were all booked.) 5. Nada (Nothing will get in the way of our victory.) 6. ajuda alguma (He didn't ask for any help.) 7. notícia alguma (The reporter still hasn't gotten any news.) 8. entrevista alguma (The athletes haven't given any interviews.) 9. clube algum (They aren't members of any club.) 10. filme algum (China doesn't have any films in the competition.)

PRACTICE 2: 1. She's always tired during the day because she's always going out at night. **2.** His performance is worse because he stopped going to practice. **3.** The Museum of Modern Art is incredible; you shouldn't miss visiting it. **4.** He almost failed and now he tries to study day and night. **5.** The elevator isn't working; there's no point in pressing the button. **6.** Sorry I was late; I'll try to arrive on time from now on. **7.** There's no point in calling him. He left his cell phone at home. **8.** Boys and girls: be sure to study chapters three and four for the test tomorrow. **9.** Why did you give up playing tennis? You were so good! **10.** They're always fighting, but in fact, they love each other very much.

Lesson 38 (phrases)

PHRASE LIST 1

a quadra poliesportiva	*sports court or grounds*
a hidroginástica	*aquatic exercise, water sports*
o taco de golfe	*golf club*
a bola de basquetebol	*basketball*
o campo de futebol	*soccer field*
a quadra de tênis de saibro	*clay tennis court*
a equipe de natação	*swimming team*
o time de futebol de salão	*indoor soccer team*
a pista de atletismo	*sports track*
a luva de goleiro	*goalie glove*
a piscina aquecida	*heated pool*
praticar esportes	*to practice sports*
jogar vôlei	*to play volleyball*
o segundo tempo	*halftime*
a locação de quadra de squash	*squash court rental*
fazer jogging	*to jog*

NUTS & BOLTS 1
Relative pronouns

A relative pronoun is a word used to link two sentences, like *that* in *I read the book that you recommended.* There are three invarialble relative pronouns in Portuguese: **que** *(which, who, that)*, **onde** *(where)*, and **quem** *(who/whom)*. Let's start with **que,** which functions as a relative pronoun referring to either a person or a thing:

O filme que eu assisti é bom.
The film I watched is good.

Os ingressos que você comprou são caros.
The tickets that you bought are expensive.

Você viu a atriz que estava aqui?
Did you see the actress who was here?

Quem *(whom)* is used to refer to a person after a preposition such as **com** *(with)*, **contra** *(against)*, **entre** *(between/among)*, **para** *(to)*, **por** *(for)*, **sobre** *(about)*, etc.

O rapaz com quem eu saio é bonito.
The guy with whom I go out is cute./The guy who I go out with is cute.

A jogadora contra quem joguei ontem quebrou o braço.
The player against whom I played yesterday broke her arm./The player who I played against yesterday broke her arm.

O gerente sobre quem falamos foi promovido.
The manager about whom we talked was promoted./The manager who we talked about was promoted.

Use **onde** *(where)* to refer to places.

O hotel onde ficamos é perto daqui.
The hotel where we stayed is near here.

A rua onde ele mora não é segura.

The street where he lives isn't safe.

The relative pronouns **qual** *(which)* and **cujo** *(whose)* vary according to the preposition that follows them. Use **o qual, a qual, os quais,** and **as quais** to refer to people or things after a preposition. Notice that these pronouns can usually be replaced by **que, quem,** and **onde** in conversation.

Não gostei da peça na qual ela atua. (Não gostei da peça em que ela atua.)

I didn't like the play she acts in.

O homem com o qual viajei não falava inglês. (O homem com quem viajei não falava inglês.)

The man I traveled with didn't speak English.

As ruas pelas quais passamos eram escuras. (As ruas por onde passamos eram escuras.)

The streets we passed by were dark.

Os livros sobre os quais eu falei estão aqui. (Os livros de que eu falei estão aqui.)

The books I talked about are here.

Use **cujo, cuja, cujos,** or **cujas** *(whose)* when referring to possession. This pronoun also varies according to the noun that follows it.

O carro, cuja porta está quebrada, é meu.

The car, whose door is broken, is mine.

A minha amiga, cujo pai é senador, chegou.

My friend, whose father is a senator, arrived.

Os jogadores, cujas camisetas estão sujas, precisam se trocar.

The players whose jerseys are dirty need to get changed.

Os veículos, cujos proprietários estão no restaurante, podem permanecer aqui.
The vehicles, whose owners are in the restaurant, can remain here.

It's important to note that, unlike in English, you cannot omit relative pronouns in Portuguese.

O preço que você quer é alto.
The price (that) you want is high.

PRACTICE 1
Join the pairs of sentences to form one longer one using the relative pronoun in parentheses, making any changes to the pronoun if necessary. Translate your answers.

1. Eu recebi um e-mail. Ele escreveu o e-mail. (que)

2. Eu comprei uma revista. A revista é cara. (que)

3. Você deu uma festa. A festa foi boa. (que)

4. Vocês ficaram em um hotel. O hotel é fantástico. (onde)

5. Ele nasceu em um país. O país fica na África. (onde)

6. Você comprou uma bolsa em uma loja. A loja é francesa. (onde)

7. Eu estudo com a professora. A professora é japonesa. (quem)

8. Ela se casou com o homem. O homem é arquiteto. (quem)

9. A mulher do meu amigo é atriz de teatro. O meu amigo vem aqui hoje. (cujo)

10. Os motoristas foram multados. Os carros dos motoristas estavam em lugar proibido. (cujo)

PHRASE LIST 2
o clube de campo	*country club*
o leilão de antigüidades	*antiques auction*

o museu de história natural	natural history museum
o desenho animado	cartoons (animated films)
o programa de rádio	radio program
a entrevista coletiva	press conference
a dança de salão	ballroom dancing
a peça de teatro	theater play
a galeria de arte	art gallery
comprar um ingresso	to buy a ticket
reservar umas entradas	to reserve some tickets
o lugar marcado/o lugar numerado	marked seat/numbered seat
proibido para menores de dezoito anos	under 18 not allowed
as palavras cruzadas	crossword puzzles
a revista em quadrinhos	comic books
as manchetes do jornal	newspaper headlines

NUTS & BOLTS 2
THE PERFECT TENSES

In English, the past participle is the verb form such as *spoken, written, shown, talked,* or *swum,* which can be used with the auxiliary *have* to form the perfect tenses, as in *have spoken, had swum,* and so on. In Portuguese, too, the past participle is used in perfect verb tenses. First, let's see how the past participle is formed. For verbs ending in -**ar,** remove the -**ar** and add -**ado.** For verbs ending in -**er** and -**ir** remove the -**er** or -**ir** and add -**ido.**

falar–falado *(to speak–spoken)*	beber–bebido *(to drink–drunk)*
andar–andado *(to walk–walked)*	dormir–dormido *(to sleep–slept)*
comer–comido *(to eat–eaten)*	decidir–decidido *(to decide–decided)*

There are also a lot of irregular past participles. Here's a list of some of the more common ones: **abrir–aberto** *(to open–opened)*, **cobrir–coberto** *(to cover–covered)*, **dizer–dito** *(to say/to tell–said/told)*, **escrever–escrito** *(to write–written)*, **fazer–feito** *(to do/to make–done/made)*, **ganhar–ganho** *(to win–won)*, **gastar–gasto** *(to spend–spent)*, **pagar–pago** *(to pay–paid)*, **pôr–posto** *(to put–put)*, **ver–visto** *(to see–seen)*, **vir–vindo** *(to come–come)*.

To form the present perfect tense, use the verb **ter** *(to have)* as an auxiliary, along with the past participle. This tense expresses an action that started in the past and continues into the present, much like the English *have been doing* (present perfect progressive) or *have done* (present perfect). The adverb **ultimamente** *(lately)* is often used with this tense.

Eu tenho estudado muito ultimamente.
I've been studying a lot lately./I've studied a lot lately.

Eles não têm ido ao cinema ultimamente.
They haven't been going to the movies lately./They haven't gone to the movies lately.

Você tem visto os jogos do campeonato?
Have you seen the championship games?

Nós não temos saído muito, temos ficado em casa.
We haven't gone out much; we've been staying at home.

The past perfect is formed with the imperfect of the verb **ter** *(to have)* and the past participle. It expresses an action in the past that happened before a more recent past action, like the English past perfect *(had done)*. This tense sometimes goes with the adverb **já** *(already)*.

Quando nós chegamos o jogo já tinha começado.
When we arrived, the game had already begun.

Ele já tinha feito a reserva para o teatro.
He had already made the theater reservation.

Vocês já tinham saído quando eu telefonei.
You had already left when I called.

Onde eles tinham ido quando nós chegamos?
Where had they gone when we arrived?

Note that when you use an object pronoun, it comes between the verb **ter** *(to have)* and the participle.

Ele tem me telefonado ultimamente.
He has called me lately.

Nós não tínhamos lhes avisado.
We hadn't warned them.

PRACTICE 2
Complete the following with the participle of the verb in parentheses, and translate.

1. Pedro não tem _____ (comparecer) às aulas ultimamente.

2. Eu não tenho _____ (parar) o dia todo.

3. Vocês têm _____ (ver) a Vera ultimamente?

4. As crianças têm _____ (estar) muito doentes.

5. O meu carro só tem me _____ (dar) problemas ultimamente.

6. O namorado já tinha _____ (pagar) quando ela ofereceu para rachar a conta.

7. Quando chegou o fim do mês, eles já tinham _____ (gastar) todo o salário.

8. Quando o atacante passou a bola, o arbitro já tinha _____ (apitar).

9. Quando nós chegamos ao cinema, o filme já tinha _____ (começar).

10. A polícia já tinha _____ (fazer) as perguntas quando o detetive chegou.

ANSWERS

PRACTICE 1: 1. Eu recebi o e-mail que ele escreveu. (I got the e-mail that he wrote.) **2.** A revista que eu comprei é cara. (The magazine that I bought is expensive.) **3.** A festa que você deu foi boa. (The party that you gave was good.) **4.** O hotel onde vocês ficaram é fantástico. (The hotel where you stayed is fantastic.) **5.** O país onde ele nasceu fica na África. (The country where he was born is in Africa.) **6.** A loja onde você comprou a bolsa é francesa. (The store where you bought your bag is French.) **7.** A professora com quem eu estudo é japonesa. (The teacher who I study with is Japanese.) **8.** O homem com que ela se casou é arquiteto. (The man who she got married with/to is an architect.) **9.** O meu amigo, cuja mulher é atriz de teatro, vem aqui hoje. (My friend whose wife is a theater actress is coming here today.) **10.** Os motoristas, cujos carros estavam em lugar proibido, forma multados. (The cars, whose drivers were fined, were parked illegally.)

PRACTICE 2: 1. comparecido (Pedro hasn't attended class lately.) **2.** parado (I haven't stopped all day.) **3.** visto (Have you seen Vera lately?) **4.** estado (The children have been very sick.) **5.** dado (My car has been giving me trouble lately.) **6.** pago (The boyfriend had already paid when she offered to share the bill.) **7.** gasto (When the end of the month arrived, they had already spent the entire salary.) **8.** apitado (When the striker/forward passed the ball, the referee had already blown the whistle.) **9.** começado (When we arrived at the cinema, the film had already begun.) **10.** feito (The police had already asked the questions when the detective arrived.)

SENTENCE LIST 1

Não tem ninguém na defesa.	*There's no one on defense.*
O time adversário não marcou nenhum gol.	*The opposing team didn't score a single goal.*
Aquele goleiro não pega nada!	*That goalie doesn't catch anything.*
Não adianta tentar; eles vão perder.	*There's no use trying; they're going to lose.*
O time local está tentando empatar a partida.	*The home team is trying to tie the match.*
Os meus amigos vivem me pedindo para usar a minha cadeira cativa.	*My friends are always asking me to use my season ticket.*
Pelé é o jogador que recebeu o título de Atleta do Século.	*Pelé is the player who received the title of Athlete of the Century.*
Maria Ester Bueno foi a jogadora de tênis brasileira que ganhou dezenove Grand Slam.	*Maria Ester Bueno was the Brazilian tennis player who won 19 Grand Slams.*
O Maracanã é o estádio onde serão realizados os jogos pan-americanos.	*Maracanã is the stadium where the Pan-American games will be held.*
Eu e Pedro temos jogado squash ultimamente.	*Pedro and I have played squash lately.*
Eles já tinham reservado as quadras.	*They had already booked the courts.*
Eu tenho treinado para a maratona dia e noite.	*I have trained for the marathon day and night.*
Eles competirão contra a melhor equipe.	*They will compete with the best team.*
Você participará da competição?	*Will you participate in the competition?*

NUTS & BOLTS 1
THE FUTURE TENSE

In lesson 28 you learned how to talk about the future using the immediate future tense with **ir** + verb *(be going to* + verb). **Eu vou conversar com o gerente amanhã.** *(I'm going to talk to the manager tomorrow.)* Portuguese also has a future tense, which corresponds to the English future with *will*. This future tense is more formal than the immediate future with **ir,** and it is in fact preferred in written Portuguese. In informal conversation, you can always use the immediate future with **ir.** To form the future tense, add the endings **-ei, -á, -emos, -ão** onto the infinitive of the verb.

falar *(to speak)*	vender *(to sell)*	partir *(to leave)*
eu falarei	eu escreverei	eu partirei
você falará	você escreverá	você partirá
ele/ela falará	ele/ela escreverá	ele/ela partirá
nós falaremos	nós escreveremos	nós partiremos
vocês falarão	vocês escreverão	vocês partirão
eles/elas falarão	eles/elas escreverão	eles/elas partirão

The verbs **dizer** *(to say/tell)*, **fazer** *(to do/make)*, and **trazer** *(to bring)* have irregular future stems: **eu direi, você dirá, ele/ela dirá, nós diremos, vocês dirão, eles/elas dirão; eu farei, você fará, ele/ela fará, nós faremos, vocês farão, eles/elas farão; eu trarei, você trará, ele/ela trará, nós traremos, vocês trarão, eles/elas trarão.**

Eu não irei à reunião de amanhã.

I won't go to the meeting tomorrow.

Eles pegarão os ingressos mais tarde.
They will get the tickets later.

Nós ficaremos no hotel até a próxima semana.
We will stay at the hotel until next week.

Quando o avião partirá?
When will the plane leave?

Quando será a sua festa?
When will your party be?

To say *in* plus a time period, use **daqui a/dentro de**:

Isso acontecerá daqui a/dentro de duas semanas.
This will happen in two weeks.

A encomenda chegará daqui a três dias.
The order will arrive in three days.

Os estudantes farão os exames daqui a um mês.
The students will take the exams in one month.

A minha festa será daqui a um mês.
My party will be in a month.

It's worth mentioning, by contrast, that **há** means *ago* and is used with the past tense.

Isso aconteceu há duas semanas.
This happened two weeks ago.

PRACTICE 1

Complete the passage with the following verbs in the future: **fazer, ter, assistir, ficar, ser, participar, comer, visitar, ir, durar.** Then translate.

Suzana 1_____ uma viagem de férias para Salvador, Bahia. O namorado dela também 2_____, mas só depois de dois dias porque ele 3_____ uma reunião de negócios importante. A viajem 4_____ quinze dias. Suzana e o namorado 5_____ em um hotel cinco estrelas. Eles 6_____de uma excursão às praias locais e 7_____um museu de artes. Eles 8_____ à uma peça de teatro. Eles 9_____ em restaurantes de frutos do mar da região. 10_____ uma viagem incrível!

Now change the following sentences from the immediate future tense into the future tense, then translate your answers.

11. Você vai fazer aula de português até o próximo mês?

12. O carteiro não vai entregar cartas no próximo sábado porque vai ser feriado.

13. Eu vou pagar o meu cartão de crédito na semana que vem.

14. Nós vamos trazer uma garrafa de vinho para a festa na semana que vem.

15. O que nós vamos dizer na reunião daqui a duas horas?

16. As empresas vão gastar mais dinheiro com energia elétrica no ano que vem.

17. Eu vou estar na primeira fila do cinema.

18. O tempo vai estar nublado amanhã.

SENTENCE LIST 2

Eu preferiria assistir uma comédia.	*I'd rather watch a comedy.*
Você poderia tomar conta das crianças?	*Could you take care of the children?*
Eu não queria viajar, mas preciso.	*I didn't want to travel, but I have to.*
Quem seria o nosso guia?	*Who would be our guide?*

O teatro onde fomos ontem é muito chique.	*The theater that we went to was very elegant.*
Não deixe de ver a peça que está no Teatro Picadeiro.	*Don't miss the play that's showing at the Picadeiro Theater.*
Nós iremos ao estádio, vocês gostariam de ir juntos?	*We'll go to the stadium; would you like to go with us?*
O jogo será transmitido pela TV a cabo?	*Will the game be transmitted on cable TV?*
Se você não devolver os DVDs no prazo, terá que pagar multa.	*If you don't return the DVDs on the due date, you'll have to pay a fine.*
Por mim, nós alugaríamos um filme e ficaríamos em casa.	*If it were up to me, we'd rent a movie and stay at home.*
Eu me recuso a comprar ingressos de cambista.	*I refuse to buy tickets from scalpers.*
Você já leu a crítica sobre o novo filme daquele diretor francês?	*Have you read the review about that French director's new film?*
Ele sempre consulta a previsão do tempo antes de fazer planos para o fim de semana.	*He always consults the weather forecast before making plans for the weekend.*

NOTES

These are some common expressions for talking about the weather.

Hoje teremos sol pela manhã e chuvas no final da tarde.
Today we will have sun in the morning and rain at the end of the afternoon.

A previsão para amanhã é de temporais com trovoadas e relâmpagos.
The forecast for tomorrow is for storms with thunder and lightning.

A manhã começa com nuvens esparsas.
The morning begins with scattered clouds.

O dia amanhecerá nublado com chuvas isoladas.

The day will start overcast with isolated showers.

O nascer do sol será às seis e o pôr do sol será às seis e trinta e cinco.

Sunrise will be at 6:00 and sunset will be at 6:35.

Está ventando forte hoje, acho que vai chover.

There's a strong wind; I think it's going to rain.

NUTS & BOLTS 2
THE PRESENT CONDITIONAL

The present conditional corresponds to the English *would* + verb, as in *I would go*. You use this tense to express hypothetical situations, and also to soften commands. You've actually already seen an example of this, in the polite expression **eu gostaria** *(I would like)*. Here are some examples of full conjugations in the conditional.

comprar *(to buy)*	escrever *(to write)*	abrir *(to open)*
eu compraria	eu escreveria	eu abriria
você compraria	você escreveria	você abriria
ele/ela compraria	ele/ela escreveria	ele/ela abriria
nós compraríamos	nós escreveríamos	nós abriríamos
vocês comprariam	vocês escreveriam	vocês abririam
eles/elas comprariam	eles/elas escreveriam	eles/elas abririam

As with the future tense, the conditional forms of **dizer** *(to say/to tell)*, **fazer** *(to do/to make)*, and **trazer** *(to bring)* are irregular: **eu** diria, você diria, ele/ela diria, nós diríamos, vocês diriam, eles/elas diriam; eu faria, você faria, ele/ela faria, nós faríamos, vocês fariam, eles/elas fariam; eu traria, você traria, ele/ela traria, nós traríamos, vocês trariam, eles/elas trariam.

Você ficaria neste hotel caro?
Would you stay in this expensive hotel?

Ele não diria mentiras.
He wouldn't tell lies.

Nós faríamos o necessário.
We would do whatever it takes.

Quem atenderia ao telefone?
Who would answer the telephone?

Ela telefonaria, mas não tem cartão.
She would call, but she doesn't have a card.

Eu viajaria, mas não tenho dinheiro.
I'd travel, but I don't have money.

Here are some more examples of polite requests with the conditional.

Ele nos daria uma carona?
Would he give us a ride?

Você me faria esse favor?
Would you do this favor for me?

Also note that the conditional of the verb **poder** *(to be able to/can)* is translated as *could*.

Vocês poderiam esperar um pouco?
Could you wait a little?

Eu poderia ficar até mais tarde.

I could stay until later.

PRACTICE 2

Complete the following sentences with the present conditional of the verbs in parentheses.

1. Eu _____ (ficar) mais alguns dias.

2. Nós não _____ (ser) felizes sem as crianças.

3. Você _____ (estar) livre amanhã à tarde?

4. Mariana _____ (escrever) mais para os pais, mas precisa estudar demais.

5. Geralmente, eles não _____ (mandar) as encomendas pelo correio, mas não podem entregá-las pessoalmente.

6. Eu acho que vocês _____ (ouvir) melhor o discurso daquele lado da sala.

7. Marco _____ (ter) mais amigos, mas ele é tímido.

8. Assim as alunas _____ (ter) melhor desempenho.

9. Eu não _____ (dizer) onde fui.

10. Geralmente, nós não _____ (fazer) tanto esforço.

11. O que a sua filha _____ (comer)?

12. Por que nós _____ (comprar) aquela casa?

ANSWERS

PRACTICE 1: 1. fará; **2.** irá; **3.** terá; **4.** durará; **5.** ficarão;
6. participarão; **7** visitarão; **8.** assistirão; **9.** comerão; **10.** Será
(Suzana will take a vacation in Salvador, Bahia. Her boyfriend
will also go, but only after a couple of days because he will have
an important business meeting. The trip will last fifteen days.
Suzana and her boyfriend will stay at a five-star hotel. They will
take part in a tour to the local beaches, and will visit an art
museum. They will watch a play at the theater. They will eat in
regional seafood restaurants. It will be an incredible trip!)
11. fará (Will you have Portuguese lessons until next month?)
12. entregará (The letter carrier won't deliver letters next
Saturday because it will be a holiday.) **13.** pagarei (I'll pay my
credit card [bill] next week.) **14.** traremos (We'll bring a bottle of
wine to the party next week.) **15.** diremos (What will we say at
the meeting in two hours?) **16.** gastarão (Companies will spend
more money on energy next year.) **17.** estará (I'll be in the front
row at the movies.) **18.** estará (The weather will be cloudy
tomorrow.)

PRACTICE 2: 1. ficaria (I would stay some more days.)
2. seríamos (We wouldn't be happy without the children.)
3. estaria (Would you be free tomorrow afternoon?) **4.** escreveria
(Mariana would write more to her parents, but she has too
much to study.) **5.** mandaríamos (Usually they wouldn't send
the orders by mail, but they can't deliver them personally.)
6. ouviriam (I think you'd hear the speech better from that side
of the room.) **7.** teria (Marco would have more friends, but he's
shy.) **8.** teriam (This way the students would have a better
performance.) **9.** diria (I wouldn't say where I went.)
10. faríamos (We usually don't make such an effort.) **11.** comeria
(What would your daughter eat?) **12.** compraríamos (Why
would we buy that house?)

CONVERSATION 1

Felipe: Você vai ao jogo amanhã?

Pedro: Eu duvido que a gente consiga ingressos assim, em cima da hora.

Felipe: Um amigo meu disse que, se eu quisesse, ele arrumaria ingressos com um cambista.

Pedro: Não, obrigado. Eu me recuso a pagar para cambista: seria um assalto à mão armada!

Felipe: Você tem razão. Mas qual a alternativa? Eu estou morrendo de vontade de ver a final do campeonato.

Pedro: Bem, que tal assisti-lo num telão de um bar? Poderemos ver a partida enquanto tomamos umas cervejas, e batemos um papo.

Felipe: Não é uma má idéia—convidaríamos mais algumas pessoas . . . Talvez a Andréa vá também. Tomara que ela traga a amiga dela, a Vera, ela vive dizendo que quer conhecer você.

Pedro: Legal! Parece que o jogo vai acabar sendo uma boa desculpa para paquerar!

Felipe: Are you going to the game tomorrow?

Pedro: I doubt we'll get tickets this late.

Felipe: A friend of mine said that if I wanted, he'd get tickets from a scalper.

Pedro: No thanks, I refuse to pay to a scalper: it'd be a rip-off.

Felipe: You're right. But what's the alternative? I'm dying to watch the final championship game.

Pedro: Well, how about watching it on a big screen at a bar? We could watch the match while we have some beers and chat.

Felipe: That's not a bad idea; we'd invite some other people . . . Maybe Andréa will come. I hope she brings her friend, Vera; she's always saying that she wants to meet you.

> Pedro: It seems that the game will end up being a good excuse
> to flirt!

NUTS & BOLTS 1
THE PRESENT SUBJUNCTIVE

You've already learned several different verb tenses, as well as the infinitive, gerund, and past participle. Verbs are also divided into categories called moods, and Portuguese verbs have three moods: the indicative, the imperative, and the subjunctive. So far, you've studied the indicative, which is the mood used to express facts and states that are real and well-defined. You've learned several tenses in the indicative—the simple present, the preterite, the future, and the perfect tenses. You also know the imperative, which is used to express commands. The subjunctive mood expresses actions or states that are uncertain or unreal. It is sometimes called the mood of possibility. As an example, take a look at the following pair. The first example is in the indicative (**é,** *is),* and the second is in the subjunctive (**seja,** *might/could be).*

Eu digo que é assim.

I say it's like that.

Pode ser que seja assim.

It could be that it's that way.

But before we get into its meaning, let's look at how to form the subjunctive. Start with the first person (**eu**) form of the indicative, and take off the **-o** ending. Then, in its place, add to **-ar** verbs **-e** in the singular, and **-emos** and **-em** in the plural. For **-er** and **-ir** verbs, add **-a** in the singular, and **-amos** and **-am** in the plural.

falar (fal-o)	escrever (escrev-o)	partir (part-o)
eu fale	eu escreva	eu parta
você fale	você escreva	você parta

ele/ela fale	ele/ela escreva	ele/ela parta
nós falemos	nós escrevamos	nós partamos
vocês falem	vocês escrevam	vocês partam
eles/elas falem	eles/elas escrevam	eles/elas partam

This rule also holds for most irregular verbs.

dizer (dig-o)	fazer (faç-o)	ver (vej-o)	pôr (ponh-o)
eu diga	eu faça	eu veja	eu ponha
você diga	você faça	você veja	você ponha
ele/ela diga	ele/ela faça	ele/ela veja	ele/ela ponha
nós digamos	nós façamos	nós vejamos	nós ponhamos
vocês digam	vocês façam	vocês vejam	vocês ponham
eles/elas digam	eles/elas façam	eles/elas vejam	eles/elas ponham

The following verbs are irregular in the present subjunctive.

dar *(to give)*: **eu dê, você dê, ele/ela dê, nós demos, vocês dêem, eles/elas dêem**

estar *(to be)*: **eu esteja, você esteja, ele/ela esteja, nós estejamos, vocês estejam, eles/elas estejam**

ir *(to go)*: **eu vá, você vá, ele/ela vá, nós vamos, vocês vão, eles/elas vão**

querer *(to want)*: **eu queira, você queira, ele/ela queira, nós queiramos, vocês queiram, eles/elas queiram**

saber *(to know)*: **eu saiba, você saiba, ele/ela saiba, nós saibamos, vocês saibam, eles/elas saibam**

ser *(to be)*: **eu seja, você seja, ele/ela seja, nós sejamos, vocês sejam, eles/elas sejam**

Don't forget about consonant changes, **c** to **qu** and **g** to **gu**, to preserve hard **c** or **g**. For example, the verb **ficar** *(to stay)* changes the **-co** ending to **-qu: eu fique, nós fiquemos, elas fiquem.** And the verb **chegar** *(to arrive)* changes the **-go** ending to **-gu: eu chegue, nós cheguemos, eles cheguem.**

Now that we've seen how to form the subjunctive, let's take a look at how it's used. The subjunctive is always in a secondary clause, or mini-sentence, introduced by verbs of desire or doubt, or by verbs that express feelings, or by commands. Here are several examples.

Eu desejo que ele venha à festa.
I yearn for him to come to the party.

Ele quer que você saiba a verdade.
He wants you to know the truth.

Nós esperamos que ela esteja melhor.
We hope that she's better.

Eu prefiro que nós fiquemos aqui.
I prefer us to stay here.

Tomara que eles cheguem cedo.
I hope they arrive on time.

O governo proíbe que nós viajemos sem visto.
The government prohibits us from traveling without a visa.

A polícia manda que vocês abram a porta.
The police order you to open the door.

A empresa exige que vocês trabalhem mais.
The company demands that you work more.

Ela pede que vocês sejam pontuais.
She asks you to be punctual.

Não estou certo que possa ir ao jogo.
I'm not sure I can go to the game.

Não temos certeza que faça bom tempo.
We're not sure the weather will be good.

Duvido que ele venha.
I doubt he'll come.

Não acho que elas ganhem o campeonato.
I don't think they'll win the championship.

Não pensamos que o filme seja bom.
We don't think the film will be good.

Talvez eu não chegue a tempo.
Maybe I won't arrive on time.

Eu estou contente que você venha também.
I'm glad you are coming too.

Ele está triste que você fique sozinha.
He's sad you are alone.

Receio que você esteja errado.
I'm afraid you're wrong.

Temos medo que ela esteja perdida.
We fear she's lost.

Lamento que ele não venha.

I'm sorry he won't come.

Sinto que nós não possamos ficar mais.

I'm sorry that we can't stay any longer.

Que pena que vocês não venham mais vezes.

What a pity you don't come more often.

É pena que o quarto não esteja pronto.

It's a pity the room isn't ready.

PRACTICE 1
Complete the following sentences with the subjunctive form of the verbs in parentheses. The English translations are given to help you.

1. Que pena que você não _____ (vir). *(What a pity that you can't come.)*

2. Espero que Carolina _____ (aprender) inglês nas férias. *(I hope that Carolina learns English during the vacation.)*

3. O que você quer que nós ___ (fazer)? *(What do you want us to do?)*

4. Tomara que não _____ (chover) amanhã. *(I hope it doesn't rain tomorrow.)*

5. Nós preferimos que elas _____ (receber) a encomenda daqui a dois dias. *(We prefer that they receive the order in two days.)*

6. Eles desejam que você_____ (ser) feliz no seu empreendimento. *(They wish that you be happy in your endeavor.)*

7. Eu duvido que a empresa _____ (pagar) o que me deve. *(I doubt that the company will pay what it owes me.)*

8. A lei proíbe que vocês _____ (fumar) em locais públicos. *(The law prohibits you from smoking in public places.)*

9. Não acho que Gustavo _____ (estar) bem. *(I don't think Gustavo is all right.)*

10. Talvez eles não _____ (escrever) o relatório a tempo. *(Maybe they won't write the report on time.)*

11. Receio que ela não _____ (ter) um visto válido. *(I'm afraid she doesn't have a valid visa.)*

12. Estamos felizes que as crianças _____ (dizer) a verdade. *(We're happy the children tell the truth.)*

CONVERSATION 2

José Carlos: O que você gostaria de fazer esse fim de semana?

Mariana: Eu gostaria de ir velejar no sábado, mas eu duvido que faça bom tempo. Assim mesmo, eu pedi para a babá ficar com as crianças no sábado. Ela disse que ficará se dermos folga para ela no fim de semana que vem.

José Carlos: Por mim tudo bem. Mas o que faremos se chover?

Mariana: Bem, se o tempo não estiver bom, daremos o dia de folga para a babá, iremos à locadora, e passaremos a noite em casa, assistindo vídeos e comendo pipocas.

José Carlos: Até que não seria ruim, e durante o dia eu poderia fazer alguns concertos pela casa.

Mariana: É verdade, eu poderei ajudá-lo a arrumar a garagem quando as crianças estiverem brincando. E depois, se você tiver tempo, você poderá cortar a grama também.

José Carlos: Ai! Tomara que faça sol. Ficar em casa trabalhando no fim de semana não me agrada nem um pouco.

Mariana: A mim tampouco. Eu vou fazer figa para que sábado amanheça ensolarado e nós possamos passar o dia velejando.

José Carlos:	What would you like to do this weekend?	
Mariana:	I'd like to go sailing on Saturday, but I doubt the weather will be nice. In any case, I asked the nanny to stay with the kids on Saturday. She said she'll stay if we give her next weekend off.	
José Carlos:	It's fine with me. But, what will we do if it rains?	
Mariana:	Well, if the weather's not good, we'll give the nanny the day off, we'll go to the video store, and we'll all spend the evening at home, watching TV and eating popcorn.	
José Carlos:	It won't be that bad; I could fix some things around the house.	
Mariana:	That's true; I could help you put the garage in order while the children are playing. And then, if you have time, you can also mow the lawn.	
José Carlos:	Oh! I hope it will be sunny. Working at home on the weekend doesn't please me at all.	
Mariana:	Me neither. I'll keep my fingers crossed for a sunny Saturday so we can spend the day sailing.	

NUTS & BOLTS 2

THE FUTURE SUBJUNCTIVE

To form the future subjunctive, start with the third person plural of the preterite, for example, **eles falaram** *(they spoke)* for both regular and irregular verbs. Take off the **-am** ending, and add nothing in the singular, and **-mos** and **-em** for the plural.

acordar (acordar-am)	entender (entender-am)	abrir (abrir-am)
eu acordar	eu entender	eu abri
você acordar	você entender	você abrir
ele/ela acordar	ele/ela entender	ele/ela abrir
nós acordarmos	nós entendermos	nós abrirmos

vocês acordarem	vocês entenderem	vocês abrirem
eles/elas acordarem	eles/elas entenderem	eles/elas abrirem

By looking at the examples above you might think that the future subjunctive is formed by just adding -**mos**, and -**em** endings (for the plural) to the infinitive. But notice, in the examples below using irregular verbs, that the base is actually the third person plural of the preterite. And it's also worth noting that although the verb in the preterite might be irregular, it is still formed regularly in the future subjunctive.

estar (estiver-am)	ter (tiver-am)	vir (vier-am)
eu estiver	eu tiver	eu vier
você estiver	você tiver	você vier
ele/ela estiver	ele/ela tiver	ele/ela vier
nós estivermos	nós tivermos	nós viremos
vocês estiveram	vocês tiveram	vocês vieram
eles/elas estiveram	eles/elas tiveram	eles/elas vieram

Remember that the third person plural preterite of the verb **ser** *(to be)* is **foram,** which is the same as the third person preterite of the verb **ir** *(to go).* So in the future subjunctive, both verbs are: **eu for, você for, ele/ela for, nós formos, vocês forem, eles/elas forem.**

The future subjunctive is used in clauses after the following conjunctions: **quando** *(when),* **enquanto** *(as long as),* **logo que** *(as* *soon as)*, **assim que** *(as soon as)*, **depois que** *(after)*, **se** *(if)*, **se não** *(unless)*, **como** *(as)*, **sempre que** *(whenever)*, **à medida que** *(as/while)*, and **conforme** *(as/while)*. Notice that the action it expresses is a possible future condition, upon which some other action (usually expressed by the future) hinges.

Eu escreverei quando puder.
I'll write when I can.

Eles ficarão aqui enquanto quiserem.
They'll stay here as long as they want.

Você ficará para trás se não se apressar.
You'll stay behind unless you hurry.

Nós viajaremos logo que comprarmos as passagens.
We'll travel as soon as we buy the tickets.

Ela não tomará banho depois que acordar.
She won't take a bath after she wakes up.

Você irá ao jogo se tiver tempo?
Will you go to the game if you have time?

A empresa crescerá à medida que o tempo passar.
The company will grow as time goes by.

Pedro e as crianças irão aos jogos sempre que encontrarem ingressos.
Pedro and the children will go to the games whenever they find tickets.

The future subjunctive is also used after clauses that express commands.

Faça o que quiser.
Do as you want.

Venha quando for melhor para você.
Come when it's best for you.

Esperem somente se não tiverem outra opção.
Wait only if you don't have another option.

Aproveitem enquanto estiverem de férias.
Take advantage while you're on vacation.

Compre as entradas se encontrar preço bom.
Buy the tickets if you find a good price.

The future subjunctive is also used after relative clauses.

Ele só virá quando estiver pronto.
He'll only come when he's ready.

Encontrarei você onde você quiser.
I'll meet you wherever you want.

Falaremos com quem comparecer.
We'll talk to whoever attends.

Vocês poderão trazer quantas pessoas quiserem.
You can bring as many people as you want.

Nós não faremos tudo que vocês pedirem.
We won't do whatever you ask.

Você fará como eu ensinar?
Will you do as I instruct?

PRACTICE 2
Complete the following sentences using the future subjunctive of the verbs in parentheses. The translation is provided to help you.

1. Nós reservaremos esse quarto enquanto os senhores _____ (estar) aqui conosco. *(We'll reserve this room for as long as you're here with us.)*

2. Elas não irão se Pedro e Marco não _____ (ir) também. *(They won't go if Pedro and Marco don't go either.)*

3. Isso não dará certo se você _____ (ser) impaciente. *(This won't work out if you're not patient.)*

4. O entregador deixará a mercadoria onde a senhora _____ (querer). *(The delivery person will leave the merchandise wherever you want.)*

5. O que vocês farão depois que o programa _____ (terminar)? *(What will you do after the program ends?)*

6. Telefone para mim sempre que _____ (ter) um problema com essa máquina. *(Call me whenever you have a problem with this machine.)*

7. As crianças ficarão felizes se nós _____ (vir) com elas. *(The children will be happy if we go with them.)*

8. Eu não ficarei triste se não o _____ (ver) nunca mais! *(I won't be sad if I never see him again!)*

9. Vocês poderão assistir TV assim que _____ (acabar) o jantar. *(You can watch TV as soon as you finish dinner.)*

10. Venha me visitar quando _____ (poder). *(Come and visit me when you can.)*

11. Só abram a caixa depois que _____ (chegar) em casa. *(Open the box only after you arrive home.)*

12. Os seus pais irão quando _____ nós (fazer) as reservas? *(Will your parents go when we make the reservation?)*

ANSWERS
PRACTICE 1: 1. venha; 2. aprenda; 3. façamos; 4. chova;
5. recebam; 6. seja; 7. pague; 8. fumam; 9. esteja; 10. escrevam;
11. tenha; 12. digam

PRACTICE 2: 1. estiverem; 2. forem; 3. for; 4. quiser;
5. terminar; 6. tiver; 7. viermos; 8. vir; 9. acabarem; 10. puder;
11. chegarem; 12. fizermos

UNIT 10 ESSENTIALS

Eu não fui à festa porque ninguém me convidou.

I didn't go to the party because no one invited me.

Nós não queremos nada.

We don't want anything.

Eu não tive nenhuma dificuldade.

I didn't have any difficulties.

Ele não quer sair, não adianta insistir.

He doesn't want to go out; there's no point in insisting.

Não deixe de ir ao jogo.

Don't miss the game.

Ela vive inventando desculpas.

She's always making up excuses.

Os ingressos que você comprou são caros.

The tickets you bought are expensive.

O gerente de quem falei foi promovido.

The manager I talked about was promoted.

Eles não têm ido ao cinema ultimamente.

They haven't gone to the movies lately.

Eu tenho treinado para a maratona dia e noite.

I've trained for the marathon day and night.

Nós ficaremos no hotel até a próxima semana.

We'll stay in the hotel until next week.

O dia amanhecerá nublado com chuvas isoladas.

The day will be overcast with isolated showers.

Eu viajaria, mas não tenho dinheiro.

I'd travel, but I don't have any money.

Não acho que elas ganhem o campeonato.

I don't think they'll win the championship.

Nós viajaremos logo que comprarmos as passagens.

We'll travel as soon as we buy the tickets.

A. HOTEL BROCHURE

O Resort Hotel Itaparica, em Ilha Grande, Rio de Janeiro, oferece vários tipos de pacotes com três ou quatro diárias para o feriado de 7, de setembro a partir de R$ 1.358 para o casal.

O pacote especial de 7 de setembro inclui:

Um drinque de boas-vindas no check-in e, como cortesia, um passeio de caiaque (por pessoa), durante meia hora, pela praia Aroeira.

O hotel, situado na preservada praia de Aroeira, põe à disposição dos hóspedes várias opções de lazer: quadra poliesportiva, quadras de tênis, piscinas, playground, salão de jogos, sala de TV e Internet, academia de ginástica com instrutor, quiosques com churrasqueira, restaurantes, lanchonete, e butique. Há também equipes de monitores infantis e adultos que desenvolvem atividades como caminhadas por trilhas ecológicas, aulas de tênis, passeios de caiaque, e jogos de entretenimento e integração.

Para tornar a experiência realmente inesquecível, O Resort Hotel Itaparica também oferece um spa, localizado em meio à vegetação, com vista incomparável para a praia de Aroeira. Ali, completamente integrado à natureza, o SPA Itaparica conta com profissionais especializados para massagens relaxantes, shiatsu, reflexologia, e também aulas de ioga.

Durante o feriado de 7 de setembro, o casal também poderá usufruir da Academia Itaparica, aparelhada com os mais modernos equipamentos de musculação e monitorada por professores de Educação Física.

Preço de pacotes no feriado de 7 de setembro para três diárias para duas pessoas, de 7 a 9 de setembro:

Bangalô: R$1.358,00

Apartamento Luxo: R$1.558,00

Apartamento Super Luxo: R$1.798,00

quatro diárias para duas pessoas, de 6 a 9 de setembro:

Bangalô: R$1.508,00

Apartamento Luxo: R$1.728,00

Apartamento Super Luxo: R$1.988,00

Os apartamentos e bangalôs acomodam no máximo 4 pessoas. Crianças até sete anos, poderão ficar no quarto dos pais como cortesia.

Café da manhã incluído no preço.

The Resort Hotel Itaparica, in Ilha Grande, Rio de Janeiro, offers couples 3- or 4-day package deals for the September 7 holiday beginning at R$1,358.00.

The special September 7 package includes:

A welcome drink at check-in as well as a courtesy half-hour kayak ride (per person) along the Aroeira beach.

The hotel, located at the preserve of the Aroeira beach, offers several leisure alternatives for its guests: sports courts, tennis courts, swimming pools, playground for children, indoor activities center, TV and internet rooms, gym with instructors, kiosks with barbecue grills, restaurants, snack bars, and a boutique. There are also groups of monitors for children and adults who carefully plan activities such as hikes on eco trails, tennis lessons, kayak rides, and games for entertainment and integration.

To make the experience a really unforgettable one, The Resort Hotel Itaparica also offers a spa, situated in the middle of the natural vegetation with an incomparable view to Aroeira beach. There, completely integrated with nature, the Itaparica SPA relies on specialized professionals for relaxing massages, shiatsu, and reflexology, as well as yoga classes.

During the September 7 holiday, the couple will also be able to use the Itaparica Fitness Center, equipped with the most modern workout machines and monitored by Physical Education teachers.

Prices for the September 7 holiday package

3 nights for 2 people, from September 7 through 9:

Bungalow: R$1,358.00

Luxury Apartment: R$1,558.00

Super Luxury Apartment: R$1,798.00

4 nights for 2 people, from September 6 through 9:

Bungalow: R$1,5008.00

Luxury Apartment: R$1,728.00

Super Luxury Apartment: R$1,988.00

All apartments and bungalows lodge up to 4 people. Children up to 7 can stay in the same room as their parents for no additional charge.

Breakfast is included in the price.

B. FRIENDLY E-MAIL CHAIN

Oi Júlia,

Eu não pude enviar o documento para o Sérgio.

Jordano

Hi, Julia,

I couldn't send the document to Sérgio.

Jordano

RESPOSTA

Eu tbm[1] mandei e voltou para mim. Ele tem outro endereço. Vou testar para ver se funciona.

Julia

REPLY

I did, too, and it bounced back to me. He's got another e-mail address. I'll test that to see if it works.

Julia

RETORNO

Oi,

Pode ser isso, mas você pode enviar novamente para ele? Talvez seja o meu computador ...

Jordano

REPLY

Hi,

It could be, but can you resend it to him? Maybe it's my computer ...

Jordano

RE-RETORNO

Eu acho que o problema é com arquivos grandes. Eles devem ter um filtro no sistema de email na escola.

Julia

[1]Notice the abbreviation **tbm**, meaning **também** *(also)*.

RE-REPLY
I think the problem is with large files. They must have a filter on the
e-mail system at the school.

Julia

C. BUSINESS LETTERS

Rua Tobias Barreto, 1326
São Paulo, S. P.
5 de julho de 2010

Sr. Júlio Matos
Avenida Rio Branco, 213
Rio de Janeiro, R. J.

Ilmo. Sr:
Anexo remeto-lhe um cheque de R$60.00 para obtenção de
uma assinatura anual da revista *Branco e Negro,* que é dirigida
por V. Sª.[1]

Atenciosamente,
João Carlos Martins

Rua Tobias Barreto, 1326
São Paulo. S. P.
July 5, 2010

Mr. Júlio Matos
Avenida Rio Branco, 213
Rio de Janeiro, R. J.

Dear Sir:
Enclosed please find a check for 60 real for a year's subscription to your
magazine Branco e Negro.

Very truly yours,
João Carlos Martins

---

[1]**V. Sª.** stands for **Vossa Senhoria,** a correspondence term for *you.*

Lopes, Nunes & Cia.
Rua de Madalena, 154
Lisboa, Portugal
2 de maio de 2009

Aos Srs.
Gomes, Lima & Cia.
Rua Nova d'Alfândega, 110
Porto

Prezados Senhores:

Temos a satisfação de apresentar-lhes o portador desta, o Sr. Alberto Rocha, nosso gerente de vendas, que visitará as principais cidades dessa região.

Não é preciso dizer-lhes que ficaremos imensamente gratos pelas atenções que lhe dispensarem.

Aproveitamos a oportunidade para agradecer-lhes antecipadamente o que fizerem pelo Sr. Rocha, e subscrevemo-nos muito atenciosamente.

De VV.SS.
Atos. e Obos.
Lopes, Nunes & Cia.
João Lopes
Presidente

Lopes, Nunes & Co.
Rua de Madalena, 154
Lisbon, Portugal
May 2, 2009

Gomes, Lima & Co.
Rua Nova d'Alfândega, 110
Oporto

Gentlemen:
We have the pleasure of introducing to you the bearer of this letter, Mr. Alberto Rocha, our sales manager, who will be visiting the principal cities of your region.
Needless to say, we will greatly appreciate any courtesy you may extend to him.
Thanking you in advance, we remain

Very truly yours,
Lopes, Nunes & Cia.
João Lopes
President

D. LETTER

2 de fevereiro

Meu caro José,
Foi com grande prazer que recebi a sua última carta. Para ir direto ao assunto, vou contar-lhe a grande notícia.
Finalmente decidimos fazer a projetada viagem a Lisboa, onde pretendemos ficar todo o mês de julho.
Naturalmente Maria está encantada, muito ansiosa de visitar o país dos seus avós e de conhecer você e sua amável esposa. Temos muitas coisas que comentar e espero que você possa livrar-se de outros compromissos durante esses dias.

Os negócios vão bem por agora e espero que continuem assim, de vento em popa. Na semana passada estive com o Alberto, e ele perguntou por você.

Ficarei muito agradecido se você puder reservar-nos um quarto num hotel, pertinho do prédio em que mora.

Escreva-me contando o que tem acontecido ultimamente, e o que lhe parece esta notícia.

Mando lembranças a Helena, e você, receba um abraço de seu amigo

João

February 2

Dear José,

I was very happy to get your last letter. Without further delay I'm going to spring the big news. We've finally decided to take the trip to Lisbon, where we expect to spend all of July.

Naturally, Maria's thrilled, being really anxious to visit her grandparents' country and to meet you and your charming wife. We have a lot to talk about, and I hope you'll be able to free yourself of other obligations during that period.

Business is good now, and I hope we'll continue to have smooth sailing. I saw Alberto last week, and he asked about you.

I'd appreciate it very much if you could reserve a room for us in a hotel near the building where you live.

Write and let me know what's been going on lately and what you think of the news.

Give my regards to Helena.

Yours,
João

1: WEATHER

o clima	*weather*
Está chovendo.	*It's raining.*
Está nevando.	*It's snowing.*
Está chovendo granizo.	*It's hailing.*
Está ventando.	*It's windy.*
Está quente.	*It's hot.*
Está frio.	*It's cold.*
Está ensolarado.	*It's sunny.*
Está nublado.	*It's cloudy.*
Está muito bonito.	*It's beautiful.*
a tempestade	*storm*
o vento	*wind*
o sol	*sun*
o trovão	*thunder*
o relâmpago	*lightning*
o furacão	*hurricane*
a temperatura	*temperature*
o grau	*degree*
a chuva	*rain*
a neve	*snow*
a nuvem, as nuvens	*cloud*
a neblina	*fog*
a nuvem de poluição	*smog*
o guarda-chuva, a sombrinha	*umbrella*

2: FOOD

os alimentos	*food*
o jantar, a janta	*dinner*

o almoço	*lunch*
o café da manhã	*breakfast*
a carne	*meat*
o frango, a galinha	*chicken*
a carne de vaca	*beef*
o porco	*pork*
o peixe	*fish*
o camarão	*shrimp*
a lagosta	*lobster*
o pão, os pães	*bread*
o ovo	*egg*
o queijo	*cheese*
o arroz	*rice*
o vegetal	*vegetable*
a alface	*lettuce*
o tomate	*tomato*
a cenoura	*carrot*
o pepino	*cucumber*
o pimentão	*(green) pepper*
a fruta	*fruit*
a maçã	*apple*
a laranja	*orange*
a banana	*banana*
a pera	*pear*
as uvas	*grapes*
a bebida	*drink*
a água	*water*
o leite	*milk*
o suco	*juice*
o café	*coffee*
o chá	*tea*

o vinho	*wine*
a cerveja	*beer*
o refrigerante	*soft drink, soda*
o sal	*salt*
a pimenta	*pepper*
o açúcar	*sugar*
o mel	*honey*
quente/frio, fria	*hot/cold*
doce/amargo, amarga	*sweet/sour*

3: PEOPLE

as pessoas, a gente	*people*
a pessoa	*person*
o homem	*man*
a mulher	*woman*
o adulto, a adulta	*adult*
a criança	*child*
o menino, o garoto, o guri	*boy*
a menina, a garota	*girl*
o/a adolescente	*teenager*
alto, alta/baixo, baixa	*tall/short*
velho, velha/novo, nova	*old/young*
gordo, gorda/magro, magra	*fat/thin*
amigável, simpático/antipático, antipática	*friendly/unfriendly*
feliz, alegre/infeliz, triste	*happy/sad*
bonito, bonita or belo, bela/feio, feia	*beautiful/ugly*
doente/saudável	*sick/healthy*

forte/fraco, fraca	*strong/weak*
famoso, famosa	*famous*
inteligente	*intelligent*
talentoso, talentosa	*talented*

4: AT HOME

em casa, no lar	*at home*
a casa	*house*
o apartamento	*apartment*
a sala, o aposento	*room*
a sala de estar, o living	*living room*
a sala de jantar	*dining room*
a cozinha	*kitchen*
o quarto	*bedroom*
o banheiro	*bathroom*
o corredor, o hall	*hall*
o armário	*closet*
a janela	*window*
a porta	*door*
a mesa	*table*
a cadeira	*chair*
o sofá	*sofa, couch*
a cortina	*curtain*
o carpete	*carpet*
o tapete	*rug*
a televisão, o televisor	*television*
o toca CD	*CD player*
o abajur, a luminária	*lamp*
o toca DVD	*DVD player*
o aparelho de som, o som	*sound system*
a pintura, a fotografia	*painting, picture*

a prateleira	*shelf*
a(s) escada(s)	*stairs*
o teto	*ceiling*
a parede	*wall*
o chão	*floor*
o térreo	*first floor*
segundo andar	*second floor*
grande/pequeno	*big/small*
novo, nova/velho, velha	*new/old*
a madeira/de madeira	*wood/wooden*
o plástico/de plástico	*plastic/made of plastic*

5: THE HUMAN BODY

o corpo humano	*the human body*
a cabeça	*head*
o rosto, a face	*face*
a testa	*forehead*
o olho	*eye*
a sombracelha	*eyebrow*
os cílios	*eyelashes*
o ouvido	*ear*
o nariz	*nose*
a boca	*mouth*
o dente	*tooth*
a língua	*tongue*
a bochecha	*cheek*
o queixo	*chin*
o cabelo	*hair*
o pescoço	*neck*
o peito	*chest*
os seios, as mamas	*breasts*
os ombros	*shoulders*

o braço	*arm*
o cotovelo	*elbow*
o pulso	*wrist*
a mão	*hand*
a barriga, o estômago, o abdome, o abdômen	*stomach, abdomen*
o pênis	*penis*
a vagina	*vagina*
a perna	*leg*
o joelho	*knee*
o tornozelo	*ankle*
o pé	*foot*
o dedo	*finger*
o dedo do pé (o artelho)	*toe*
a pele	*skin*
o sangue	*blood*
o cérebro	*brain*
o coração	*heart*
os pulmões	*lungs*
o osso	*bone*
o músculo	*muscle*
o tendão	*tendon*

6: TRAVEL AND TOURISM

a viagem de turismo	*travel and tourism*
o/a turista	*tourist*
o hotel	*hotel*
o albergue	*youth hostel*
a recepção	*reception desk*
o check-in	*check-in*
fechar a conta	*to check out*
a reserva	*reservation*

o passaporte	passport
a tour de ônibus	bus tour
com guia	guided tour
a câmara	camera
o centro de informação/informações	information center
o mapa	map
o guia de mão	brochure
o monumento	monument
fazer um passeio com guia	to go sightseeing (with a guide)
tirar fotografia	to take a picture
Pode tirar minha/nossa foto?	Can you take my/our picture?

7: IN THE OFFICE

no escritório	in the office
o escritório	office
a mesa, o gabinete	desk
o computador	computer
o telefone	telephone
a fax	fax machine
a estante	bookshelf
o arquivo	file, file cabinet
a pasta	file, folder
o chefe	boss
o/a colega	colleague
o trabalhador, a trabalhadora, o empregado, a empregada	employee, worker
o estafe, a equipe	staff
a companhia, a firma	company
o negócio	business
a fábrica	factory

a sala de reunião	*meeting room*
a reunião	*meeting*
o encontro, a hora marcada	*appointment*
o salário	*salary*
o trabalho	*job*
ocupado, ocupada	*busy*
trabalhar	*to work*
ganhar	*to earn*

8: AT SCHOOL

na escola	*at school*
a escola	*school*
a universidade	*university*
a sala de aula	*classroom*
o curso	*course*
o professor, a professora	*teacher*
o professor, a professora	*professor*
o/a estudante	*student*
o tema, o assunto, o tópico	*subject*
o caderno	*notebook*
o livro de texto	*textbook*
a matemática	*math*
a história	*history*
a química	*chemistry*
a biologia	*biology*
a literatura	*literature*
a língua	*language*
a arte	*art*
a música	*music*
a ginástica, a educação física	*gym*

o intervalo, o recreio	*recess*
a prova	*test*
a nota	*grade*
o boletim	*report card*
o diploma	*diploma*
o grau	*degree, grade*
difícil/fácil	*difficult/easy*
estudar	*to study*
aprender	*to learn*
passar	*to pass*
repetir	*to fail*

9: SPORTS AND RECREATION

os esportes e a recreação	*sports and recreation*
o futebol	*soccer*
o basquete, o basquetebol	*basketball*
o basebol	*baseball*
o futebol americano	*American football*
o hóquei	*hockey*
o tênis	*tennis*
o voleibol	*volleyball*
o futebol de salão	*footsal*
o jogo	*game*
o time	*team*
o estádio	*stadium*
o técnico	*coach*
o jogador	*player*
o campeão	*champion*
a bola	*ball*
caminhar, ir passear	*(to go) hiking*
acampar	*(to go) camping*
jogar	*to play*

vencer	*to win*
perder	*to lose*
empatar	*to draw, to tie*
as cartas, o baralho	*cards, deck*
sinuca	*pool, billiards*

10: NATURE

a natureza	*nature*
a árvore	*tree*
a flor	*flower*
a floresta	*forest*
a montanha	*mountain*
o campo, a campina	*field*
o rio	*river*
o lago	*lake*
o oceano	*ocean*
o mar	*sea*
a praia	*beach*
o deserto	*desert*
a pedra	*rock*
a areia	*sand*
o céu	*sky*
o sol	*sun*
a lua	*moon*
a estrela	*star*
a água	*water*
a terra	*land*
a planta	*plant*
a subida, a colina	*hill*
o lago	*pond*

11: COMPUTERS AND THE INTERNET

os computadores e a internet	*computers and the internet*
o computador	*computer*
o teclado	*keyboard*
o monitor, a tela	*monitor, screen*
a impressora	*printer*
o mouse	*mouse*
o modem	*modem*
a memória	*memory*
o cd-rom	*CD-ROM*
o drive de cd-rom	*CD-ROM drive*
o arquivo	*file*
o documento	*document*
o cabo de internet rápida	*cable (DSL)*
a internet	*internet*
o site	*website*
a página da internet	*webpage*
o blogue, o blog	*weblog*
o correio eletrônico, o e-mail	*e-mail*
a sala de bate-papo	*chatroom*
a mensagem instantânea	*instant message*
o anexo	*attachment*
enviar correio eletrônico/e-mail	*to send an e-mail*
enviar um arquivo	*to send a file*
reenviar	*to forward*
responder	*to reply*
deletar	*to delete*
salvar um documento	*to save a document*
abrir um arquivo	*to open a file*
fechar um arquivo	*to close a file*
anexar um arquivo	*to attach a file*

12: FAMILY AND RELATIONSHIPS

a família e o parentesco	*family and relationships*
a mãe	*mother*
o pai	*father*
o filho	*son*
a filha	*daughter*
a irmã	*sister*
o/a bebê	*baby*
o irmão, os irmãos	*brother(s)*
o marido	*husband*
a esposa	*wife*
a tia	*aunt*
o tio	*uncle*
a avó	*grandmother*
o avô	*grandfather*
o primo, a prima	*cousin*
a sogra	*mother-in-law*
o sogro	*father-in-law*
a madrasta	*stepmother*
o padrastro	*stepfather*
o enteado	*stepson*
a enteada	*stepdaughter*
o namorado	*boyfriend*
a namorada	*girlfriend*
o noivo, a noiva	*fiancé(e)*
o amigo, a amiga	*friend*
o/a parente	*relative*
amar	*to love*
conhecer, apresentar-se	*to know (a person)*
encontrar, apresentar-se	*to meet (a person)*
casar com	*to marry (someone)*
divorciar de	*to divorce (someone)*

divorciar-se	*to get a divorce*
herdar	*to inherit*

13: ON THE JOB

a ocupação, o trabalho	*job*
o/a polícia	*policeman, policewoman*
o advogado, a advogada	*lawyer*
o doutor, a doutora	*doctor*
o engenheiro, a engenheira	*engineer*
o/a homem/mulher de negócios	*businessman, businesswoman*
o vendedor, a vendedora	*salesman, saleswoman*
o professor, a professora	*teacher, professor*
o banqueiro, a banqueira	*banker*
o arquiteto, a arquiteta	*architect*
o veterinário, a veterinária	*veterinarian*
o/a dentista	*dentist*
o carpinteiro, a carpinteira	*carpenter*
o pedreiro, a pedreira	*construction worker, mason*
o/a taxista	*taxi driver*
o/a artista	*artist*
o escritor, a escritora	*writer*
o encanador, a encanadora	*plumber*
o/a eletricista	*electrician*
o/a jornalista	*journalist*
o ator, a atriz	*actor, actress*
o músico, a música	*musician*
o fazendeiro, a fazendeira	*farmer*
o secretário, a secretária/ o/a assistente	*secretary/assistant*
o desempregado, a desempregada	*unemployed*

o aposentado, a aposentada	*retired*
o/a trabalhador/a de tempo integral	*full-time employee*
o meio período	*part-time*
trabalho permanente	*steady job*
trabalho temporário	*summer (temporary) job*

14: CLOTHING

as vestimentas, as roupas	*clothing*
a camisa	*shirt*
as calças	*pants*
os jeans	*jeans*
a camiseta	*T-shirt*
os sapatos	*shoes*
as meias	*socks*
o cinto, a cinta	*belt*
o tênis	*sneakers, tennis shoes*
o vestido	*dress*
a saia	*skirt*
a blusa	*blouse*
o terno	*suit*
o chapéu	*hat*
as luvas	*gloves*
o cachecol	*scarf*
o paletó, a jaqueta	*jacket*
a capa	*coat*
o brinco	*earring*
o bracelete	*bracelet*
o colar	*necklace*
os óculos	*eyeglasses*
os óculos de sol	*sunglasses*

o relógio de pulso	*watch*
o anel	*ring*
a cueca, a roupa de baixo	*underpants*
a camiseta, a roupa de baixo	*undershirt*
o maiô	*bathing suit*
o calção, a sunga	*bathing trunks*
o pijama	*pajamas*
o algodão	*cotton*
o couro	*leather*
a seda	*silk*
o tamanho	*size*
usar	*to wear*

15: IN THE KITCHEN

na cozinha	*in the kitchen*
o refrigerador, a geladeira	*refrigerator*
a pia	*sink*
o balcão	*counter*
o fogão	*stove*
o forno	*oven*
o microondas	*microwave*
a cristaleira	*cupboard*
a gaveta	*drawer*
o prato	*plate*
a xícara	*cup*
a tigela	*bowl*
o copo (vidro)	*glass*
a colher	*spoon*
a faca	*knife*
a lata	*can*
a caixa	*box*

a garrafa	*bottle*
o pacote (a caixa)	*carton*
a cafeteira	*coffeemaker*
o bule de chá	*teakettle*
o liquidificador	*blender*
o ferro	*iron*
a tábua de passar roupa	*ironing board*
a vassoura	*broom*
a lavadora de prato	*dishwasher*
a máquina de lavar	*washing machine*
a secadora	*dryer*
cozinhar	*to cook*
lavar os pratos	*to do the dishes*
lavar a roupa	*to do the laundry*
sabão de máquina de lavar prato	*dishwashing detergent*
sabão em pó	*laundry detergent powder*
cloro	*bleach*
limpo, limpa/sujo, suja	*clean/dirty*

16: IN THE BATHROOM

no banheiro	*in the bathroom*
a privada, o vaso sanitário	*toilet*
a pia	*sink (washbasin)*
a banheira	*bathtub*
o chuveiro, a ducha	*shower*
o espelho	*mirror*
o armarinho do banheiro	*medicine cabinet*
a toalha	*towel*
o papel higiênico	*toilet paper*
o champu	*shampoo*
o sabão, sabonete	*soap*

o gel de banho	*bath gel*
o creme de barbear	*shaving cream*
a lâmina, a navalha	*razor*
lavar-se	*to wash oneself*
tomar banho	*to take a shower/bath*
barbear-se	*to shave*
a colônia	*cologne*
o perfume	*perfume*
o desodorante	*deodorant*
a bandagem	*bandage*
o pó	*powder*

17: AROUND TOWN

pela cidade, a cidade	*around town*
a cidade	*town, city*
a vila	*village*
o carro	*car*
o ônibus	*bus*
o trem	*train*
o táxi	*taxi*
o metrô	*subway, metro*
a estação do metrô	*subway station*
o tráfego	*traffic*
o edifício	*building*
o condomínio, o prédio de apartamento	*apartment building*
a biblioteca	*library*
o restaurante	*restaurant*
a loja	*store*
a rua	*street*
o parque	*park*
a estação de trem	*train station*

o aeroporto	*airport*
o avião	*airplane*
o cruzamento, a intersecção	*intersection*
o poste de luz	*lamppost*
a luz da rua	*streetlight*
o banco	*bank*
a igreja	*church*
o templo	*temple*
a mesquita	*mosque*
a calçada	*sidewalk*
a padaria	*bakery*
o açougue	*butcher shop*
o bar, o restaurante	*diner, restaurant*
a drogaria, a famácia	*drugstore, pharmacy*
o supermercado	*supermarket*
o mercado	*market*
a sapataria	*shoe store*
a loja de roupas	*clothing store*
a loja de eletrônicos	*electronics store*
a livraria	*bookstore*
a loja de departamentos	*department store*
o prefeito	*mayor*
a prefeitura	*city hall, municipal building*
comprar	*to buy*
ir às compras	*to go shopping*
perto/longe	*near/far*
urbano, urbana	*urban*
suburbano, suburbana	*suburban*
rural	*rural*

18: ENTERTAINMENT

a diversão, o divertimento	*entertainment*
o cinema, o filme	*movie, film*
ir ao cinema	*to go to the movies*
assistir um filme	*to see a movie*
o teatro	*theater*
assistir a uma peça	*to see a play*
a ópera	*opera*
o concerto	*concert*
o clube	*club*
o circo	*circus*
o ingresso	*ticket*
o museu	*museum*
a galeria	*gallery*
a pintura	*painting*
a escultura	*sculpture*
o programa de televisão	*television program*
assistir televisão	*to watch television*
o documentário	*documentary*
o drama	*drama*
o livro	*book*
a revista	*magazine*
ler um livro	*to read a book*
ler uma revista	*to read a magazine*
ouvir música	*to listen to music*
a música, a canção	*song*
o grupo musical, a banda	*band*
o noticiário	*the news*
o show de entrevista	*talk show*
mudar/procurar o canal	*to flip channels*
divertir-se	*to have fun*
ficar chateado	*to be bored*

engraçado/a	*funny*
interessante	*interesting*
assustador/a	*scary*
a festa	*party*
o restaurante	*restaurant*
ir a uma festa	*to go to a party*
fazer uma festa	*to have a party*
dançar	*to dance*

The following is a list of Portuguese language websites that students of Portuguese will find interesting and useful.

www.livinglanguage.com	Living Language's site offers online courses, descriptions of supplemental learning material, resources for teachers and librarians, and much more.
www.google.com.br	Google's Brazil site.
news.google.com.br	Google news in Portuguese.
br.yahoo.com	Yahoo! for users in Brazil.
www.ectaco.co.uk/ English-Portuguese-Dictionary	Online English-Portuguese dictionary.
www.brasilemb.org	Brazilian Embassy.
www.brazilny.org	Brazilian consulate in New York.
pt.embassyinformation.com	Portuguese Embassy information.
www.onlinenewspapers.com	A site that will link you to newspapers from all around the world.
www.brazzil.com	English language magazine about Brazil.
cbn.globoradio.globo.com	Radio, in Portuguese.

www.portugal.org	General travel, tourism, business, and cultural information.
www2.usp.br	University of São Paulo, Brazil.
www.uc.pt/	University of Coimbra, Portugal.

1. THE ALPHABET

LETTER	NAME	LETTER	NAME	LETTER	NAME
a	*a (á)*	j	*jota*	s	*ésse*
b	*bê*	k	*cá/capa*	t	*tê*
c	*cê*	l	*ele*	u	*u*
d	*dê*	m	*eme*	v	*vê*
e	*e/é*	n	*ene*	w	*dábliu*
f	*efe*	o	*ó*	x	*xis*
g	*gê*	p	*pê*	y	*ípsilon*
h	*agá*	q	*quê*	z	*zê*
i	*i*	r	*erre*		

2. PRONUNCIATION
SIMPLE VOWELS

a

In a stressed position, it is "open," as in *ah* or *father.* In unstressed positions and in the case of the article *a* and its plural, *as* (the), it tends to be more "closed," like the final *a* in *America* (this is particularly true in Portugal and in general with unstressed final *a*).

e

"Open" *e* is as in *best; é* has this sound. "Closed" *e* is between the sound of *a* in *case* and *e* in *fez; ê* has this sound, as does nasal *e*. Variations occur in different areas. In a final unstressed position, in Brazil, it varies between the sound of *i* in *did* and the *i* in *machine;* in Portugal, it is often clipped sharply, like a mute *e,* or it is dropped. Stressed *e* before *j, ch, lh,* or *nh* in Portugal can have the sound of the final *a* in *America* or of closed *e*. In an unstressed position, it is sometimes pronounced like *e* in *be* in parts of Brazil, as mute *e* in Portugal, or like *i* in *did* in both Portugal and Brazil.

i

Like *i* in *machine*.

o

"Open" *o* is like *o* in *off; ó* has this sound. "Closed" *o* is as in *rose; ô* has this sound, and so does nasal *o*. In an unstressed position and in the case of the definite article *o, os* (the), it is also pronounced like *oo* in *boot*.

u

Approximates *u* in *rule*.

Vowel Combinations

ai	*ai* as in *aisle*
au	*ou* as in *out*
ei	*ey* as in *they*
éi	similar to open *e*
eu	*ey* of *they* plus *u* of *lute*
éu	similar but with open *e*
ia	*ya* as in *yard*
ié	*ye* as in *yes*
ie	similar but with closed *e*
io	*yo* as in *yoke*
iu	*e* plus *u* of *lute*
oi	*oy* as in *boy*
ói	similar but with open *o*
ou	*ou* as in *soul*
ua	*wah*, like *ua* in *quadrangle*

ué	*we* as in *wet*
ui	*we* (if main stress is on *u*, however, like *u* of *lute* plus *e*)
uo	*wo* as in *woe*, or as *uó*

Consonants

Those consonants not mentioned are approximately like English.

c	Before *a, o,* and *u,* and before another consonant, like *c* in *cut.*
c	Before *e* and *i,* like *c* in *center.*
ch	Like *ch* in *machine.*
d	As *d* in *dog* but before *e* or *i* it approximates the *j* in *just.*
g	Before *e* and *i,* somewhat like *s* in *measure.*
g	Otherwise, like *g* in *go.*
h	Not pronounced.
j	Like a soft *j* (see *g,* above).
l	Formed with the tongue forward, with the tip of the tongue near the upper teeth.
l	In final position is quite soft, similar to *-w.*
lh	Like *lli* in *million.*
m	In initial position in a word or syllable, like English *m;* in final position in a syllable or word, it tends to nasalize the preceding vowel; this nasal quality is especially strong in Brazil, but it may be more subtle or even absent in Continental Portuguese. (Lips should not be closed when pronouncing *m* at the end of a word.)
n	In initial position, like English *n;* in word- or syllable-final positions, same as for *m,* above.
nh	Like *ni* in *onion.*
qu	Before *a* or *o,* like *qu* in *quota.*

qu	Before *e* or *i*, usually like *k*.
qü	Before *e* or *i*, like *qu* in *quota*.
r	Pronounced by tapping the tip of the tongue against the gum ridge behind the upper teeth; initial *r* and *rr* are trilled with the tongue vibrating in this position. This pronunciation is heard in Portugal. In Brazil, *r* is pronounced at the back of the mouth (similar to a French back *r*); initial *r* is pronounced like a cross between *h* and German *ch*, with some variation by region.
s	Between vowels, *z*, like *s* in *rose*.
s	Before a voiced consonant (a consonant sound produced with a vibration of the cords: *b, d, ge, gi, j, l, m, n, r, v, z*), tends to be like *z* in *azure*.
s	Before a voiceless consonant (a consonant sound produced without a vibration of the vocal cords: hard *c*, hard *g, f, p, qu, t*) and in the final position, like *s* in *see* in São Paulo and like *sh* in *shine* in Portugal and by *cariocas* and other Northerners in Brazil.
s	In initial position, or after a consonant, like *s* in *see*.
ss	Like *ss* in *passage*.
t	Much like English *t*; before *e* or *i*, it is pronounced very forcefully by some *cariocas*, being palatalized and approximating the *ch* in *church*.
x	Like *z* in some words *(exame)*, like *sh* in some words *(caixa)*, like *s* in *see* in some words *(máximo)*, and like *x* in *wax* in some words *(táxi)*.
z	Generally, like *z* in *zeal*. However, in final position or before a voiceless consonant, *s* is also heard in Brazil; *sh* is the common pronunciation in Portugal and in a few parts of Brazil, and before a voiced consonant, it is like *z* in *azure* in Portugal.

STRESS

Words ending in *-a, -e,* or *-o* (or in one of these vowels and *-s, -m,* or *-ns*) are stressed on the next-to-last syllable.

casa	house
estudante	student
jovem	young

Some words ending in *l* or in a nasal vowel or diphthong (two vowels pronounced in union) are stressed on the last syllable.

papel	paper
manhã	morning
descansei	I rested

Words not following the above rules generally have a written accent mark that indicates the stressed syllable.

café	coffee
América	America
Itália	Italy
difícil	difficult
órfão	orphan

3. PUNCTUATION

In general, Portuguese punctuation is similar to English. This section only includes important differences.

The dash is used in dialogues to indicate the words of the speakers.

> *- Como vai o senhor?*

> *- Muito bem, obrigado.*

Capital letters are not used as frequently as in English. They are not used with adjectives of nationality, the days of the week, or months (in Portugal, the months and the seasons are capitalized), nor is the pronoun *eu* (I) capitalized.

Eles são russos.	They are Russians.
Ela chegará na quinta.	She will arrive on Thursday.
Comprei o tapete em setembro (Setembro).	I bought the carpet in September.

Suspension points (. . .) are used more frequently than in English to indicate interruption, etc.

Notice the difference from English in the use of the decimal point.

3.000.000 de habitantes	3,000,000 inhabitants
5.289 metros	5,289 meters
R$8.300,00	8,300 reals

4. SOME ORTHOGRAPHIC SIGNS

The tilde *(til)* (˜) over a vowel indicates a nasal sound.

posição	position

The dieresis *(trema)* (¨) is used in Brazil but not in Portugal in modern spelling over the letter *u* when it occurs after *q* or *g* and before *e* or *i* and is pronounced.

eloqüente (eloquente)	eloquent

The cedilla *(cedilha)* is used with *c* (*ç*) when it is pronounced *s* before *a, o,* or *u.*

pedaço	piece, bit

Written accent marks are used to indicate the stressed syllable in words not following the regular rules (see Section 2 of the grammar summary). They also help distinguish between words that are spelled alike but have different meanings and between different forms of the same verb.

pôr	to put	*por*	for, by
pôde	he/she was able to, he/she could	*pode*	he/she is able to, he/she can
pára	he stops	*para*	for, to

The circumflex accent *(acento circunflexo)* (ˆ) is used over stressed closed *e* and *o*; the acute accent *(acento agudo)* (ˊ) is used over stressed open *a, e,* and *o*.

conhecê-lo	to know him	*câmera*	camera
avô	grandfather	*avó*	grandmother
célebre	famous	*fé*	faith

The acute accent (ˊ) is used over stressed *i* and *u* when they are not combined with the preceding vowel.

país	country	*pais*	parents
saúde	health	*saída*	departure

The grave accent *(acento grave)* (ˋ) indicates the contraction of preposition *a* and the definite articles *a* and *as*. Also, the same combination happens when the prepositions are followed by the demonstratives *aquele, aquela,* and *aquilo*. It is important to observe that, in speech, there is no distinction in stress between *a* and *à* in the Portuguese spoken in Brazil, although in Portugal, *a* and *à* are pronounced differently. In Brazil, the listener will be able to tell from the semantic context that a contraction has occurred.

Ele vai à biblioteca.	He's going to the library.
Vamos àqueles parques.	Let's go to those parks.
Ele deu o livro às meninas.	He gave the book to the girls.

Notice that the circumflex or acute accent is dropped when suffixes such as *-mente, -zinho, -íssimo*, etc., are added to a word because there is a change in the stressed syllable.

café-cafezinho	small cup of coffee
só-somente	only
útil-utilíssimo	very useful
câmera-camerazinha	little camera
ângulo-angulozinho	little angle

The grave accent indicates a combination of *a* and a word beginning with *a* (demonstratives, such as *aquele*, etc.) or with the definite article *a*.

àqueles	to those	*à*	to the

5. SYLLABLE DIVISION
A single consonant goes with the following vowel.

a-fi-nal	finally

Two similar consonants usually split.

in-ter-rom-per	to interrupt

The consonant combinations *ch, lh,* and *nh* do not split.

bor-ra-cha	rubber, eraser
o-re-lha	ear
so-nhar	to dream

Two vowels that are pronounced separately are split.

vi-ú-va	widow
ca-ir	to fall
vo-ar	to fly

6. THE DEFINITE ARTICLE

	Singular	Plural
Masculine	*o*	*os*
Feminine	*a*	*as*

o menino	the boy
a menina	the girl
os meninos	the boys
as meninas	the girls

The definite article is used with abstract or generic nouns.

A verdade vale mais que o dinheiro.	Truth is worth more than money.
A mulher brasileira se veste (-se) bem.	Brazilian women dress well.
As mulheres americanas se vestem (-se) bem.	American women dress well.
O óleo é muito útil.	Oil is very useful.

It is also used with the names of languages (except when immediately after *falar, de,* or *em;* the article is often not used with languages in some situations).

O português é fácil.	Portuguese is easy.
Falo inglês.	I speak English.
Tenho um livro de espanhol.	I have a Spanish book.

It is used with expressions of time, days of the week, and seasons.

a semana passada	last week
às duas horas	at two o'clock
na segunda-feira	on Monday
a primavera (Primavera)	spring

It is used with the names of most countries[1] and with other geographical names. On the other hand, names of most cities do not require the use of articles.[2]

o Brasil	Brazil
a Itália	Italy
a África	Africa

It is used with first names at times.

o Carlos	Carlos

It is used with titles or other words modifying a proper noun.

Ele jantou com o professor Silva.	He dined with Professor Silva.
O senhor Ramos não está em casa.	Mr. Ramos is not home.

It is used with possessive pronouns and adjectives, although less frequently with possessive adjectives in Brazil than in Portugal.

Este não é (o) meu lenço;	This is not my handkerchief; it's
é (o) seu.	yours.

It is also used with parts of the body and articles of clothing, instead of the possessive form.

[1]Main exceptions that do not need an article: *Portugal, Moçambique, Angola, Cuba, Israel, Porto Rico.*
[2]Main exceptions that need an article: *o Rio de Janeiro, o Porto.*

O menino lavou as mãos.	The boy washed his hands.
Ela perdeu as luvas.	She lost her gloves.

7. THE INDEFINITE ARTICLE

	Singular	Plural
Masculine	*um*	*uns*
Feminine	*uma*	*umas*

um homem	a man
uma mulher	a woman
uns homens	some (a few) men
umas mulheres	some (a few) women

The indefinite article is omitted before a noun of occupation, nationality, etc., coming after the verb, especially if the noun is not modified.

Ele é capitão.	He is a captain.
Ela é aluna.	She is a student.

It is also omitted before *cem* (a hundred) and *mil* (a thousand) and the preposition *sem* (without).

cem entrevistas	a hundred interviews
mil esperanças	a thousand hopes
Ele saiu sem chapéu.	He left without a hat.

8. CONTRACTIONS

Contractions of *de* with the definite article (*o/a* and its other forms):

de + o = do	*de + os = dos*	of the, from the
de + a = da	*de + as = das*	

$a + o = ao$	$a + os = aos$	to the
$a + a = \grave{a}s$	$a + as = \grave{a}s$	
$em + o = no$	$em + os = nos$	in the, on the
$em + a = na$	$em + as = nas$	
$por + o = pelo$	$por + os = pelos$	by, through the
$por + a = pela$	$por + as = pelas$	

do menino	*dos meninos*	the boy's, the boys'
da menina	*das meninas*	the girl's, the girls'
ao menino	*aos meninos*	to the boy, to the boys
à menina	*às meninas*	to the girl, to the girls
no lago	*nos lagos*	in (on) the lake, in (on) the lakes
na pátria	*nas pátrias*	in the homeland, in the homelands
pelo menino	*pelos meninos*	by the boy, by the boys
pela praça	*pelas praças*	through the square, through the squares

Contractions of *de* and *em* with the indefinite article (*um* and its other forms) are optional, both contracted and noncontracted forms being used.

de um artigo or dum artigo	of an article
de uma árvore or duma árvore	of a tree
em umas aldeias or numas aldeias	in some villages

Por never makes contractions with indefinite articles.

De and *em* combine with the demonstrative forms.

daquela	of that one
naquele	in that one

The preposition *a* combines with the initial *a* of the demonstratives *aquele,* etc., and with the definite article *a.*

àquela	to that one
à baía	to the bay

9. DAYS OF THE WEEK

The days of the week are not capitalized. *Sábado* (Saturday) and *domingo* (Sunday) are masculine; the other days are feminine. The article is generally used, except after *ser.*

segunda-feira or *segunda*	Monday
terça-feira or *terça*	Tuesday
quarta-feira or *quarta*	Wednesday
quinta-feira or *quinta*	Thursday
sexta-feira or *sexta*	Friday
sábado	Saturday
domingo	Sunday
Vou vê-lo na segunda.	I'm going to see him Monday.
Hoje é terça.	Today is Tuesday.

"On Monday," "on Mondays," etc.:

na segunda-feira	on Monday
nas segundas-feiras	on Mondays

10. MONTHS

The names of the months are masculine and usually are not capitalized in Brazil (but they are in Portugal: *Janeiro,* etc.). They are usually used without the definite article.

janeiro	January
fevereiro	February
março	March
abril	April
maio	May
junho	June
julho	July
agosto	August
setembro	September
outubro	October
novembro	November
dezembro	December

11. SEASONS

a primavera (a Primavera)	spring
o verão (o Verão)	summer
o outono (o Outono)	autumn
o inverno (o Inverno)	winter

The names of the seasons are usually not capitalized in Brazil (but they are in Portugal). They are usually used with the definite article.

Ninguém vai lá no inverno.	Nobody goes there in the winter.

12. GENDER
Nouns referring to males are masculine; nouns referring to females are feminine.

o pai	the father	*a mãe*	the mother
o filho	the son	*a filha*	the daughter
o homem	the man	*a mulher*	the woman
o leão	the lion	*a leoa*	the lioness

The masculine plural of certain nouns can include both genders.

os pais	the parents, the father and mother
os irmãos	the brothers, the brother and sister, the brothers and sisters

Masculine Nouns

Nouns ending in diphthongs (vowel combinations pronounced together), *-m* (but not *-em*), *-s,* and *-o* are usually masculine.

o grau	the degree
o elogio	the praise
o dom	the gift
o lápis	the pencil
um abraço	an embrace, a hug

Names of months, seas, rivers, mountains, and letters of the alphabet are generally masculine.

Janeiro é o primeiro mês.	January is the first month.
o Atlântico	the Atlantic
o Amazonas	the Amazon (River)
o dê	the d

Feminine Nouns

Nouns ending in *-a, -ie, -em, -ade, -ede,* and *-ice* are usually feminine.

a boca	the mouth
a ordem	the order
a amizade	friendship
a parede	the wall
a velhice	old age

Common exceptions:

o homem	the man
a avó	the grandmother

A good number of words ending in *-a* (or *-ma),* especially words of Greek origin, are masculine.

o programa	the program
o problema	the problem
o cinema	the cinema
o drama	the drama
o clima	the climate
o dia	the day
o mapa	the map
o idioma	the language

-a is added to some masculine nouns ending in *-r* to form the feminine.

leitor	*leitora*	reader
diretor	*diretora*[3]	director
orador	*oradora*	speaker, orator

Names of islands and continents are usually feminine.

a Europa	Europe
a Sicília	Sicily
a América	America

13. THE PLURAL

Nouns ending in a vowel (including nasal vowels) or in a diphthong usually add *-s* to form the plural.

[3]In Portugal: *director, directora.*

um ato	one act	*dois atos*[4]	two acts
a maçã	the apple	*as maçãs*	the apples
a lei	the law	*as leis*	the laws

Words ending in *-ão* form the plural with *-ões*.

a ambição	ambition	*as ambições*	ambitions
o avião	airplane	*os aviões*	airplanes
a posição	position	*as posições*	positions

However, there are a few exceptions to the above rule, and these words should be learned individually. Some change *-ão* to *-ães* in the plural.

o capitão	*os capitães*	the captain(s)
o alemão	*os alemães*	the German(s)
o pão	*os pães*	the bread(s)
o cão	*os cães*	the dog(s)

Others form the plural by just adding an *-s.*

o irmão	*os irmãos*	brother(s)
a mão	*as mãos*	hand(s)
o cidadão	*os cidadãos*	citizen(s)
o órfão	*os órfãos*	orphan(s)
o grão	*os grãos*	grain(s)

Words that end in *-m* change the *m* into *n* before adding *-s*. This change has no effect on the pronunciation.

o homem	man	*os homens*	men
o fim	end	*os fins*	end
jovem	young	*jovens*	young *(adj.)*
bom	good	*bons*	good *(adj.)*

[4]In Portugal: *acto, actos*

Words ending in *-r, -z,* and *-s* add *-es.*

o doutor	doctor	*os doutores*	doctors
a luz	light	*as luzes*	lights
o mês	month	*os meses*	months

Words ending in unstressed *-s* retain the same form in the plural.

o ônibus (o autocarro)	*os ônibus*	the bus(es)
o lápis	*os lápis*	the pencil(s)
o campus	*os campus* (or *os campi*)	the campus(es)
simples	*simples*	simple *(adj.)*

Words ending in *-l* drop the *l* and add *-is.* Note that the endings *-éis* and *-óis* bear a written accent.

a capital	*as capitais*	capital(s)
o jornal	*os jornais*	newspaper(s)
o papel	*os papéis*	paper(s)
o hotel	*os hotéis*	hotel(s)
espanhol	*espanhóis*	Spanish *(adj.)*
azul	*azuis*	blue *(adj.)*

Words ending in *-il* drop the *l* and add *-s.*

o barril	*os barris*	barrel(s)
civil	*civis*	civil *(adj.)*

But a few words ending in unstressed *-il* or *-vel* have irregular plurals that end in *-eis.*

fácil	*fáceis*	easy *(adj.)*
difícil	*difíceis*	difficult *(adj.)*
útil	*úteis*	useful *(adj.)*
fútil	*fúteis*	futile *(adj.)*
horrível	*horríveis*	horrible *(adj.)*
detestável	*detestáveis*	dislikeable *(adj.)*

14. THE POSSESSIVE

Possession is shown with the preposition *de* (of).

o neto de Dona Maria	Dona Maria's grandson

Possessive adjectives and pronouns agree in number and gender with the object possessed. The possessive adjective usually comes before the word it modifies.

meu livro	my book
meus livros	my books
minha sobrinha	my niece
minhas sobrinhas	my nieces

In conversation, *seu* tends to refer to the person spoken to and can be translated as "your." However, *seu* can also be used to mean "his," "her," or "their." For greater clarity, the prepositional form with *de* may be used.

Eles falaram de seu amigo.	They spoke of your (his, her, their) friend.
Eles falaram do amigo dele/do amigo dela/do amigo deles/do amigo delas.	They spoke of his friend/of her friend/of their friend.

15. ADJECTIVES

Adjectives agree with the nouns they modify in gender and number.

um menino alto	a tall boy
uma menina alta	a tall girl
dois meninos altos	two tall boys
duas meninas altas	two tall girls

The feminine is formed with the ending *-a* instead of the *-o* of the masculine form.

Masculine		Feminine
antigo	old, ancient	*antiga*
rico	rich	*rica*
baixo	short, low	*baixa*

If the masculine form ends in *-u*, the feminine form ends in *-a*.

Masculine		Feminine
nu	nude, bare	*nua*
mau	bad	*má*

There is no change between genders if the masculine form ends in *-e*.

Masculine		Feminine
contente	happy, content	*contente*

Common exceptions:

este	this	*esta*
aquele	that	*aquela*

The feminine ending *-ã* is substituted for the *-ão* of the masculine form.

Masculine		Feminine
alemão	German	*alemã*
cristão	Christian	*cristã*

With augmentatives, *-ona* replaces *-ão*.

bonitão	handsome, pretty	*bonitona*

Adjectives ending in a consonant tend to have the same form for the masculine and the feminine.

Masculine		Feminine
capaz	capable	*capaz*
comum	common	*comum*
formidável	formidable	*formidável*
simples	simple	*simples*

Ela não é capaz de fazê-lo.	She is not able to do it.
A lição é muito simples.	The lesson is quite simple.

With adjectives of nationality, *-a* is usually added to the masculine form.

francês	French	*francesa*
português	Portuguese	*portuguesa*

Santo is used before names beginning with a vowel and before *Gral,* and *São* is used before most other names; *Santa* is used before feminine names.

Santo Antônio (Antônio)	Saint Anthony
o Santo Gral	the Holy Grail
São Paulo	Saint Paul
São Francisco	Saint Francis
Santa Bárbara	Saint Barbara

16. POSITION OF ADJECTIVES

Descriptive adjectives (which tend to distinguish people or things from others of the same type or class) and adjectives of nationality usually come after the noun they modify.

uma casa branca	a white house
uma piada (anedota) engraçada	a funny anecdote, a joke
um bairro residencial	a residential district, a suburb
romances contemporâneos	contemporary novels

Adjectives that indicate a characteristic quality of the type or class usually precede the noun.

o poderoso ditador	the powerful dictator
a melhor cidade	the best city

Limiting adjectives, such as demonstrative adjectives, possessive adjectives, numerals, and adjectives of quantity, usually precede the noun they modify.

este conselho	this advice
nossa conversa	our conversation
a primeira decisão	the first decision
dez dedos	ten fingers
muitas lutas	many struggles

Some adjectives have a different meaning according to their position. After the noun modified, they have their literal (usual) meaning, and before the noun, they have a figurative (extended) meaning.

um homem pobre	a poor (financially) man
um pobre homem	a poor (to be pitied) man
presentes caros	expensive gifts
meu caro amigo	my dear friend
a cidade toda	all the city
toda cidade	every city
um carro novo	a new car (a brand new one)
um novo carro	a new car (a different one)
uma grande cidade	a great city
uma cidade grande	a big city
meu amigo velho	my old (not young) friend
meu velho amigo	my old (long-standing) friend

17. COMPARISON
Regular comparison is formed with *mais* (more) or *menos* (less). The definite article produces the superlative (most or least).

fácil	easy
mais fácil	easier
menos fácil	less easy
o mais fácil	the easiest
o menos fácil	the least easy

There are some common irregulars.

bom	good	*melhor*	better, best
mau	bad	*pior*	worse, worst
ruim	bad	*pior*	worse, worst
muito	much	*mais*	more, most
pouco	little	*menos*	less, least

grande	big, large	*maior*	bigger, biggest
pequeno	small	*menor*	smaller, smallest
bem	well	*melhor*	better, best
mal	badly	*pior*	worse, worst

Este livro é bom mas o outro é melhor.	This book is good, but the other is better.

Que is used to mean "than."

O português não é mais fácil que o inglês.	Portuguese isn't easier than English.
Ele é mais inteligente do que parece.	He is more intelligent than he looks.

To give an equal comparison, *tão . . . quanto . . .* is used.

Tão fácil quanto . . .	As easy as . . .
Ela fala português tão bem quanto ele.	She speaks Portuguese as well as he does.

With equal comparisons of nouns, *tanto* agrees for gender and number.

Este teatro não tem tantas entradas quanto aquele.	This theater does not have as many entrances as that one.

Before numerals, *mais de* and *menos* de are used.

Eles têm mais de duzentas vacas.	They have more than two hundred cows.

An adjective may be qualified in degree with a modifying word.

Ela está cansada.	She is tired.
Ela está muito cansada.	She is very tired.

The meaning "very" is also given by adding the proper form of *-íssimo* to a word (this cannot always be done).

Ela está cansadíssima.	She is very tired.
Estamos cansadíssimos.	We are very tired.

18. PRONOUNS

Pronouns have varying forms depending on whether they are the subject of a verb, used after a preposition, the object of a verb, used as indirect objects, used with reflexive verbs, or used to join parts of a sentence (relative pronouns).

SUBJECT PRONOUNS
Singular

eu	I
(tu)	(you) *(familiar)* (used in Portugal)
ele	he
ela	she
o senhor	you *(masc., polite)*
a senhora	you *(fem., polite)*
você	you *(friendly)*

Plural

nós	we
(vós)	(you) (rarely used)
eles	they *(masc.)*

elas	they *(fem.)*
os senhores	you *(masc., polite)*
as senhoras	you *(fem., polite)*
vocês	you *(friendly)*

Pronouns Used after Prepositions

para mim	for me
(para ti)	(for you) *(familiar)* (Portugal)
para ele	for him
para ela	for her
para o senhor	for you *(masc., polite)*
para a senhora	for you *(fem., polite)*
para você	for you *(friendly)*
para nós	for us
(para vós)	(for you) (rarely used)
para eles	for them *(masc.)*
para elas	for them *(fem.)*
para os senhores	for you *(masc., polite)*
para as senhoras	for you *(fem., polite)*
para vocês	for you *(friendly)*

Notice that the form of the pronoun used after a preposition is the same as the form of the pronoun used as a subject, except for *mim* (me) and *ti* (you, *familiar*).

There are special forms for "with me," *comigo,* "with us," *conosco,* "with you" *(familiar), contigo,* and "with you," "with him," "with her," etc., *consigo,* although the last form is not used as frequently as *com o senhor, com ele,* etc.

Direct Object Pronouns

me	me
te	you *(familiar)* (Portugal)

o	him
a	her
o	you *(masc., polite)*
a	you *(fem., polite)*
nos	us
(vos)	(you) (rarely used)
os	them *(masc.)*
as	them *(fem.)*
os	you *(masc., polite)*
as	you *(fem., polite)*

Indirect Object Pronouns

me	to me
te	to you *(familiar)* *(Portugal)*
lhe	to him, to her, to you *(polite)*
nos	to us
(vos)	(to you) (rarely used)
lhes	to them *(masc.* and *fem.)*, to you *(polite)*

Note that the subject pronouns *nós* and *vós* and the forms used after prepositions have the accent mark, but the corresponding direct and indirect object pronouns do not have the accent mark and are pronounced differently.

Since *lhe* and *lhes* can have several meanings, a prepositional form can be used for clarity.

Eu lhe mandei uma carta.	I sent him (her, you) a letter.
Eu mandei a ela uma carta.	I sent her a letter.

Reflexive Pronouns
These pronouns are used with reflexive verbs to indicate an action the subject performs on itself.

me	myself
te	yourself *(familiar)* (Portugal)
se	himself, herself, yourself *(polite)*
nos	ourselves
(vos)	yourselves (rarely used)
se	themselves, yourselves *(polite)*

Relative Pronouns
These pronouns are used more in Portuguese than in English because they are normally required, even in cases where English usage is optional. *Que* is by far the most common form used for "that," "which," and even "who" and "whom," although *quem* may be used for the last two with a preposition. Both of these forms are invariable, not changing for gender or number.

Ela disse que viria mais tarde.	She said (that) she would come later.
Ele não é o homem que falou comigo ontem.	He is not the man who spoke to me yesterday.
Isto é para quem eu gosto.	This is for (the person) whom I like.

19. POSITION OF PRONOUNS
The position of object pronouns is not fixed, and variations will be noted in different areas. The following rules are given as a general guide.

Object pronouns usually follow the verb and are attached to the verb with a hyphen in commands, with a present participle, and to avoid beginning a sentence with an object pronoun.

Prometa-me isso.	Promise me that.
oferecendo-nos mais	offering us more
Abracei-o.	I embraced him.

In popular speech, Brazilians put the pronoun before the verb in these cases.

Me deu o livro.	He gave me the book.
Me faz um favor.	Do me a favor.

Object pronouns may come before or after the verb if the sentence begins with a pronoun or noun subject and with infinitives.

Ele me perdoou.	He pardoned me.
Ele perdoou-me.	He pardoned me.
Ela veio para me dizer a verdade.	She came to tell me the truth.
Ela veio para dizer-me a verdade.	She came to tell me the truth.

In these cases, speakers of Brazilian Portuguese tend to prefer the position before the verb, and speakers in Portugal tend to prefer the position after the verb.

Remember that if the direct object pronouns *o, a, os,* or *as* follow an infinitive or a verb form ending in -*s* or -*z*, the -*r* of the infinitive is dropped, and the letter *l* is added to the object pronoun *(lo, la, los,* or *las).* The -*ar* and -*er* verbs take a written accent (*á* and *ê,* respectively) and -*uir* verbs end in -*í.* This is not the case with -*guir* verbs.

Vou comprá-lo.	I'm going to buy it.
Precisamos vê-los.	We must see them.
Quero abri-lo.	I want to open it.
Vou construí-la.	I will build it.

In negative sentences and negative commands, the object pronouns precede the verb; in most other cases, they tend to come before the verb.

Não o traduzimos.	We did not translate it.
Não me escreva mais.	Don't write me anymore.
Eles decidiram que nos mandariam o dinheiro.	They decided that they would send us the money.
Onde o vimos?	Where did we see him?

In Portugal, if two object pronouns, one direct and the other indirect, are used as objects of the same verb, the indirect comes before the direct object. This would cause the following contractions. These contractions are rarely used in Brazil.

me + o, a, os, as	*mo, ma, mos, mas*
te + o, a, os, as	*to, ta, tos, tas*
lhe + o, a, os, as	*lho, lha, lhos, lhas*
nos + o, a, os, as	*no-lo, no-la, no-los, no-las*
vos + o, a, os, as	*vo-lo, vo-la, vo-los, vo-las*
lhes + o, a, os, as	*lho, lha, lhos, lhas*

Contractions can be avoided by using the prepositional form for the indirect object or by sometimes omitting the direct object pronoun, especially in conversation in Brazil.

Eu lho dei.	I gave it to him.
Eu o dei a ele.	I gave it to him.
Eu lhe dei.	I gave (it) to him.
Eu dei a ele.	I gave (it) to him.

If a direct object pronoun comes after a verb form ending in -*r*, -*s*, or -*z*, the last letter is dropped and *l*- is prefixed to the direct object form.

| *Ele fê-lo.* | He did it. (The verb is *fez* from *fazer.*) |
| *Ela vai comprá-los.* | She is going to buy them. (The verb is *comprar,* and the pronoun is *os.*) |

In conversation, these combinations, except after an infinitive, are avoided.

| *Ele o fez.* | He did it. |

If a direct object pronoun comes after a verb form that ends in a nasal sound (a vowel plus *m*), *n-* is prefixed to the object pronoun.

| *Eles abandonaram-no.* | They abandoned him. |
| *Ela põe-na.* | She puts it on. |

These combinations are also avoided in conversation by placing the pronoun before the verb.

| *Eles o abandonaram.* | They abandoned him. |
| *Ela a põe.* | She puts it on. |

20. CONJUNCTIONS

Some common conjunctions are *e* (and), *mas* (but), *ou* (or), and *porque* (because).

Ele é alto e magro.	He is tall and thin.
Quero ir mas não posso.	I want to go, but I can't.
mais ou menos	more or less
cinco ou seis reais	five or six reals
Gosto dele porque é muito simpático.	I like him because he is very nice.

Other conjunctions are:

ainda que	although
assim que	as soon as
até que	until
como	as, since
conforme	as
de maneira que	so, so that
depois que	after
embora	although
logo que	as soon as
para que	so that, in order that
quando	when
se	if
segundo	as, according to
a menos que	unless

21. QUESTION WORDS
What?

When alone, or in an emphatic position, as at the end of a sentence, these forms have an accent mark.

Quê?/O quê?/Que é que . . . ?	What?
Que disse ele?/Que é que ele disse?	What did he say?

Why?

Por quê?	Why?
Por que ela não chegou antes das nove?	Why didn't she arrive before nine?

How?

Como?	How?
Como se diz em português?	How do you say (it) in Portuguese?

How much?/How many?

Quanto?/Quanta?	How much?
Quanto dinheiro temos?	How much money do we have?
Quantas irmãs João tem?	How many sisters does João have?

Which?/What?

Qual?/Quais?	Which?/What?
Qual é o seu?	Which one is yours?
Quais são os seus?	Which ones are yours?

Who?

Quem?	Who?
Quem veio com ela?	Who came with her?

Where?

Onde?	Where?
Onde estão os livros?	Where are the books?

When?

Quando?	When?
Quando aconteceu?	When did it happen?

22. ADVERBS

Some Portuguese adverbs are formed by adding *-mente* (-ly) to the feminine singular form of the adjective.

exclusivamente	exclusively

If there are two or more adverbs with this same ending, *-mente* is given only with the last one.

clara e concisamente	clearly and concisely

If the word has a written accent, the accent is dropped after adding *-mente*.

só—somente	only
fácil—facilmente	easily
último—ultimamente	lately

Adverbs are generally compared like adjectives, with *mais* (more) or *menos* (less).

Positive	*claramente*	clearly
Comparative	*mais claramente*	more clearly
Superlative	*o mais claramente*	the most clearly

There are some common irregular comparative adverbs.

bem	well	*melhor*	better, best
mal	badly	*pior*	worse, worst
muito	much	*mais*	more, most
pouco	little	*menos*	less, least

Many adverbs become prepositions when *de* is added.

| *depois* | afterward(s) | *depois de* | after (something) |
| *antes* | formerly | *antes de* | before (something) |

Other words that act similarly: *atrás* (behind), *debaixo* (under), *longe* (far), *mais* (more), *menos* (less), *perto* (near).

When *que* is added to some of these, they act as conjunctions.

Depois que eles chegarem falaremos. After they arrive, we'll talk.

ADVERBS OF TIME

hoje	today
ontem	yesterday
amanhã	tomorrow
cedo	early
tarde	late
muitas vezes, freqüentemente (*frequentemente*)	often
sempre	always
nunca	never
depois	afterward
antes	before, formerly
depressa	quickly
devagar	slowly
imediatamente	immediately
raramente	seldom, rarely
agora	now

ADVERBS OF PLACE

aqui	here
cá	here (motion)
aí	there
ali	there (farther away)

lá (acolá)	there (more remote)
adiante	forward, ahead
atrás	behind
dentro	inside
fora	outside
debaixo (x = sh)	below, down
perto	near
longe	far
abaixo (x = sh)	below, under
acima	above

ADVERBS OF QUANTITY OR INTENSITY

muito	very, much
pouco	little
mais	more
menos	less
quanto	how much
tão	so
tanto	so much
demais, muito	too much
só, somente	only
apenas	only, hardly
quase	almost
bastante	enough

ADVERBS EXPRESSING AFFIRMATION

sim	yes
também	also
verdadeiramente	truly
certamente	truly, certainly
claro	certainly, of course
Pois não!	Certainly!/ Of course!

ADVERBS EXPRESSING NEGATION

não	no, not
nunca	never
já não	no longer, not now
ainda não	not yet
nem	nor
nem . . . nem	neither . . . nor

"Here" and "there" are expressed in a few different ways. *Aqui* (here) refers to something near the speaker, and *aí* (there) refers to something near the person spoken to. *Cá* (here) expresses motion toward the speaker, and *ali* (there) refers to something away from the speaker and from the person spoken to. *Lá (acolá)* (there) refers to something more remote.

23. DIMINUTIVES AND AUGMENTATIVES

Certain endings, such as *-inho, -ote, -ete,* and *-ilho,* imply smallness, daintiness, or even affection.

um pouco	a little
um pouquinho	a little bit
gato	cat
gatinha	kitten *(fem.)*
sabão	soap
sabonete	a bar of soap
velho	old man
velhinho	little old man
avô	grandfather
avozinho	(dear) grandfather
avó	grandmother
avozinha	(dear) grandmother
cedo	soon
cedinho	quite soon

Circumflex and acute accents are dropped because there is also a shift in stress.

pé–pezinho	little feet
café–cafezinho	demitasse (small cup of coffee)
árvore–arvorezinha	little tree
prêmio (prémio)–premiozinho	little prize

Other endings, such as *-ão, -arrão,* and *-aço,* indicate large size, but they can also be uncomplimentary, indicating clumsiness, etc.

gato	cat	*gatão*	big cat
homem	man	*homenzarrão*	very large man
casa	house	*casarão*	large house, mansion
drama	drama, play	*dramalhão*	melodrama
mulher	woman	*mulheraça*	big woman
mulher	woman	*mulherona*	big woman

Although you should notice the difference in meaning given by these endings, you should be careful in using them and be sure that you know the form and meaning before employing words with these endings.

24. DEMONSTRATIVES
DEMONSTRATIVE ADJECTIVES

Masculine	Feminine	
este	*esta*	this
esse	*essa*	that
aquele	*aquela*	that (farther removed)
estes	*estas*	these
esses	*essas*	those
aqueles	*aquelas*	those (farther removed)

Portuguese demonstrative adjectives usually precede the nouns they modify and agree with them in gender and number.

este menino	this boy
aqueles vizinhos	those neighbors

Esse and *aquele* both mean "that." *Esse* refers to something near or related to the person spoken to; *aquele* refers to something more remote.

Não gosto desse livro.	I don't like that book (near you or mentioned by you).
É aquele senhor que chegou ontem.	He's that gentleman who arrived yesterday.

DEMONSTRATIVE PRONOUNS

The same forms are also used as demonstrative pronouns.

Não quero este sem aquele.	I don't want this one without that one.

Este and *aquele* also mean "the latter" and "the former."

Acabam de chegar o embaixador (x = sh) e (o) seu secretário; este é jovem e aquele é velho.	The ambassador and his secretary just arrived; the former is old and the latter is young.

Notice that the order in Portuguese is the opposite of the usual English order: *este . . . aquele* ("the latter . . . the former").

There are also some neuter forms.

isto	this, this (one)
isso	that, that (one) (near person spoken to, or mentioned by that person)
aquilo	that, that (one) (farther removed)

The neuter forms are more general, referring to an idea or statement, or to an object or several items in a general way, more as "this" than "this one" or "these."

Isto é melhor que (or do que) aquilo. This is better than that.

Demonstratives form contractions with the prepositions *a* (to), *de* (of), and *em* (in).

àquele	*àqueles*	*àquela*	*àquelas*	*àquilo*
deste	*destes*	*desta*	*destas*	*disto*
desse	*desses*	*dessa*	*dessas*	*disso*
daquele	*daqueles*	*daquela*	*daquelas*	*daquilo*
neste	*nestes*	*nesta*	*nestas*	*nisto*
nesse	*nesses*	*nessa*	*nessas*	*nisso*
naquele	*naqueles*	*naquela*	*naquelas*	*naquilo*

25. INDEFINITE ADJECTIVES AND PRONOUNS

todos	all
tal (tais, pl.)	such (a)
outro	another, other
alguém	somebody, someone
ninguém	nobody, no one
alguma coisa	something
nenhum	no one, none
algum	some
vários	several, some
nada	nothing
cada	each, every
tudo	all, everything
tanto	as much
certo	certain, a certain

mais	more
menos	less
qualquer	any, whatever, whoever
os demais	the rest

The adjectives above generally vary in form to agree with the word modified; *tal (tais)*, *alguém*, *ninguém*, *nada*, *cada*, *tudo*, *mais*, and *menos* are invariable.

26. NEGATION
Não (not) comes before the verb.

Não falo italiano.	I don't speak Italian.

There are two forms for "nothing," "never," "nobody," etc.—one with *não*, which is used more frequently, and one without *não*, which is less common.

Não vejo nada.	I don't see anything.
Não vou nunca.	I never go.
Não vem ninguém.	Nobody is coming./No one comes.

Nada vejo.	I don't see anything.
Nunca vou.	I never go.
Ninguém vem.	Nobody is coming./No one comes.

27. WORD ORDER
The usual order tends to be subject-verb-adverb-object.

João comprou lá os livros de português.	John bought the Portuguese books there.

The tendency in Portuguese is to put the longer element of the sentence (or the emphasized part, at times) last.

| *João viu os seus amigos no restaurante espanhol que é na esquina.* | John saw his friends in the Spanish restaurant that is on the corner. |

To ask a question, the same word order as for a statement can be used. This is the more common form in conversation.

| *João comprou lá os livros de português?* | Did John buy his Portuguese books there? |

A change of intonation indicates the difference between a statement and a question. A question can also be formed by adding *É que . . .* (lit., Is it [the case] that . . .) in front of a statement.

Adjectives come right after forms of the verb *ser.*

É tarde?	Is it late?
É bom?	Is it good?
A lição é fácil?	Is the lesson easy?

28. VERB TENSES

Portuguese verbs are organized in three classes or conjugations according to their infinitival endings:

-ar:	*falar* (to speak)
-er:	*aprender* (to learn)
-ir:	*partir* (to leave)

In the present tense, regular verbs have the following endings added to the stem of the verb (the infinitive minus the *-ar/-er/-ir* ending). The *tu* forms are used primarily in Portugal, and the *vos* forms are used very rarely.

	-ar	*-er*	*-ir*
eu	*-o*	*-o*	*-o*

(tu)	(-as)	(-es)	(-es)
ele, ela, você, o senhor, a senhora	-a	-e	-e
nós	-amos	-emos	-imos
(vós)	(-ais)	(-eis)	(-is)
vocês, os senhores, as senhoras	-am	-em	-em

falar (to speak)	aprender (to learn)	partir (to leave)
falo	aprendo	parto
(falas)	(aprendes)	(partes)
fala	aprende	parte
falamos	aprendemos	partimos
(falais)	(aprendeis)	(partis)
falam	aprendem	partem

The present can be translated in several ways.

Falo português. I speak Portuguese.
I am speaking Portuguese.
I do speak Portuguese.

In the imperfect tense, regular verbs have the following endings added to the stem of the verb.

-ar	-er and -ir
-ava	-ia
(-avas)	(-ias)
-ava	-ia
-ávamos	-íamos
(-áveis)	(-íeis)
-avam	-iam

The imperfect is used to indicate continued or customary action or physical, mental, or emotional states in the past. It is also used to describe past conditions such as weather, time, and age.

Quando eu era estudante, morava aqui.	When I was a student, I used to live here.
Ele não estava em casa.	He was not at home.
Ele sempre me telefonava.	He always used to call me.
Fazia muito calor.	It was very hot.
Eram cinco e meia da manhã.	It was 5:30 A.M.

The imperfect also indicates an action in progress at the time of another past action, or two actions in progress simultaneously.

Eu dormia quando você telefonou.	I was sleeping when you called me.
Eu dormia enquanto ele falava ao telefone.	I was sleeping while he was talking on the phone.

In spoken language, the imperfect can also be used in place of the conditional (expressed in English by "would").

Eu queria ficar aqui, mas ela disse que ia embora.	I'd like to stay here, but she said she'd go.
Eu podia ir com ele.	I'd be able to go with him.

There are four verbs in Portuguese that are irregular in the imperfect.

pôr (to put)

punha	*púnhamos*
(punhas)	*(púnheis)*
punha	*punham*

ser (to be)

era	*éramos*
(eras)	*(éreis)*
era	*eram*

ter (to have)

tinha	*tínhamos*
(tinhas)	*(tínheis)*
tinha	*tinham*

vir (to come)

vinha	*vínhamos*
(vinhas)	*(vínheis)*
vinha	*vinham*

The future of regular verbs is formed by adding the endings *-ei, (-ás), -á, -emos, (-eis)*, and *-ão* to the infinitive.

falar (to speak)	*aprender* (to learn)	*partir* (to leave)
falarei	*aprenderei*	*partirei*
(falarás)	*(aprenderás)*	*(partirás)*
falará	*apprenderá*	*partirá*
falaremos	*aprenderemos*	*partiremos*
(falareis)	*(aprendereis)*	*(partireis)*
falarão	*aprenderão*	*partirão*

There are three verbs that are irregular in the future.

dizer (to say)

direi	*diremos*
(dirás)	*(direis)*
dirá	*dirão*

fazer (to do)

farei	*faremos*
(farás)	*(fareis)*
fará	*farão*

trazer (to bring)

trarei	*traremos*
(trarás)	*(trareis)*
trará	*trarão*

The future generally expresses a future action, but it may also express conjecture or probability in the present.

Chegarei às nove.	I'll arrive at nine.
Que horas serão?	What time can it be?
Serão sete horas?	Is it seven o'clock?
Ele provavelmente estará em casa.	He's probably at home.

The preterite (also called simple past tense) of regular verbs is formed by adding the following endings to the stem of the verb.

-ar	-er	-ir
-ei	*-i*	*-i*
(-aste)	*(-este)*	*(-iste)*
-ou	*-eu*	*-iu*

-amos (-ámos)	-emos	-imos
(-astes)	(-estes)	(-istes)
-aram	-eram	-iram

Note that the first person plural of regular verbs has the same form in the present and in the preterite. In Portugal, there is an accent in the preterite *(-ámos)* to differentiate it from the present tense. Brazilians do not make this distinction.

Nós estudamos muito.   We study a lot (today).
Nós estudamos (estudámos)   We studied yesterday.
ontem.

For phonetic reasons, there are a few spelling changes in the first person singular of some verbs. Verbs ending in *-car* change the *c* to *qu* before the ending *-ei*.

explicar (to explain)   *eu expliquei* (I explained)
praticar (to practice)   *eu pratiquei* (I practiced)

Verbs ending in *-çar* change the *ç* to *c* before the ending *-ei*.

dançar (to dance)   *eu dancei* (I danced)
almoçar (to have lunch) *eu almocei* (I had lunch)

Verbs ending in *-gar* change the *g* to *gu* before the ending *-ei*.

pagar (to pay)   *eu paguei* (I paid)
chegar (to arrive) *eu cheguei* (I arrived)

The preterite expresses an action completed in the past, with emphasis on the fact rather than on the duration, repetition, or description.

Carlos falou comigo ontem.	Charles spoke to me yesterday.
Ele me disse (disse-me) tudo.	He told me everything.
Fomos ao cinema.	We went to the movies.
Ela nos viu (viu-nos).	She saw us.
Escrevi uma carta.	I wrote a letter.
Choveu todo o dia.	It rained all day.
Ficaram lá dois meses.	They stayed there two months.

It is important to note that the simple past (preterite) in Portuguese is the tense that indicates the same idea expressed by the present perfect in English. Sometimes the verb is preceded by the adverb *já* (already).

Você já comeu?	Have you eaten?
Ele já saiu.	He has already left.
Eles me disseram isto.	They have told me this.
Você leu este livro?	Have you read this book?
Ele vendeu muitos livros.	He has sold many books.
Onde você foi?	Where have you gone?

The perfect tenses are formed with the simple tenses of *ter* (to have), or *haver* in literary style, and the past participle of the main verb. Most perfect tenses in English correspond to the perfect tenses in Portuguese; however, there are some differences.

The present perfect in Portuguese often expresses a situation that requires the progressive form of the present perfect in English.

Nós temos estudado português.	We have been studying Portuguese.
O que é que você tem feito?	What have you been doing?
Não tenho ido ao parque ultimamente.	I haven't been going to the park lately.

Remember that the English present perfect is translated as the simple past (preterite) in Portuguese.

I have studied Portuguese.	*Eu estudei português.*
I have already been to Brazil.	*Eu já fui ao Brasil.*

The pluperfect, or past perfect, is formed with the imperfect of *ter* or *haver* and the past participle of the main verb. It is used as in English and implies an action that took place prior to the main action of the statement. It translates into English as "had" plus a past participle.

Quando eu cheguei, ele já tinha partido.	When I arrived, he had already left.
Esqueci que você tinha comprado o presente.	I forgot that you had bought the gift.

The future perfect is formed with the future of *ter* (rarely *haver*) and the past participle of the main verb. It is used to express a future action that will take place before another future action. Sometimes it indicates probability.

Quando eu chegar, ele já terá partido.	When I arrive, he will already have left.
Eles já terão chegado.	They probably have already arrived.

29. THE SUBJUNCTIVE
The tenses given in the preceding section are called tenses of the indicative mood. There is another set of tenses for the subjunctive mood. The subjunctive mood expresses, among other things, hypothetical states or actions, feelings, commands, suggestions, or wishes. The subjunctive is used in a dependent clause introduced by a conjunction, most frequently *que* (except in sentences with *talvez* and in indirect commands). In Portuguese, there are present, imperfect, and future forms of the subjunctive, as well as compound forms.

The present subjunctive is formed by removing the final *-o* of the first person singular of the present indicative (*eu* form) and then adding the endings *-e, (-es), -e, -emos, (-eis), -em* to *-ar* verbs, and *-a, (as), -a, -amos, (-ais), -am* to *-er* and *-ir* verbs.

falar (to speak)—present indicative: *eu falo*

que eu fale	*que nós falemos*
(que tu fales)	*(que vos faleis)*
que você, ele, ela fale	*que vocês, eles, elas falem*

ter (to have)—*eu tenho*	Pres. Subj.: *tenha, tenhamos, tenham*
vir (to come)—*eu venho*	Pres. Subj.: *venha, venhamos, venham*
pôr (to put)—*eu ponho*	Pres. Subj.: *ponha, ponhamos, ponham*

There are seven verbs that have irregular forms and do not follow the above rule.

ser (to be)	*seja, sejamos, sejam*
estar (to be)	*esteja, estejamos, estejam*
haver (to have)	*haja, hajamos, hajam*
ir (to go)	*vá, vamos, vão*
dar (to give)	*dê, demos, dêem*
saber (to know)	*saiba, saibamos, saibam*
querer (to want)	*queira, queiramos, queiram*

The present subjunctive is used after any verb or phrase that expresses the imposition of desire, request, permission, approval, disapproval, etc., of one person (or people) on another (or others). Some of these verbs of volition are *querer* (to want), *proibir* (to forbid), *aconselhar* (to advise), *esperar* (to hope), *permitir* (to permit, to allow), *insistir* (to insist), *exigir* (to require), *desejar* (to wish), *pedir* (to ask, to demand), *preferir* (to prefer), and *sugerir* (to suggest). Note that, at times, the subjunctive is used in Portuguese when an infinitive is used in English.

Eu quero que ele venha cedo.	I want him to come early (lit., I want that he comes early).
Nós esperamos que eles façam isto.	We hope that they do this.
O que você quer que eu diga?	What do you want me to say?
Aconselho que você vá lá.	I advise you to go there.

The subjunctive is used after verbs or expressions of emotion (to be happy that . . . , to be sorry that . . . , etc.).

Sinto muito que ela não possa vir.	I am very sorry that she can't come.
Estou contente que ela venha.	I am happy that she is coming.
Estou com medo que ela não venha.	I'm afraid she won't come.
Lamento que ela não venha.	I regret that she can't come.

The subjunctive is used after verbs or expressions of doubt or denial. It is also used after verbs in the negative that express an opinion or thought.

Duvido que eles estejam em casa.	I doubt they are at home.
Não acho que seja verdade.	I don't believe it is true.
Não é certo que ela venha.	It's not sure/definite that she will come.
Pode ser que ela queira.	Maybe (It can be that) she wants it.

Note that the adverb *talvez* (perhaps) expresses possibility or doubt, so it requires the subjunctive, but *que* (that) is not used.

| *Talvez eles não o conheçam.* | Perhaps they don't know him. |
| *Talvez ela vá ao Brasil o ano que vem.* | Perhaps she will go to Brazil next year. |

However, if the verb in the main clause expresses certainty, the indicative is used instead of the subjunctive.

| *Estou certo que ela tem o dinheiro.* | I'm sure that she has the money. |
| *Eu acho que é verdade.* | I believe it is true. |

The subjunctive is used after most impersonal expressions (except those that express certainty).

É pouco provável que ele o faça.	It's hardly probable that he will do it.
É importante que tragamos dinheiro.	It's important that we bring money.
É melhor que ela não fume.	It's better that she not smoke.
É necessário que você me ajude.	It's necessary that you help me.
É preferível que ele não fume.	It's preferable that he not smoke.

If the statement is general and there is no specific need to use a subject for the second verb, the infinitive can be used by eliminating the conjunction *que*.

É possível fazê-lo.	It's possible to do it.
É preciso chegar cedo.	It's necessary to arrive early.
É necessário ajudar o professor.	It's necessary to help the teacher.
É melhor não fumar aqui.	It's better not to smoke here.

The subjunctive is used in indirect commands.

Não digamos mais nada.	Let's not say another word.
Deixe que eles venham cedo.	Let them come early.
Deixe que ele vá!	Let him go!
Deixe que ele pague a conta.	Let him pay the bill.
Comamos!	Let's eat.
Vejamos . . .	Let's see . . .
Vamos!	Let's go!

The subjunctive is also used when the antecedent of the word *que* is not known. Words such as *alguém, ninguém, nenhum, um,* etc., imply indefinite things, and because there is doubt, the subjunctive is needed.

Não conheço nenhum hotel que seja mais barato.	I don't know any hotel that is cheaper.
Há alguém aqui que possa me ajudar?	Is there anyone here who could help me?
Quero um livro que me explique isto.	I want a book that will explain this to me.

But if the subject is something definite, the indicative is used.

Conheço um hotel barato.	I know a cheap hotel.
Aquele moço pode lhe ajudar.	That young man can help you.
Este livro explica bem isto.	This book explains this well.

The subjunctive is always used following adverbial conjunctions of concession, time, condition, or purpose.

embora . . .	although . . .
se bem que . . .	although, even if . . .
ainda que . . .	although, even if . . .
nem que . . .	even if . . .
mesmo que . . .	even if . . .
antes que . . .	before . . .
até que . . .	until . . .
sem que . . .	without . . .
a menos que . . .	unless . . .
para que . . .	in order to
a fim de que . . .	in order to . . .
de maneira que . . .	so that . . .

Embora não tenha dinheiro, irei.	Although I don't have any money, I'll go.

Mesmo que faça frio, nós iremos.	Even if it's cold, we'll go.
Vou comprar um antes que vendam todos.	I'm going to buy one before they sell them all.
Para que aprendamos bem, temos que praticar.	In order for us to learn (it) well, we have to practice (it).
Vamos ficar aqui até que eles retornem.	We are going to stay here until they come back.

In the imperfect subjunctive, there is just one set of endings for all the conjugations. The stem is obtained by removing the letters *-ram* from the third person plural of the preterite and by adding the endings *-sse, (-sses), -sse, -ssemos, (-sseis), -ssem.*

falar (to speak)—preterite: *eles falaram*

que eu falasse	*que nós falássemos*
(que tu falasses)	*(que vos falásseis)*
que você, ele, ela falasse	*que vocês, eles, elas falassem*

ter (to have)—*eles tiveram*	*tivesse, tivéssemos, tivessem*
vir (to come)—*eles vieram*	*viesse, viéssemos, viessem*
pôr (to put)—*eles puseram*	*pusesse, puséssemos, pusessem*

The imperfect subjunctive is used in the dependent clause instead of the present or future subjunctive if the verb of the main clause is in a past tense or in the conditional. Because the circumstances still denote a hypothetical state of affairs, its use is basically a matter of sequence of tenses.

Eu queria que ela ficasse.	I wanted her to stay (lit., I wanted that she stayed).
Embora estudasse muito, aprendi pouco.	Although I studied a lot, I learned little.
Talvez ele fosse lá ontem.	Perhaps he went there yesterday.

Eu compraria esta casa se tivesse dinheiro.	I would buy this house if I had money.
Se eu fosse você, não iria.	If I were you, I wouldn't go.

In the future subjunctive, there is just one set of endings for all the conjugations. The form is also derived by removing the letters *-ram* from the third person plural of the preterite and by adding the endings *-r, (-res), -r, -rmos, (-rdes), -rem.*

falar (to speak)—preterite: *eles falaram*

eu falar	*nós falarmos*
(tu falares)	*(vos falardes)*
você ele, ela falar	*vocês eles, elas falarem*

ter (to have)—*eles tiveram*	Fut. Subj.: *tiver, tivermos, tiverem*
vir (to come)—*eles vieram*	Fut. Subj.: *vier, viermos, vierem*
pôr (to put)—*eles puseram*	Fut. Subj.: *puser, pusermos, puserem*

The future subjunctive is a peculiarity of Portuguese. It is required in situations in which the uncertainty of future actions is implied. It is used when words that imply uncertainty, such as *se* (if), *quando* (when), *assim que* (as soon as), *logo que* (as soon as), and *depois que* (after), introduce a conditional clause. Note that these words refer primarily to a condition that "may" exist.

Eu vou (or *irei*) *se você quiser.*	I will go if you want me to.
Eu lhe pagarei (pagar-lhe-ei) quando puder.	I will pay when I can.
Eu lhe telefonarei (telefonar-lhe-ei) quando chegar em (à) casa.	I will call you up when I arrive at home.
Assim que tivermos dinheiro, viremos.	As soon as we have money, we will come.
Eu lhe mando (mando-lhe) o livro se ele me mandar o dinheiro.	I will send him the book if he sends me the money.

Depois que vocês acabarem de comer, venham para cá.	After you finish eating, come here.

The future subjunctive is also used with the "ever" expressions: whatever *(o que)*, whenever *(quando)*, whoever *(quem)*, and wherever *(onde)*.

Faça o que puder.	Do whatever you can.
Vá para onde quiser.	Go wherever you want.
Estude quando tiver tempo.	Study whenever you have time.

Finally, it is important to observe that the choice between the present and future subjunctive in the dependent clause does not depend exactly on the tense of the main clause. Rather, the choice depends on certain conditions, such as doubt, the use of impersonal expressions, and the use of specific expressions, such as *embora* (although), *talvez* (perhaps), etc. In these cases, the dependent clause requires the present subjunctive, even if the verb in the main clause is in the future, or even if the action referred to will take place in the future.

Será preciso que você fique.	It will be necessary for you to stay. (It will be necessary that you stay.)
Estou contente que ele não venha no próximo ano.	I am happy that he will not come next year.
Ele comprará o carro embora não tenha dinheiro.	He will buy the car although he doesn't have money.
Eu proibirei que você vá.	I will forbid you to go. (I will forbid that you go.)
Talvez ele faça isto no próximo ano.	Perhaps he will do this next year.

Likewise, the future subjunctive must be used following those words mentioned previously *(se, quando, assim/logo que, depois que)* whenever they refer to an uncertain action, even if the verb in the main clause is in the present tense.

Eu faço isto se tiver tempo.	I do this if I have time.
Eu dou o livro para ele quando puder.	I will give the book to him when I can.
Você pode vir comigo se tiver tempo.	You can come with me if you have time.
Compro se quiser.	I'll buy (it) if I want to.
Venha quando puder.	Come when you can.

After *quando* (when), *assim que/logo que* (as soon as), and *depois que* (after), the past subjunctive is used only if the verb in the main clause is the conditional tense. Remember that the statement must imply a hypothesis in order for the subjunctive to be used.

Eu lhe compraria (comprar-lhe-ia) o carro quando tivesse dinheiro.	I'd buy you the car if I had the money. (I didn't buy it.)
Ele não ficaria aqui depois que você chegasse.	He would not stay here after your arrival. (hypothesis)

However, if the verb in the main clause is the simple past, those words must be followed by a tense in the indicative mood because the clause expresses an accepted fact and no longer a hypothesis.

Eu comprei quando tinha dinheiro.	I bought (it) when I had money. (I did buy . . .)
Eu fui assim que pude.	I went as soon as I was able to. (I did go . . .)
Ele saiu depois que você chegou.	He left after you arrived. (fact)

30. SEQUENCE OF TENSES

If the main verb is in the present or future, the subjunctive, if required, will be in the present if its time is present or future.

Duvido que ele venha.	I doubt that he will come.
Duvido que elas estejam em casa.	I doubt that they are home.

The subjunctive will be in the imperfect if its time is past.

Duvido que ele viesse.   I doubt that he came.

If the main verb is in the past, the subjunctive, if required, will be in the imperfect if it reflects action at the same time or later; it will be in the pluperfect (past perfect subjunctive) if it indicates previous action.

Eu duvidava que ele viesse.   I doubted that he would come.
Eu duvidava que ele tivesse vindo. I doubted that he had come.

31. THE INFINITIVE

Portuguese has two types of infinitives: impersonal and personal. The impersonal infinitive is used in most cases calling for an infinitive. Practically all infinitives end in *-ar* (first conjugation): *falar* (to speak), *-er* (second conjugation): *comer* (to eat), or *-ir* (third conjugation): *partir* (to leave). There is just one verb that ends in *-or: pôr* (to put), and it is not considered to be one conjugation by itself but instead belongs to the second conjugation (*-er*). The same is true of compound verbs formed from it: *compôr* (to compose), *supôr* (to suppose), *impôr* (to impose), *opôr* (to oppose), etc.

Os alunos não querem estudar.   The students don't want to study.
Eles preferem ficar aqui.   They prefer to stay here.
Ele deve pagar a conta.   He must pay the bill.
Vou pôr o dinheiro aqui.   I'm going to put the money here.

The personal infinitive is a distinct feature of the Portuguese language. It is the infinitive that has a logical subject and endings as follows.

eu falar   *nós falarmos*
(tu falares)   *(vós falardes)*

você falar   *vocês falarem*
ele/ela falar   *eles/elas falarem*

The personal infinitive is usually used to avoid ambiguity or for clarity.

Vão jantar depois de chegar. (impersonal)	They're going to have dinner after (someone) arrives.
Vão jantar depois de eu chegar.	They're going to have dinner after I arrive.
Vão jantar depois de nós chegarmos.	They're going to have dinner after we arrive.
Eles partiram sem nós sabermos.	They left without our knowing

Mostly in the plural, the subject pronoun can be deleted because the verbal ending itself indicates the subject.

É preciso trabalhar para ganharmos dinheiro.	It's necessary for us to work to earn money.
Depois de estudarmos este livro, vamos saber falar português.	After studying this book, we will know how to speak Portuguese.

The personal infinitive in Portuguese is used quite frequently in conversation. In several instances, it can replace some uses of the subjunctive. For example, conjunctions that require the present (or imperfect) subjunctive have prepositional counterparts that can be used with the personal infinitives.

Conjunction + (present) subjunctive	Preposition + personal infinitive
sem que	*sem*
para que	*para*
até que	*para*

Ela pede para que nós fiquemos mais um pouco.	She is asking us to stay a little longer.

Ela pede para nós ficarmos mais um pouco.	She's asking us to stay a little longer.
Não vamos sair até que vocês digam a verdade.	We're not going to leave until you tell the truth.
Não vamos sair até vocês dizerem a verdade.	We're not going to leave until you tell (us) the truth.

Impersonal expressions that will require the present (or imperfect) subjunctive may also be used with impersonal infinitives if *que* is deleted.

É necessário que nós digamos e façamos isto.	It's necessary that we say and do this.
É necessário nós dizermos e fazermos isto.	It's necessary for us to say and do that.
Era preciso que vocês fossem lá e comprassem isto.	It was necessary that you go and do this.
Era preciso vocês irem lá e comprarem isto.	She needs you to go there and buy this.

In some instances, the personal infinitive can also replace the future subjunctive.

Depois que nós fizermos isto, vamos sair.	After we do this, we are going to leave.
Depois de nós fazermos isto, vamos sair.	After we do this, we are going to leave.

Note that with regular verbs, the future subjunctive and personal infinitive have the same forms.

Depois que nós falarmos com ele, vamos sair.	After we talk to him, we will leave.
Depois de nós falarmos com ele, vamos sair.	After we talk to him, we will leave.

É preciso que nós estudemos.	It's necessary for us to study.
É preciso nós estudarmos.	It's necessary for us to study.
Eu fui lá sem que ela soubesse.	I went there without her knowing it.
Eu fui lá sem ela saber.	I went there without her knowing it.
Vou ficar aqui até que eles cheguem.	I'm going to stay here until they arrive.
Vou ficar aqui até eles chegarem.	I'm going to stay here until they arrive.
Nós iremos ao parque depois que você fizer isto.	We will go to the park after you do this.
Nós iremos ao parque depois de você fazer isto.	We will go to the park after you do this.

32. THE CONDITIONAL

The present conditional is formed by adding the endings *-ia, -ias, -ia, -íamos, -íeis,* and *-iam* to the infinitives of all three conjugations.

-ar	*-er*	*-ir*
falar (to speak)	*aprender* (to learn)	*partir* (to leave)
falaria	*aprenderia*	*partiria*
(falarias)	*(aprenderias)*	*(partirias)*
falaria	*aprenderia*	*partiria*
falaríamos	*aprederíamos*	*partiríamos*
(falaríeis)	*(aprenderíeis)*	*(partiríeis)*
falariam	*aprenderiam*	*partiriam*

The verbs *dizer, fazer,* and *trazer* add these endings to a shortened stem: *diria, faria, traria,* etc.

The conditional is used to express the future from a past point, usually translated as "would" plus the meaning of the verb.

Ele me disse que chegaria às sete.	He told me that he would arrive at seven.

It also expresses probability or conjecture in the past.

Seriam oito horas, quando ele chegou.	It was probably eight o'clock when he arrived.
Que horas seriam quando ele chegou?	What time could it have been (I wonder what time it was) when he arrived?

It can also soften a statement.

Eu gostaria de vê-lo.	I would like to see him.

The perfect conditional is formed with the conditional of *ter* (*haver* is used sometimes) and the past participle of the main verb.

Ele me teria falado . . .	He would have spoken to me . . .
Elas não teriam ido . . .	They would not have gone . . .

33. CONDITIONAL SENTENCES

Conditional sentences have two parts, the conditional, or "if" clause, and the conclusion. A simple condition can be expressed with both verbs in the indicative. Sometimes the "if" clause is equivalent to "when" or "whenever."

Se estiver (está) chovendo não vamos.	If it is raining, we won't go.
Se ele entrou eu não o vi.	If he came in, I didn't see him.
Se ele chegava cedo vinha me ver.	If (whenever) he arrived early, he came to see me.

When the "if" clause expresses a simple condition (not a doubtful one) in the future, the future subjunctive is used in the "if" clause and the future indicative (or the present indicative) is used in the conclusion.

Se chover não iremos (vamos).   If it rains, we won't go.

When the "if" clause expresses a doubtful condition in the future, the imperfect subjunctive is used in the "if" clause and the conditional or the imperfect indicative is used in the conclusion. The imperfect indicative is usually preferred in conversation.

Se chovesse não iríamos (íamos).   If it were to rain, we would not go.

The same sequence is used to indicate a doubtful or contrary-to-fact situation in the present.

Se eu fosse rico viajaria (viajava)   If I were rich, I would travel every
todos os verões.   summer.

When the "if" clause expresses a condition contrary to fact in the past, the pluperfect (past perfect) subjunctive is used in the "if" clause and the conditional perfect (or the pluperfect indicative) is used in the conclusion. The pluperfect indicative is preferred in conversation.

Se tivesse chovido não teríamos   If it had rained, we would not have
(tínhamos) ido.   gone.

34. COMMANDS AND REQUESTS
English uses the imperative (command) form more often and in more instances than Portuguese. Remember that commands imply "you," in either the singular or the plural sense. There are two types of commands in Portuguese: formal and informal.

FORMAL COMMANDS

Practically all Portuguese commands, affirmative or negative, will be given with the third person singular and plural forms of the present subjunctive. Remove the final -o of the first person singular of the present indicative *(eu)* form, and add *e* and *-em* for *-ar* verbs, and *-a* and *-am* for *-er* and *-ir* verbs.

Infinitive	Present Indicative	Singular Imperative	Plural Imperative	English
falar	*eu falo*	*Fale!*	*Falem!*	Speak!
fazer	*eu faço*	*Faça!*	*Façam!*	Do!
vir	*eu venho*	*Venha!*	*Venham!*	Come!
pôr	*eu ponho*	*Ponha!*	*Ponham!*	Put!

The following verbs have irregular command forms. Note that *querer* (to want) is used to soften the imperative, meaning "please."

ser: seja, sejam	*Seja feliz!*	Be happy!
estar: esteja, estejam	*Estejam à vontade!*	Make yourself comfortable!
ir: vá, vão	*Não vá lá.*	Don't go there.
dar: dê, dêem	*Dê-me mais um.*	Give me one more.
saber: saiba, saibam	*Saiba o endereço dele.*	Know his address.
querer: queira, queiram	*Queiram sentar-se.*	Please sit down.
valer: valha, valham	*Valha-me.*	Protect me.

There are a few spelling changes in some verbs in order to maintain the original sound.

Verbs ending in *-car* change the *c* to *qu* before the ending *-e*.

explicar: Explique./Expliquem.   Explain.

Verbs ending in -*çar* change the *ç* to *c* before the ending -*e*.

dançar: Dance./Dancem.   Dance.

Verbs ending in -*gar* change the *g* to *gu* before the ending -*e*.

pagar: Pague./Paguem.   Pay.

Verbs ending in -*cer* change the *c* to *ç* before the ending -*a*.

esquecer: Esqueça./Esqueçam.   Forget.

Commands with reflexive verbs use the reflexive pronoun. When the pronoun follows the verb, it is attached to it with a hyphen.

Infinitive	Present Indicative	Singular Imperative	Plural Imperative	English
Sentar-se	*(eu me sento)*	*Sente-se!*	*Sentem-se!*	Sit down!
Vestir-se	*(eu me visto)*	*Vista-se!*	*Vistam-se!*	Get dressed!

But in the negative, the pronoun comes before the verb.

Não se corte.   Don't cut yourself.

Não se sente aqui.   Don't sit down here.

In commands with object pronouns, the object pronoun must follow the verb. However, whenever a vowel pronoun *(o, a, os,* or *as)* occurs after the plural command, *n* is added to it. But remember that with the negative command, the pronoun is placed without the *n* before the verb (because the verb is no longer the first element).

Mostre-lhes o quarto.   Show them the room.

Diga-me a verdade.   Tell me the truth.

Tragam-no.   Bring it.

Levem-nas.   Take them.

In Brazil, these forms are avoided in speech. It's more common to use the expressed object instead: *Tragam o livro. Levem as crianças ao parque.* (Bring the book. Take the children to the park.)

But in the negative, the pronoun comes before the verb.

Não o traga ao meu lar.	Don't bring him to my home.
Não o tragam.	Don't bring it.
Não lhes mostre.	Don't show them.

Here are some other examples of commands.

Escreva-o.	Write it.
Escute!	Listen!
Termine tudo.	Finish everything.
Não venha antes das cinco.	Don't come before five.
Não lhe diga isto.	Don't tell him/her this.
Dê-lhe o troco.	Give her/him the change.
Traga-nos um café.	Bring us a (cup of) coffee.
Peça-lhe para ficar.	Ask him to stay.
Deite-se cedo.	Go to bed early.

In informal, conversational style, the third person singular of the present indicative is used as the imperative. In this way, the "formal" command is more grammatically correct, whereas the indicative used as an imperative is preferred in Brazil as a kind of "soft" command. One will hear this form among Brazilians in almost all informal situations.

Fala com ele. (for *Fale . . .*)	Talk to him.
Vai lá. (for *Vá . . .*)	Go there.
Dá um café, por favor. (for *Dê . . .*)	Give (us, me) a coffee, please.
Fica quieto. (for *Fique . . .*)	Be quiet.

| *Não diz nada para ele.* (for *Não lhe diga nada.*) | Don't tell him anything. |
| *Faz o favor . . .* (for *Faça . . .*) | Do me a favor . . . |

Also in Brazil, the verb *querer* (or *poder*) followed by an infinitive is often used as an alternative to soften a request. *Poder* is more commonly used in Portugal than *querer*.

Você pode virar à esquerda, por favor?	Turn to the left, please?
Quer me dar um café, por favor?	Give me a (cup of) coffee, please?
Você pode esperar lá fora, por favor?	Wait outside, please?
Você quer repetir mais uma vez, por favor?	Repeat (it) once more, please?

It may be helpful to understand another common expression: *vê se você*. In informal conversation, for stronger emphasis, these words denote more the sense of a command than that of a request. The tone of voice in which the words are said will reveal them as a command without sounding like an order.

Vê se você chega cedo. (for *Chegue . . .*)	Make sure you get there early.
Vê se vocês não fazem barulho. (for *Não façam . . .*)	Don't make noise.
Vê se não gasta muito. (for *Não gaste . . .*)	Don't spend too much.
Vê se me deixa em paz. (for *Deixe-me . . .*)	Leave me alone.

35. PARTICIPLES
The present participle is formed by adding *-ndo* to the infinitive minus the final *-r.*

	-ar		-er		-ir	
falar	to speak	*aprender*	to learn	*partir*	to leave
falando	speaking	*aprendendo*	learning	*partindo*	leaving

If an object pronoun follows the present participle, the two are joined with a hyphen.

falando-nos	speaking to us
escrevendo-lhe	writing to him
vendo-o	seeing him

The present participle is used in the progressive tenses.

Vi-o na praia, dormindo.	I saw him sleeping on the beach.
Partindo (Ao partir), ele me deu seu cartão.	When leaving, he gave me his card.

This form is also used in "gerundization," which is an informal kind of speech, limited to relaxed, conversational contexts. In fact, it is considered incorrect and improper by many speakers of Portuguese.

The standard form:

(Te) Ligo mais tarde.	I will call you later.
Vou (te) ligar mais tarde.	I will call you later.
Conversamos amanhã.	We'll talk tomorrow.

The gerundicized form:

Vou estar (te) ligando mais tarde.	I am going to be calling you later.
Vamos estar conversando amanhã.	We are going to be talking tomorrow.

The past participle is formed by adding *-ado*, *-ido*, or *-ido* to the stems of verbs of the three conjugations.

	-ar		-er		-ir	
	falar	to speak	*aprender*	to learn	*partir*	to leave
	falado	spoken	*aprendido*	learned	*partido*	left

Some common verbs have irregular past participles.

Infinitive		Irregular Past Participle
abrir	to open	*aberto*
cobrir	to cover	*coberto*
dizer	to say	*dito*
escrever	to write	*escrito*
fazer	to do, to make	*feito*
pôr	to put	*posto*
ver	to see	*visto*
vir	to come	*vindo*

Some verbs have a regular participle and also a shortened form.

Infinitive		Regular	Irregular
aceitar	to accept	*aceitado*	*aceito, aceite*
entregar	to deliver, to give	*entregado*	*entregue*
ganhar	to earn, to gain	*ganhado*	*ganho*
gastar	to spend	*gastado*	*gasto*
pagar	to pay	*pagado*	*pago*
morrer	to die	*morrido*	*morto*

Although both forms are used, there is a tendency for the regular form to be favored as the past participle of the perfect tenses (with *haver*) and for the shortened form to be favored as an adjective.

Tínhamos aceitado todo o dinheiro.	We had accepted all the money.
O dinheiro não foi aceito.	The money was not accepted.

36. PROGRESSIVE TENSES

The Portuguese progressive tenses are formed with the present participle and the tenses of *estar* (although other verbs, such as *ir*, may also be used as the auxiliary verb).

Estou estudando.	I am studying.
Quando eles entraram na sala nós estávamos lendo o jornal.	When they entered the room, we were reading the newspaper.
Elas estão divertindo-se.	They are having a good time.
Eles iam cantando.	They were singing. ("They went on singing.")

In Portugal, *estar a* plus the infinitive is also used: *Estou a estudar.* (I am studying.)

37. THE PASSIVE VOICE

The passive voice is formed with *ser* and the past participle.

O Brasil foi descoberto pelos portuguesesem 1500 (mil e quinhentos).	Brazil was discovered by the Portuguese in 1500.

The passive voice is used the same way as in English. Very often, however, Portuguese uses *se* to express the passive.

Descobriu-se o Brasil em 1500.	Brazil was discovered in 1500.

38. TO BE

Ser and *estar* both mean "to be" in Portuguese. In general, *ser* indicates a characteristic or permanent state, and *estar* indicates a temporary condition or state. However, one should note the different uses of these verbs.

ser	estar	
eu sou	*eu estou*	I am
(tu és)	*(tu estás)*	you are *(familiar)*
o senhor é	*o senhor está*	you are *(masc.)*
a senhora é	*a senhora está*	you are *(fem.)*
você é	*você está*	you are
ele é	*ele está*	he is
ela é	*ela está*	she is
nós somos	*nós estamos*	we are
(vós sois)	*(vós estais)*	(you are)
os senhores são	*os senhores estão*	you are
as senhoras são	*as senhoras estão*	you are
vocês são	*vocês estão*	you are
eles são	*eles estão*	they are
elas são	*elas estão*	they are

Ser indicates a characteristic or inherent quality.

Meu irmão é alto.	My brother is tall.
O livro é vermelho.	The book is red.
Ela é jovem.	She is young.
O gelo é frio.	Ice is cold.
Ele é inteligente.	He is intelligent.

It also indicates an established or permanent location.

A capital é no Distrito Federal.	The capital is in the Federal District.
A escola é longe daqui.	The school is far from here.

It is used with a predicate noun or pronoun.

Ele é professor.	He is a professor.
Ela é aluna.	She is a student.
Somos americanos.	We are Americans.
É ele.	It is he/him.
Sou eu.	It is I/me.

It indicates origin or source.

Ele é de Lisboa.	He's from Lisbon.
Esta madeira é do Brasil.	This wood is from Brazil.

It is used with materials.

A casa é de pedra.	The house is made of stone.

It indicates possession.

Os livros são dele.	The books are his.
De quem é?	Whose is it?
É meu.	It is mine.

It is used to indicate the time.

São duas horas.	It is two o'clock.
É meio-dia.	It is noon.

It is also used in impersonal expressions.

É tarde.	It is late.
É cedo.	It is early.
É possível.	It is possible.
É pena.	It's a pity.
Não é verdade?	Isn't it so?

Estar expresses position or location.

Ele não está aqui.	He is not here.
Maria está em casa.	Mary is home.
Onde estão os livros?	Where are the books?
O jornal está na caixa. (x = sh)	The newspaper is in the box.

It indicates a transient quality or characteristic.

Ela está contente.	She is happy (pleased).
Estamos cansados.	We are tired.
Estou pronto.	I'm ready.
O café está frio.	The coffee is cold.
A janela está aberta (fechada).	The window is open (closed).
Ela está bonita hoje.	She looks pretty today.

It is used to form the progressive tenses.

Eles estão falando (a falar) de nós.	They are talking about us.

It is used in expressions related to the weather.

Está frio hoje.	It is cold today.
No verão estará quente.	It will be hot in the summer.

It is used in certain other expressions (especially in Brazil).

Estou com fome.	I am hungry.
Eles estão com sede.	They are thirsty.

The verb *ficar* (to be located, to become) is quite popular in Brazil and is often used in place of *ser* or *estar*.

Onde fica a estação?	Where is the station?
Fica longe daqui.	It is far from here.

Ela fica contente.   She is happy (pleased).

Ele ficou doente.   He became ill.

39. REGULAR VERB FORMS

PRESENT INFINITIVE

falar (to speak)   *aprender* (to learn)   *partir* (to leave)

PERSONAL INFINITIVE

falar	*aprender*	*partir*
(falares)	*(aprenderes)*	*(partires)*
falar	*aprender*	*partir*
falarmos	*aprendermos*	*partirmos*
(falardes)	*(aprenderdes)*	*(partirdes)*
falarem	*aprenderem*	*partirem*

PAST INFINITIVE

ter falado	*ter aprendido*	*ter partido*
to have spoken	to have learned	to have left

PRESENT PARTICIPLE

falando	*aprendendo*	*partindo*
speaking	learning	leaving

PAST PARTICIPLE

falado spoken	*aprendido* learned	*partido* left

PRESENT INDICATIVE

falo	*aprendo*	*parto*
(falas)	*(aprendes)*	*(partes)*

fala	aprende	parte
falamos	aprendemos	partimos
(falais)	(aprendeis)	(partis)
falam	aprendem	partem

IMPERFECT INDICATIVE

falava	aprendia	partia
(falavas)	(aprendias)	(partias)
falava	aprendia	partia
falávamos	aprendíamos	partíamos
(faláveis)	(aprendíeis)	(partíeis)
falavam	aprendiam	partiam

PRETERITE (SIMPLE PAST)

falei	aprendi	parti
(falaste)	(aprendeste)	(partiste)
falou	aprendeu	partiu
falamos (falámos)	aprendemos	partimos
(falastes)	(aprendestes)	(partistes)
falaram	aprenderam	partiram

FUTURE

falarei	aprenderei	partirei
(falarás)	(aprenderás)	(partirás)
falará	aprenderá	partirá
falaremos	aprenderemos	partiremos
(falareis)	(aprendereis)	(partireis)
falarão	aprenderão	partirão

CONDITIONAL

falaria	aprenderia	partiria
(falarias)	(aprenderias)	(partirias)
falaria	aprenderia	partiria
falaríamos	aprenderíamos	partiríamos
(falaríeis)	(aprenderíeis)	(partiríeis)
falariam	aprenderiam	partiriam

PRESENT PERFECT

tenho	+	falado	aprendido	partido
(tens)	+	falado	aprendido	partido
tem	+	falado	aprendido	partido
temos	+	falado	aprendido	partido
(tendes)	+	falado	aprendido	partido
têm	+	falado	aprendido	partido

PLUPERFECT (COMPOUND)

tinha	+	falado	aprendido	partido
(tinhas)	+	falado	aprendido	partido
tinha	+	falado	aprendido	partido
tínhamos	+	falado	aprendido	partido
(tínheis)	+	falado	aprendido	partido
tinham	+	falado	aprendido	partido

PLUPERFECT (SIMPLE)

falara	aprendera	partira
(falaras)	(aprenderas)	(partiras)
falara	aprendera	partira
faláramos	aprendêramos	partíramos
(faláreis)	(aprendêreis)	(partíreis)
falara	aprendera	partira

Note that the simple pluperfect has the same meaning as the compound pluperfect, but it is more a literary tense and is rarely used in conversation.

FUTURE PERFECT

terei	+	falado	aprendido	partido
(terás)	+	falado	aprendido	partido
terá	+	falado	aprendido	partido
teremos	+	falado	aprendido	partido
(tereis)	+	falado	aprendido	partido
terão	+	falado	aprendido	partido

CONDITIONAL PERFECT

teria	+	falado	aprendido	partido
(terias)	+	falado	aprendido	partido
teria	+	falado	aprendido	partido
teríamos	+	falado	aprendido	partido
(teríeis)	+	falado	aprendido	partido
teriam	+	falado	aprendido	partido

PRESENT SUBJUNCTIVE

fale	aprenda	parta
(fales)	(aprendas)	(partas)
fale	aprenda	parta
falemos	aprendamos	partamos
(faleis)	(aprendais)	(partais)
falem	aprendam	partam

IMPERFECT SUBJUNCTIVE

falasse	aprendesse	partisse
(falasses)	(aprendesses)	(partisses)
falasse	aprendesse	partisse

falássemos	aprendêssemos	partíssemos
(falásseis)	(aprendêsseis)	(partísseis)
falassem	aprendessem	partissem

Future Subjunctive

falar	aprender	partir
(falares)	(aprenderes)	(partires)
falar	aprender	partir
falarmos	aprendermos	partirmos
(falardes)	(aprenderdes)	(partirdes)
falarem	aprenderem	partirem

Present Perfect Subjunctive

tenha	+	falado	aprendido	partido
(tenhas)	+	falado	aprendido	partido
tenha	+	falado	aprendido	partido
tenhamos	+	falado	aprendido	partido
(tenhais)	+	falado	aprendido	partido
tenham	+	falado	aprendido	partido

Pluperfect Subjunctive

tivesse	+	falado	aprendido	partido
(tivesses)	+	falado	aprendido	partido
tivesse	+	falado	aprendido	partido
tivéssemos	+	falado	aprendido	partido
(tivésseis)	+	falado	aprendido	partido
tivessem	+	falado	aprendido	partido

Radical-Changing Verbs

The sounds of vowels vary in Portuguese, with open and closed qualities for the same vowel, as well as other variations. Certain verbs in Portuguese have variations in the stem (or radical). Only some of these changes, with a few sample verbs, are given here. Unless otherwise indicated, the change given pertains to those forms of the verb in which the stress falls on the last vowel of the stem: all three singular forms, and the third person plural, of the present indicative and of the present subjunctive. For convenience, we'll call these the *eu, tu, você,* and *vocês* forms.

-*ar* verbs

(open *e*)

levar	to take away
secar	to dry

(open *o*)

cortar	to cut
escovar	to brush
jogar	to play (a game)
morar	to dwell, to live
notar	to note
voltar	to return

(*e* changes to *ei*)

cear	to eat supper
estrear	to use, to wear for the first time
passear	to take a walk or ride
recear	to fear

(*i* changes to *ei*)

odiar	to hate
remediar	to remedy

-er verbs

(*e* changes to open *e* except in *eu* form)

dever	to owe, to have to
escrever	to write
meter	to put

(open *o* except in *eu* form)

correr	to run
mover	to move

-ir verbs

(*e* becomes *i* in *eu* form; *e* becomes open *e* in *tu, você,* and *vocês* of pres. ind.; *e* becomes *i* in all six forms of pres. subj.)

competir	to compete
conferir	to confer
conseguir	to obtain
despir (-se)	to undress (oneself)
divertir (-se)	to amuse (oneself)
ferir	to wound
preferir	to prefer
referir	to refer
repetir	to repeat
seguir	to follow
servir	to serve
vestir (-se)	to dress (oneself)

(*e* becomes *i* in *eu* of pres. ind. and in all pres. subj.)

mentir	to lie
sentir	to feel, to be sorry

(*o* becomes *u* in *eu; o* becomes open *o* in *tu, você,* and *vocês* of pres. ind.; *o* becomes *u* in all six forms of pres. subj.)

cobrir	to cover
dormir	to sleep
engolir	to swallow
tossir	to cough

(*u* becomes open *o* in *tu, você,* and *vocês* of pres. ind.)

consumir	to consume
fugir	to flee
sacudir	to shake
subir	to go up

SPELLING CHANGES IN VERBS

Some verb forms, as is true of other parts of speech, undergo spelling changes before certain endings. These changes are in the final consonant of the stem.

In verbs ending in -*car* in the infinitive, the *c* changes to *qu* before *e*. This occurs in the first person singular of the preterite and all forms of the present subjunctive.

Example: *ficar* (to remain, to be)

Preterite Indicative	Present Subjunctive
fiquei	*fique*
(*ficaste*)	(*fiques*)
ficou	*fique*
ficamos (*ficámos*)	*fiquemos*

(ficastes)   *(fiqueis)*
ficaram   fiquem

Here are some of the other verbs in -*car*.

atacar	to attack	*secar*	to dry
educar	to educate	*significar*	to signify, to mean
explicar	to explain	*tocar*	to touch, to play (music)
indicar	to indicate	*verificar*	to verify

In verbs ending in -*çar*, the *ç* changes to *c* before *e* in the same forms as those indicated above.

Example: *começar* (to begin)

Preterite Indicative	Present Subjunctive
comecei	*comece*
(começaste)	*(comeces)*
começou	*comece*
começamos (começámos)	*comecemos*
(começastes)	*(comeceis)*
começaram	*comecem*

Here are some of the other verbs in -*çar*.

abraçar	to embrace	*forçar*	to force
alcançar	to reach	*recomeçar*	to begin again
caçar	to hunt	*traçar*	to trace, to sketch

In verbs ending in -*gar*, *g* becomes *gu* before *e* in the same forms as those indicated above.

Example: *chegar* (to arrive)

Preterite Indicative	Present Subjunctive
cheguei	*chegue*
(chegaste)	*(chegues)*

chegou	*chegue*
chegamos	*cheguemos*
(chegastes)	*(chegueis)*
chegaram	*cheguem*

Here are some of the other verbs in -*gar*.

apagar	to put out, to erase
carregar	to load, to transport
entregar	to deliver
fatigar	to fatigue
jogar	to play (a game)
pegar	to seize
pagar	to pay
rogar	to beg, to ask

In verbs ending in -*cer*, *c* changes to *ç* before *o* or *a*. This occurs in the first person singular of the present indicative and all forms of the present subjunctive.

Example: *conhecer* (to know)

Present Indicative	Present Subjunctive
conheço	*conheça*
(conheces)	*(conheças)*
conhece	*conheça*
conhecemos	*conheçamos*
(conheceis)	*(conheçais)*
conhecem	*conheçam*

Here are some of the other verbs in -*cer*.

abastecer	to supply
acontecer	to happen

agradecer	to be grateful
aparecer	to appear
carecer	to lack
compadecer	to pity
desaparecer	to disappear
desobedecer	to disobey
envelhecer	to age
esquecer	to forget
falecer	to die
favorecer	to favor
fornecer	to supply
merecer	to deserve
nascer	to be born
obedecer	to obey
oferecer	to offer
padecer	to suffer
parecer	to seem
permanecer	to remain
pertencer	to belong
reconhecer	to recognize

In verbs ending in *-ger*, *g* changes to *j* before *o* or *a* in the same forms as those indicated above.

Example: *proteger* (to protect)

Present Indicative	Present Subjunctive
protejo	*proteja*
(proteges)	*(protejas)*
protege	*proteja*
protegemos	*protejamos*
(protegeis)	*(protejais)*
protegem	*protejam*

Here are some of the other verbs in *-ger.*

eleger   to elect   *reger*   to rule

Verbs ending in *-gir* have the same changes as verbs ending in *-ger.* Here are some of these verbs.

dirigir   to direct, to drive
erigir   to erect
exigir (x = z)   to demand
fugir   to flee
surgir   to emerge

In verbs ending in *-guer* or *-guir, gu* changes to *g* before *o* or *a.* This occurs in the first person singular of the present indicative and all forms of the present subjunctive.

Example: *distinguir* (to distinguish)

Present Indicative   Present Subjunctive
distingo   *distinga*
(distingues)   *(distingas)*
distingue   *distinga*
distinguimos   *distingamos*
(distinguis)   *(distingais)*
distinguem   *distingam*

Here are some verbs that end in *-guer* and *-guir.*

erguer   to raise
conseguir   to obtain
extinguir (x = sh)   to extinguish
perseguir   to pursue
seguir   to follow

Seguir is also radical-changing (see "Radical-Changing Verbs" above), and its derivatives (such as *conseguir* and *perseguir*) show these changes.

Present Indicative	Present Subjunctive
sigo	*siga*
(segues)	*(sigas)*
segue	*siga*
seguimos	*sigamos*
(seguis)	*(sigais)*
seguem	*sigam*

40. IRREGULAR VERBS

Some of the irregular verbs in Portuguese are shown below. Only tenses that have irregular forms are given. Verbs with only radical changes or orthographic changes are not given. Imperative forms are not listed. Irregular participles are indicated.

Abrir (to open)

Past Part.:	*aberto*

Caber (to fit in)

Pres. Ind.:	*caibo, cabes, cabe, cabemos, cabeis, cabem*
Pres. Subj.:	*caiba, caibas, caiba, caibamos, caibais, caibam*
Pret. Ind.:	*coube, coubeste, coube, coubemos, coubestes, couberam*
Past Perf. Ind.:	*coubera, couberas, coubera, coubéramos, coubéreis, couberam*
Impf. Subj.:	*coubesse, coubesses, coubesse, coubéssemos, coubésseis, coubessem*

Fut. Subj.:	*couber, couberes, couber, coubermos, couberdes, couberem*

Cair (to fall): Like *sair* (to leave). See below.

Cobrir (to cover)

Past Part.:	*coberto*

Conduzir (to conduct, to lead [to], to drive)

Pres. Ind.:	*conduzo, conduzes, conduz, conduzimos, conduzis, conduzem*

Construir (to construct)

Pres. Ind.:	*construo, constróis, constrói, construímos, construís, constroem*
Impf. Ind.:	*construía, construías, construía, construíamos, construíeis, construíam*
Pret. Ind.:	*construí, construíste, construiu, construímos, construístes, construíram*
Past Perf. Ind.:	*construíra, construíras, construíra, construíramos, construíreis, construíram*
Impf. Subj.:	*construísse, construísses, construísse, construíssemos, construísseis, construíssem*
Fut. Subj.:	*construir, construíres, construir, construirmos, construirdes, construírem*
Past Part.:	*construído*

Crer (to believe)

Pres. Ind.:	*creio, crês, crê, cremos, credes, crêem*
Pres. Subj.:	*creia, creias, creia, creiamos, creies, creiam*
Pret. Ind.:	*cri, creste, creu, cremos, crestes, creram*

Dar (to give)

Pres. Ind.:	*dou, dás, dá, damos, dais, dão*
Pres. Subj.:	*dê, dês, dê, demos, deis, dêem*
Pret. Ind.:	*dei, deste, deu, demos, destes, deram*
Past Perf. Ind.:	*dera, deras, dera, déramos, déreis, deram*
Impf. Subj.:	*desse, desses, desse, déssemos, désseis, dessem*
Fut. Subj.:	*der, deres, der, dermos, derdes, derem*

Despedir (to send away)

Pres. Ind.:	*despeço, despedes, despede, despedimos, despedis, despedem*
Pres. Subj.:	*despeça, despeças, despeça, despeçamos, despeçais, despeçam*

Dizer (to say)

Pres. Ind.:	*digo, dizes, diz, dizemos, dizeis, dizem*
Pres. Subj.:	*diga, digas, diga, digamos, digais, digam*
Pret. Ind.:	*disse, disseste, disse, dissemos, dissestes, disseram*
Past Perf. Ind.:	*dissera, disseras, dissera, disséramos, disséreis, disseram*
Impf. Subj.:	*dissesse, dissesses, dissesse, disséssemos, dissésseis, dissessem*
Fut. Subj.:	*disser, disseres, disser, dissermos, disserdes, disserem*
Fut. Ind.:	*direi, dirás, dirá, diremos, direis, dirão*
Cond.:	*diria, dirias, diria, diríamos, diríeis, diriam*
Past Part.:	*dito*

Eleger (to elect)

Past Part.: *elegido* and *eleito*

Erigir (to erect)

Past Part.: *erigido* and *ereto* (Portugal: *erecto*)

Escrever (to write)

Past Part.: *escrito*

Estar (to be)

Pres. Ind.: *estou, estás, está, estamos, estais, estão*

Pres. Subj.: *esteja, estejas, esteja, estejamos, estejais, estejam*

Pret. Ind.: *estive, estiveste, esteve, estivemos, estivestes, estiveram*

Past Perf. Ind.: *estivera, estiveras, estivera, estivéramos, estivéreis, estiveram*

Impf. Subj.: *estivesse, estivesses, estivesse, estivéssemos, estivésseis, estivessem*

Fut. Subj.: *estiver, estiveres, estiver, estivermos, estiverdes, estiverem*

Extinguir (to extinguish) *(x = sh)*

Past Part.: *extinguido* and *extinto*

Fazer (to do, to make)

Pres. Ind.: *faço, fazes, faz, fazemos, fazeis, fazem*

Pres. Subj.: *faça, faças, faça, façamos, façais, façam*

Pret. Ind.:	*fiz, fizeste, fez, fizemos, fizestes, fizeram*
Past Perf. Ind.:	*fizera, fizeras, fizera, fizéramos, fizéreis, fizeram*
Impf. Subj.:	*fizesse, fizesses, fizesse, fizéssemos, fizésseis, fizessem*
Fut. Subj.:	*fizer, fizeres, fizer, fizermos, fizerdes, fizerem*
Fut. Ind.:	*farei, farás, fará, faremos, fareis, farão*
Cond.:	*faria, farias, faria, faríamos, faríeis, fariam*
Past Part.:	*feito*

Haver (to have)

Pres. Ind.:	*hei, hás, há, havemos, haveis, hão*
Pres. Subj.:	*haja, hajas, haja, hajamos, hajais, hajam*
Pret. Ind.:	*houve, houveste, houve, houvemos, houvestes, houveram*
Past Perf. Ind.:	*houvera, houveras, houvera, houvéramos, houvéreis, houveram*
Impf. Subj.:	*houvesse, houvesses, houvesse, houvéssemos, houvésseis, houvessem*
Fut. Subj.:	*houver, houveres, houver, houvermos, houverdes, houverem*

Ir (to go)

Pres. Ind.:	*vou, vais, vai, vamos, ides, vão*
Pres. Subj.:	*vá, vás, vá, vamos, vades, vão*
Impf. Ind.:	*ia, ias, ia, íamos, íeis, iam*
Pret. Ind.:	*fui, foste, foi, fomos, fostes, foram*
Past Perf. Ind.:	*fora, foras, fora, fôramos, fôreis, foram*
Impf. Subj.:	*fosse, fosses, fosse, fôssemos, fôsseis, fossem*
Fut. Subj.:	*for, fores, for, formos, fordes, forem*

Ler (to read)

Pres. Ind.:	*leio, lês, lê, lemos, ledes, lêem*
Pres. Subj.:	*leia, leias, leia, leiamos, leiais, leiam*
Pret. Ind.:	*li, leste, leu, lemos, lestes, leram*

Medir (to measure)

Pres. Ind.:	*meço, medes, mede, medimos, medis, medem*
Pres. Subj.:	*meça, meças, meça, meçamos, meçais, meçam*

Ouvir (to hear)

Pres. Ind.:	*ouço, ouves, ouve, ouvimos, ouvis, ouvem*
Pres. Subj.:	*ouça, ouças, ouça, ouçamos, ouçais, ouçam*

Pedir (to ask)

Pres. Ind.:	*peço, pedes, pede, pedimos, pedis, pedem*
Pres. Subj.:	*peça, peças, peça, peçamos, peçais, peçam*

Perder (to lose)

Pres. Ind.:	*perco, perdes, perde, perdemos, perdeis, perdem*
Pres. Subj.:	*perca, percas, perca, percamos, percais, percam*

Poder (to be able to)

Pres. Ind.:	*posso, podes, pode, podemos, podeis, podem*

Pres. Subj.:	*possa, possas, possa, possamos, possais, possam*
Pret. Ind.:	*pude, pudeste, pôde, pudemos, pudestes, puderam*
Past Perf. Ind.:	*pudera, puderas, pudera, pudéramos, pudéreis, puderam*
Impf. Subj.:	*pudesse, pudesses, pudesse, pudéssemos, pudésseis, pudessem*
Fut. Subj.:	*puder, puderes, puder, pudermos, puderdes, puderem*

Pôr (to put)

Pres. Ind.:	*ponho, pões, põe, pomos, pondes, põem*
Pres. Subj.:	*ponha, ponhas, ponha, ponhamos, ponhais, ponham*
Impf. Ind.:	*punha, punhas, punha, púnhamos, púnheis, punham*
Pret. Ind.:	*pus, puseste, pôs, pusemos, pusestes, puseram*
Past Perf. Ind.:	*pusera, puseras, pusera, puséramos, puséreis, puseram*
Impf. Subj.:	*pusesse, pusesses, pusesse, puséssemos, pusésseis, pusessem*
Fut. Subj.:	*puser, puseres, puser, pusermos, puserdes, puserem*
Past Part.:	*posto*
Pres. Part.:	*pondo*

Note: *Compor* and other verbs formed from *pôr* have the same irregularities as *pôr*.

Querer (to want)

| Pres. Ind.: | *quero, queres, quer, queremos, quereis, querem* |

Pres. Subj.:	*queira, queiras, queira, queiramos, queirais, queiram*
Pret. Ind.:	quis, quiseste, quis, quisemos, quisestes, quiseram
Past Perf. Ind.:	*quisera, quiseras, quisera, quiséramos, quiséreis, quiseram*
Impf. Subj.:	*quisesse, quisesses, quisesse, quiséssemos, quisésseis, quisessem*
Fut. Subj.:	*quiser, quiseres, quiser, quisermos, quiserdes, quiserem*

Rir (to laugh)

Pres. Ind.:	*rio, ris, ri, rimos, rides, riem*
Pres. Subj.:	*ria, rias, ria, riamos, riais, riam*

Saber (to know)

Pres. Ind.:	*sei, sabes, sabe, sabemos, sabeis, sabem*
Pres. Subj.:	*saiba, saibas, saiba, saibamos, saibais, saibam*
Pret. Ind.:	*soube, soubeste, soube, soubemos, soubestes, souberam*
Past Perf. Ind.:	*soubera, souberas, soubera, soubéramos, soubéreis, souberam*
Impf. Subj.:	*soubesse, soubesses, soubesse, soubéssemos, soubésseis, soubessem*
Fut. Subj.:	*souber, souberes, souber, soubermos, souberdes, souberem*

Sair (to go out, to leave)

Pres. Ind.:	*saio, sais, sai, saímos, saís, saem*
Pres. Subj.:	*saia, saias, saia, saiamos, saias, saiam*
Impf. Ind.:	*saía, saías, saía, saíamos, saíeis, saíam*

Pret. Ind.:	*saí, saíste, saiu, saímos, saístes, saíram*
Past Perf. Ind.:	*saíra, saíras, saíra, saíramos, saíreis, saíram*
Impf. Subj.:	*saísse, saísses, saísse, saíssemos, saísseis, saíssem*
Fut. Subj.:	*sair, saíres, sair, sairmos, saírdes, saírem*
Past Part.:	*saído*

Ser (to be)

Pres. Ind.:	*sou, és, é, somos, sois, são*
Pres. Subj.:	*seja, sejas, seja, sejamos, sejais, sejam*
Impf. Ind.:	*era, eras, era, éramos, éreis, eram*
Pret. Ind.:	*fui, foste, foi, fomos, fostes, foram*
Past Perf. Ind.:	*fora, foras, fora, fôramos, fôreis, foram*
Impf. Subj.:	*fosse, fosses, fosse, fôssemos, fôsseis, fossem*
Fut. Subj.:	*for, fores, for, formos, fordes, forem*

Ter (to have)

Pres. Ind.:	*tenho, tens, tem, temos, tendes, têm*
Pres. Subj.:	*tenha, tenhas, tenha, tenhamos, tenhais, tenham*
Impf. Ind.:	*tinha, tinhas, tinha, tínhamos, tínheis, tinham*
Pret. Ind.:	*tive, tiveste, teve, tivemos, tivestes, tiveram*
Past Perf. Ind.:	*tivera, tiveras, tivera, tivéramos, tivéreis, tiveram*
Impf. Subj.:	*tivesse, tivesses, tivesse, tivéssemos, tivésseis, tivessem*
Fut. Subj.:	*tiver, tiveres, tiver, tivermos, tiverdes, tiverem*

Note: *Conter* and other verbs formed from *ter* have the same irregularities as *ter*.

Trazer (to bring)

Pres. Ind.:	*trago, trazes, traz, trazemos, trazeis, trazem*
Pres. Subj.:	*traga, tragas, traga, tragamos, tragais, tragam*
Pret. Ind.:	*trouxe, trouxeste, trouxe, trouxemos, trouxestes, trouxeram* (X = S)
Past Perf. Ind.:	*trouxera, trouxeras, trouxera, trouxéramos, trouxéreis, trouxeram* (X = S)
Impf. Subj.:	*trouxesse, trouxesses, trouxesse, trouxéssemos, trouxésseis, trouxessem* (X = S)
Fut. Subj.:	*trouxer, trouxeres, trouxer, trouxermos, trouxerdes, trouxerem* (X = S)
Fut. Ind.:	*trarei, trarás, trará, traremos, trareis, trarão*
Cond.:	*traria, trarias, traria, traríamos, traríeis, trariam*

Valer (to be worth)

Pres. Ind.:	*valho, vales, vale, valemos, valeis, valem*
Pres. Subj.:	*valha, valhas, valha, valhamos, valhais, valham*

Ver (to see)

Pres. Ind.:	*vejo, vês, vê, vemos, vedes, vêem*
Pres. Subj.:	*veja, vejas, veja, vejamos, vejais, vejam*

Pret. Ind.:	*vi, viste, viu, vimos, vistes, viram*
Past Perf. Ind.:	*vira, viras, vira, víramos, víreis, viram*
Impf. Subj.:	*visse, visses, visse, víssemos, vísseis, vissem*
Fut. Subj.:	*vir, vires, vir, virmos, virdes, virem*
Past Part.:	*visto*

Vir (to come)

Pres. Ind.:	*venho, vens, vem, vimos, vindes, vêm*
Pres. Subj.:	*venha, venhas, venha, venhamos, venhais, venham*
Impf. Ind.:	*vinha, vinhas, vinha, vínhamos, vínheis, vinham*
Pret. Ind.:	*vim, vieste, veio, viemos, viestes, vieram*
Past Perf. Ind.:	*viera, vieras, viera, viéramos, viéreis, vieram*
Impf. Subj.:	*viesse, viesses, viesse, viéssemos, viésseis, viessem*
Fut. Subj.:	*vier, vieres, vier, viermos, vierdes, vierem*
Past Part.:	*vindo*

Note: The present participle is also *vindo*. *Convir* (to suit, to agree) and other verbs formed from *vir* have the same irregularities as *vir*.

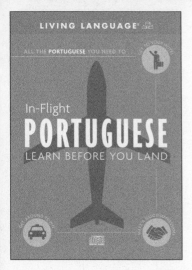